Rewriting Russia

Rewriting Russia

JACOB GORDIN'S YIDDISH DRAMA

Barbara Henry

A SAMUEL AND ALTHEA STROUM BOOK

UNIVERSITY OF WASHINGTON PRESS   *Seattle and London*

THIS BOOK IS MADE POSSIBLE BY A COLLABORATIVE GRANT
FROM THE ANDREW W. MELLON FOUNDATION.

This book is also published with the assistance of a
grant from the Samuel and Althea Stroum Endowed
Book Fund and with support from the Department
of Slavic Languages and Literatures and the College
of Arts and Sciences, University of Washington.

University of Washington Press
PO Box 50096, Seattle, WA 98145, USA
www.washington.edu/uwpress

Library of Congress Cataloging-in-Publication Data
Henry, Barbara J., 1965–
Rewriting Russia : Jacob Gordin's Yiddish drama /
Barbara J. Henry.
p. cm.
Includes bibliographical references.
ISBN 978-0-295-99132-0 (cloth : alk. paper)
ISBN 978-0-295-99133-7 (pbk. : alk. paper)
1. Gordin, Jacob, 1853–1909—Criticism and
interpretation. 2. Yiddish drama—History and
criticism. I. Title.
PJ5129.G6Z65 2011
839'.123—dc22   2011010525

The paper used in this publication is acid-free and
meets the minimum requirements of American
National Standard for Information Sciences—
Permanence of Paper for Printed Library Materials,
ANSI Z39.48–1984.

Cover image: *Bowery at Night, 1895*. Painting by
William Louis Sonntag, Jr. Museum of the City of
New York.

For Wolf and Noah, my own.

CONTENTS

ACKNOWLEDGMENTS

This book began life as a large and ungainly footnote. My wise friend and superlative doctoral supervisor, Julie Curtis, suggested that this footnote might be the start of something else. As ever, Julie was right. I will always be in Julie's debt for her scholarly guidance and friendship and for the innumerable delicious meals that she, Ray Ockenden, Sasha, and Jessica shared with us.

It was Julie who showed me that being a scholar and being a *mentsh* are closely linked, and her example has been multiplied for me many times over. I have had the great good fortune to benefit from the extraordinary kindness, generosity, and intellectual rigor of my mentors, teachers, and colleagues in the United Kingdom, the United States, and Russia. My years at Oxford University were immeasurably enriched by the advice and guidance (as well as the countless letters of recommendation) of Catriona Kelly and Gerry Smith. Philip Bullock has been a faithful friend, a brilliant scholar, and a hilarious coconspirator for many years. Judy Pallot and Jeremy Fairbank were unstintingly generous and kind at a time when my family and I needed it most.

It was at Oxford that I began studying Yiddish, and I wish to express particular gratitude to my wonderful teachers there, Anna Shternshis, Vicky Ash, and Peysakh Fiszman (z"l). Their enthusiastic and imaginative teaching was a joy and an inspiration. It was also at Oxford that I met Joel Berkowitz and Dov-Ber Kerler, who organized the first international conference on Yiddish drama and theatre in 1999, an experience that was nothing short of life changing for me. The world of Yiddish theatre scholarship is warm and fantastically generous, and I am much indebted to the friendship, guidance, humor, and outstanding scholarship of Joel, Nina Warnke, Jeremy

Dauber, Alyssa Quint, Faith Jones, and the late and very much missed John Klier.

In Russia, I am grateful to the staff of the periodicals division of the Russian State Library in Khimki, the State Archive of the Russian Federation (GARF) and the History Library in Moscow, and especially the Theatre Library in St. Petersburg, whose staff's unceasing work on behalf of the library and its magnificent collections is a model of scholarly commitment. My special thanks go to Yulia Prestenskaya, for making my time in St. Petersburg, both on this project and others, especially rewarding and fun. Yulia Ryapolova, Natasha Kraeva, Svetlana Efremova, Marina Aksyonova, and Sasha and Masha Kozyrev have been wonderful friends and hosts in my years in Russia, and their many kindnesses made much of this work possible.

In the United States, I am extremely grateful for the kindness and friendship of Andrew Wachtel and Elizabeth Calihan and to Northwestern University, which supported my research through a Mellon Fellowship and visiting professorship and generously funded summer language study in Vilna and New York. My colleagues in the Slavic Department and the Jewish Studies Program at the University of Washington in Seattle have been exceptionally kind, and it is a joy to work in such a warm and collegial environment. I would like to thank Galya Diment, Paul Burstein, and Steve Hanson in particular for their unfailing and extraordinary support. I am especially grateful also to the University of Washington Press and to Beth Fuget, whose capable, enthusiastic, and steadfast support for this book never wavered.

Among the institutions that supported this research, my thanks go to St. Antony's College, which funded my early research through the Max Hayward Fellowship in Russian Literature. I am grateful also for the support of the University of Washington's Royalty Research Fellowship; the National Endowment for the Humanities, which funded research in Russia with a Summer Stipend Grant; and the Jewish Studies Program at the University of Washington, for supporting work at the YIVO Institute for Jewish Research in New York. Rivka Schiller and Hershl Glasser made research at YIVO both personally and professionally rewarding, and I am very grateful for the vast knowledge of the staff there. I wish also to thank the *Tolstoy Studies Journal*, for permission to publish here a version of an article on *Di kreytser sonata* that originally appeared in that journal in 2005. My thanks also to Brill Academic Publishers, for permission to reprint portions of Chapter 4, which appears in *Jewish Theatre: A Global*

View, edited by Edna Nahshon (*Institute for Jewish Studies: Studies in Judaica,* Brill Academic Press, 2009). My warm thanks also to Steven Cassedy, who responded to a stranger's e-mail with tremendous generosity; to Cecile Kuznitz, for her excellent paper on Jacob Gordin's little-studied Educational League; to Alyssa Quint for her comments on and invaluable suggestions for the manuscript; and to Beth Kaplan, who fielded queries on Gordin's family life and could always be counted on to find Gordiniana as fascinating as I did.

I offer my grateful thanks to our Seattle friends: Chris and Jeff Price, Rebecca Di Nino and Gayle Childers, Amy and Brian Jeffries, Laura Streichert and Chris Roberts, Dave and L. B. Kregenow, Anne and Michael Donegan, and Hilary and Andy Dahlstrom, who offered great company, great food, a lot of laughter, and really awesome child care throughout the past six years. I don't even mind losing to them at poker (okay—and pool, and bowling).

I hope that my husband, Wolfram Latsch, and our son, Noah, know that I owe absolutely everything to them. Their love, patience, understanding, and unfailing goofy humor made all of this possible and worthwhile. It is to Wolf and Noah that this book is dedicated. Finally, I would like to thank my mother, Jane Henry; my brothers, Christopher, Thomas, Peter, and Richard Henry; and my sister, Sue Rasmussen, who never found it odd that I should be so taken with cultures, languages, and people so seemingly far from our own Irish, English, and French background. And to the memory of my late father, John, who lived with his parents only two blocks away from the Gordins in early twentieth-century Brooklyn. I like to think that maybe my grandparents and members of the Gordin clan passed each other on the street or in Prospect Park and perhaps nodded good morning, never to know the strange ways in which their descendants would connect. It can happen in America, where the warp and weft of immigrant and native born, Jewish and gentile, intersect again and again, to weave a pattern of which the very constituents are only occasionally aware.

As a result of the late orthographic standardization of Yiddish, transliteration of prewar texts presents some challenges. For ease of reading, citations within the text have been standardized to reflect YIVO guidelines. Exceptions to this rule are Yiddish names or words that have commonly accepted English transliterations, for example, "Bertha Kalich" rather than "Berta Kalish," "chutzpah" rather than "khutspe." Titles cited in the endnotes and bibliography, however, reflect their original orthography.

Russian is transliterated according to the system used by the United States Board on Geographic Names, with a few modifications. The Russian *ë* is transliterated as *yo*; for example, Fyodor, not Fëdor. The soft sign (*myagkii znak*) has been transliterated as ', but I have eliminated the soft sign in widely known names and terms used in the text, such as "Gogol" and "tsar." These transliterations are retained, however, in the endnotes and bibliography. Adjectival endings have been rendered as -y and -oy, except where this would contradict Russian spelling rules, for example, *evreiskii*, not *evreisky*. Citations and titles from prerevolutionary texts reflect modern usage; thus *Odesskiya novosti* is rendered as *Odesskie novosti*. Capitalization reflects Cyrillic convention.

Unless otherwise noted, all translations from Yiddish and Russian are my own.

UKRAINIAN

Gordin's life "in Russia" was actually in Ukraine, a territory known by different names to different people. The city where Gordin spent much of his adult life was Elisavetgrad; it became Kirovograd in the

Soviet period and now goes by its Ukrainian name, Kirovohrad. Cities are referred to by the names that they bore in the period under discussion, with present-day designations indicated in parentheses.

DATES

All dates of events in Russia before the October Revolution reflect the Old Style (OS) Julian calendar, which was twelve days behind the Western Gregorian calendar in the nineteenth century and thirteen days behind in the twentieth. Where relevant, I have supplied the Gregorian calendar date in parentheses.

Rewriting Russia

Introduction

Of all the verbal arts, only the work of the playwright appears to have anything in common with the practical crafts. The English language provisions us with shipwrights, wheelwrights, wainwrights, barrel-wrights, and . . . playwrights. The suffix suggests that the writing of plays has less in common with the mysterious alchemy of composing verse or novels than it does with forcing recalcitrant materials into useful but unnatural shapes. Just as wood must be shaped with fire, water, and force into the desired curve of wheel and prow, so too, it would seem, must language be hewn, tempered, and restrained to achieve the desired dramatic arc and heft.

The plays of Jacob Gordin (1853–1909), the dramatist credited with the "reform" of New York's raucous turn-of-the-century Yiddish theatre, certainly seem to reinforce this linguistic link with the practical arts. It is almost axiomatic that Gordin's plays served issues, actors, and box-office demands to a greater degree than they served the vaunted cause of art. Gordin's adaptations of the classics of world literature—Jewish vernacular versions of Shakespeare, Goethe, Tolstoy, and many others—are traditionally seen as vehicles for ideas and education, and Gordin as the authorial equivalent of a journeyman cartwright. Like so many barrels, Gordin's Yiddish plays contained "useful" stuff: political messages, instructive examples, and lessons about the gentile world in which Eastern European Jewish immigrants found themselves.

Yet for all their apparently workmanlike efficiency, Gordin's plays transformed the Yiddish theatre. His colloquial language replaced the stilted stage dialect (*daytshmerish*) then customary for the Jewish theatre. Instead of haphazard, vaguely historical settings, Gordin's plays were set in modern times and reflected contemporary realities. Instead of their customary ad-libbing, Gordin demanded that his actors maintain an unprecedented fidelity to the text. In less than a decade, Gordin's quest to improve the Jewish repertoire had expanded its range and ambition well beyond the costume epics and potboilers that had been the Yiddish stage's early mainstay.

For half a century Gordin's plays were seen by hundreds of thousands of audiences in North America, Latin America, and Eastern Europe. His dramas were made into half a dozen popular Yiddish films. The roles he wrote made the actors who played them legends on the Yiddish and English-language stages. Gordin's work was fundamental in defining a Jewish dramatic tradition, one valuable both in its own right and for the rebellion it sparked in the next generation. The most famous exponents of the modernist Yiddish stage—Peretz Hirshbein's Odessa "art theatre," New York's Artef (Arbeter Teater Farband), the Soviet State Jewish Theatre (GOSET), and the Warsaw Yiddish Art Theatre (VYKT)—inherited, reacted against, and transformed a Yiddish theatrical tradition that could in large part be traced to the innovations of Jacob Gordin. Yet in the century since Gordin's death there has not been a single scholarly study of his plays.

The Yiddish theatre was one of the core institutions of immigrant Jewish life. It was a popular entertainment, a commercial powerhouse, an influential public forum, a force for education and acculturation, and a battleground for ideologies, egos, and artistic credos. Because the Yiddish theatre was so closely bound up with the social, intellectual, and political ferment of immigrant life in New York, research on Jacob Gordin has tended to emphasize these very dimensions in his work. Gordin's ties with the press and radical intellectual circles and his socialist sympathies, volatile interactions with Jewish religious conservatives, and feuds with the powerful editor of the daily *Forverts*, Abraham Cahan (1860–1951), have been elucidated in scholarly and popular works in both Yiddish and English.[1] The circumstances of Gordin's plays' production and reception, especially the controversies they ignited, also make up a substantial portion of the research on his theatrical legacy, which is well documented in actors' memoirs and histories of the Yiddish stage. The plays themselves, however, have rarely been the subject of scholarly inquiry.

Gordin's many dramas have generally suffered from the perception that their merits are chiefly practical and historical rather than artistic and that they cannot reward literary analysis because their author was not a dramatist but a moralist and teacher.[2] Such a view remains helpless, however, to explain how these apparently unremarkable plays wrought the changes they did. Certainly, the force of Gordin's personality and the strategic alliances he formed with the press and with powerful actors go a long way toward explaining his outsize influence, but theatrical innovations of the kind he initiated rarely occur without parallel innovations in playwriting. This aspect of Gordin's work—the textual means by which he helped transform the raw energies of the popular American Yiddish stage into a sophisticated, modern theatre—is the subject of this study.

Gordin's Yiddish dramas were loosely adapted from works of European and Russian fiction, from which he typically borrowed themes and plot outlines and sometimes characters. Though often dismissed by later generations of playwrights and critics as poor Jewish imitations of European literature or as shameless plagiarisms, Gordin's plays were neither, and his working method was a surprisingly sophisticated one.

On a practical level, Gordin's borrowings from writers like Ibsen, Turgenev, and Hauptmann allowed him to incorporate admired gentile models into a Yiddish dramatic tradition that was keenly aware of the rudimentary condition of its own repertoire. The professional Yiddish theatre's relatively late emergence and its commercial and populist character had, in the opinion of the Jewish intelligentsia, stunted its growth as a serious dramatic art. Gordin's practice of adapting European literary models provided a structural and thematic framework for much-needed new plays, advertised Gordin's own progressive sympathies and aesthetic ambitions, and allowed the Yiddish stage to claim a degree of intellectual prestige and credibility as an educational medium—all the while generating publicity by aggravating more conservative elements of immigrant society, who found Gordin's non-Jewish sources inimical to Jewish interests.

It is the conspicuous intertextuality of Gordin's dramas, which pointedly acknowledge their debts to other literary works and invite comparison with them, that highlights his work's self-consciously literary preoccupations.[3] Gordin's characters themselves comment directly on their own source texts, further foregrounding the metadramatic dimensions of his plays, which are always concerned with the construction and perception of a reality whose meanings and structure derive in large part from literary texts. This pointed interaction of the literary and the real, and the potential for art to transform reality, is not undertaken simply with a view to "enlightening" Jewish audiences with the powers of great non-Jewish literature. Gordin's focus is on the process of adaptation itself, of transforming old world literature into new world drama, and is both a formal and metaphoric means of treating larger questions of immigration, urbanization, and assimilation. His plays encapsulate the dynamics of the Eastern European Jewish encounter with the gentile world in dramatic form and suggest that aesthetic adaptation was as essential a component of the immigrant experience as were geographic displacement and linguistic assimilation.

Gordin's plays are not translations, plagiarisms, or mechanical transpositions of European works to a Jewish milieu; they are sustained critical dialogues with his source works, which assert Jewish continuity with European literature through its reinscription as popular Yiddish drama, while always subjecting that very generative process to scrutiny. Like Aaron Halle-Wolfssohn's (1754–1835) nod to Molière in the Jewish Enlightenment (Haskalah) drama *Laykhtzin und fremelay* (*Silliness and Sanctimony*, ca.1794), S. Y. Abramovitsh's (1835–1917) to Cervantes in the early Yiddish novel *Kitser masoes binyomin hashlishi* (*The Brief Travels of Benjamin III*, 1878), and Dovid Bergelson's (1884–1952) multiple invocations of Anton Chekhov, Gordin's intertextuality is a time-tried device that signals both Jewish continuities with and divergences from non-Jewish models. Yet while Gordin's plays assert Jewish claims to the European literary tradition, it is their divergences from these precursors—evidenced by shifts in language, thematic emphases, genre, and character—that became the creative source of this new Yiddish drama.

Gordin's methods are analyzed here in three of his most successful dramas. *Der yidisher kenig lir* (*The Jewish King Lear*, 1892), *Di kreytser sonata* (*The Kreutzer Sonata*, 1902), and *Khasye di yesoyme* (*Khasye the Orphan*, 1903) are, like most of Gordin's plays, "original" adaptations. Their construction and meanings are closely linked to those of their source texts—Shakespeare's *King Lear* and Turgenev's *Stepnoi korol' Lir* (*King Lear of the Steppes*, 1870), Tolstoy's *Kreitserova sonata* (*The Kreutzer Sonata*, 1889), and Turgenev's *Asya* (1858). That all three plays derive either in part or entirely from works of Russian literature represents a very personal and deliberate strategy on Gordin's part, one that is crucial to his work as a whole.

For two decades before his immigration to the United States in 1891, Gordin had been a Russian writer; his immigration and shift to Yiddish did not diminish his attachment to his native land or its literature, but did necessitate the conversion of his literary sympathies into a more commercially viable form. Russian literature, like the English, German, and Scandinavian works that Gordin also adapted, offered a ready source of plots and themes, a radical cachet, and a provocative means of needling religious conservatives, but Gordin's "Russian" plays also recapitulate and poeticize the loss of his native country and first literary language. They establish Gordin's artistic continuity with a distant, remembered Russian ideal while in the profane land of American exile and simultaneously enact a very Jewish form of literary reclamation and sacralization, as the text became a substitute for the lost homeland. Yet Gordin's very personal, creative salvage of the Russian past through its texts also offers his audience—itself overwhelmingly composed of immigrants from the Russian empire—a means of evaluating and transforming the remembered Jewish experience of "the old country." For by literally rewriting Russian literature on Jewish terms, in a Jewish language, for the Jewish stage, Gordin's plays reframe and rewrite the Russian past itself. They render the past and the literature that shaped it knowable, mutable, and subject to revision and hold out the tantalizing possibility that by changing the story of your past, you could write your own narrative of the future.

MAN AND METHOD

Gordin's creative rewriting of the Russian past and its texts extended into his own life, as he devised a largely fictive identity for himself in New York as a Russian radical, allegedly silenced by the tsarist regime. Although he cultivated a legend that he had been cast out of his homeland for posing a threat to its political stability, his real history was much less colorful. This study is the first to dismantle Gordin's ersatz radical credentials to establish the facts of his career in

Russia as a Jewish religious reformer, creative writer, and journalist. The truth of Gordin's life in Russia begs investigation not simply as a matter of historical record but because the very process of creating a fictional past, of imposing creative control on events and individuals by rendering them as a literary narrative, helped shape Gordin's playwriting strategy itself. The malleability of all texts, be they personal, sacred, literary, or historical, and their eternal availability for revision and renewal, is a leitmotif of all Gordin's Russian and Yiddish writing.

As a religious reformer in Russia, Gordin rejected rabbinical authority and study of the Talmud and emphasized the necessity of personal interpretation of the Torah. The central and original texts of Judaism, Gordin argued, required one's personal interpretation according to the "spirit of the times." The precepts of his sect, the Spiritual-Biblical Brotherhood (Dukhovno-bibleiskoe Bratstvo), are everywhere reflected in Gordin's Yiddish plays, for which texts are not fixed in their meanings but open to interpretation and evaluation according to contemporary needs. For Gordin, this critical act was essential to the text's continued vitality, relevance, and renewal.

This study is the first to establish continuities among Gordin's religious reform movement, his Russian fiction and journalism, and his Yiddish playwriting. Gordin's Russian writing in particular offers early evidence of his fluid literary sensibility, as his short stories, feuilletons, and theatre reviews laid the groundwork for his working method as a Yiddish playwright. Gordin's Russian writing reveals that he did not spring like some bearded Yiddish Athena from the fevered brain of Jewish immigrant New York but that he had been honing his literary skills for twenty years before his first Yiddish play was ever staged.

Gordin's deep knowledge of and combative interrogation of Russian literary texts produced plays that are themselves critical readings of the Russian originals. A century ago, Gordin forced audiences and critics to contend with the European and Russian culture that he promoted; today, scholarly study of his plays demands equal attention to the non-Jewish sources that were both the object and subject of much of his work. This study's examination of how Gordin interpreted Turgenev and Tolstoy, of what he retained and what he rejected in their transformation into popular Yiddish drama, looks not only at how "high" Russian literature is rendered as "low" Yiddish theatre but also at how foreign traditions are localized and popularized.

Much as Russian dramatists in the eighteenth and the early nineteenth centuries adapted European plays for the tastes and needs of
Russian audiences (*sklonenie na nashi nravy*), Gordin does something similar in turn-of-the-century New York. Adaptations like Gordin's may look on the surface like an admission of native inability to
create an original literary work, but in fact each hybrid prompts ex
perimentation by other writers to create what appears to be a more
"native" literary work. Just as European plays adapted for a Russian
milieu prompted Russian writers like Denis Fonvizin (1745–92) and
Aleksandr Griboedov (1795–1829) to develop what they regarded as
native dramatic works, Gordin's adaptations similarly prompted his
successors like Dovid Pinski (1872–1959) to advocate a "true" Jewish drama, one faithful to the experience and culture of modern Jews.

But what is that experience, and, as ever, who are the Jews, and
what is their true culture? If Gordin's plays blur the boundaries of
high and low, novel and drama, what is Russian and what is Jewish, they ultimately must call into question the definition of a "national" literature itself. His project suggests that a national literature
is fundamentally impure—that neither form nor language defines it
and that all nations have contributed, consciously or unconsciously,
to their creation. The irony of Gordin's internationalist, integrationist ethos is that his works' vital grounding in a very specific period
and milieu is also their limitation, now that the cosmopolitan and
stateless language in which they were written is no longer the Jewish vernacular. It is Gordin's links with Russia and Russian literature that broaden the scope of his reach and merit his inclusion in a
cross-cultural and multilingual literary history, one that recognizes
that different nations may lay equal and justifiable claim to the same
literary art.

CHAPTER ORGANIZATION

The initial chapter in this monograph introduces Gordin's dramatic
revolution in the Yiddish theatre in immigrant New York through a
close reading of *Der yidisher kenig lir* and its other, less well-known
intertext, Turgenev's *Stepnoi korol' Lir*. *Der yidisher kenig lir*'s form
and philosophical implications defined Gordin's working method and
his entire adaptive process, and the play's influence on the Yiddish
theatre as a whole is difficult to overstate.

From New York, the second and third chapters work backward to

Gordin's life in Russia. Drawing on tsarist police archives and rare regional publications, I detail Gordin's heretofore shadowy Russian past, dispel the fanciful legends that he created, and establish connections between his Russian writing and his Yiddish plays. Far from being the spontaneous and hasty outpourings of a writer desperate to make a living in hardscrabble New York, Gordin's Yiddish plays were the culmination of two decades of work as a Russian writer and religious reformer, whose ideals, methods, and persistent preoccupations are echoed in all of his Yiddish writing.

My selection of *Di kreytser sonata* and *Khasye di yesoyme* for analysis in chapters 4 and 5 is dictated by the two works' use of Russian source texts, their quality and influence, and the developments they mark in Gordin's creative process. Gordin was the author of some seventy or eighty plays, not all of which survived or reward analysis. Extant plays were popular, and their popularity was closely correlated with their quality, which itself is due to the depth of their author's engagement with their source texts.

Di kreytser sonata was Gordin's most successful play. It was adapted twice for the English-language stage, made into a film in 1915, translated into Russian, and widely performed in Gordin's native land. The culmination of Gordin's many years of fraught engagement with Tolstoy's work as a writer and moralist, *Kreytser sonata* also offers an original interpretation of its Russian source text, one that questions customary readings of it as Tolstoy's dire warnings about the dangers of musical seduction. Gordin's play suggests that literature is the most dangerous and volatile of arts and presents the novel, and not the sonata, as the art form that dooms his own play's heroine and Tolstoy's protagonist.

Turgenev's *Asya* was the source text for Gordin's *Khasye di yesoyme*, which was famed not for its considerable dramatic merits but for the scandal that New York's Yiddish press initiated in response to it. *Khasye* is Gordin's most sensitive and lyrical work and. more than any other, illustrates the productive potential that his creative method had for advancing the development of the Yiddish drama. Inverting the Turgenev novel's sunny exteriors and thwarted love story, Gordin presents the Russian city as a latter-day underworld and its heroine as a Jewish Persephone, in a haunting drama that looks very much like nascent dramatic symbolism.

From the optimistic *Kenig lir* to the despairing yet innovative *Khasye* and *Kreytser sonata*, these plays also illustrate the limits of

Gordin's form of textual transformation and renewal, which, like any literary device, inevitably approached its own exhaustion. The consistently violent turns Gordin's later plays take—at a time when his material, critical, and popular success was at its peak—suggest that a point of satiety had been reached. With these works having served their purpose in producing Yiddish plays that looked to literary values as much as to theatrical values, Gordin's influence on the future course of the Yiddish theatre waned, as new forms emerged in what the Russian theorist Yuri Tynyanov characterized as the "struggle" for literary supremacy.[4] This study concludes with a discussion of the reception of Gordin's plays in prerevolutionary Russia, where they found new audiences and enjoyed a generally positive critical reception, until Gordin's plays too were superseded by the innovations of the modernist Yiddish stage.

TEXTS

The great popularity of *Der yidisher kenig lir, Di kreytser sonata,* and *Khasye di yesoyme* meant that they often circulated in pirated editions. The question of how reliable any published Gordin text is, especially one printed in the Yiddish piracy capital of Eastern Europe, Warsaw, is a vexed one. Unauthorized versions of his work caused Gordin considerable dismay, due as much to his loss of much-needed royalties as to the loss of creative control of the texts. To assert some authority over the proliferation of pirated editions, in 1909 Gordin's estate applied for membership to the imperial Russian Theatrical Society (Russkoe Teatral'noe Obshchestvo, RTO). Because of its quasi-governmental organization, the RTO jealously guarded authors' rights, ensured the payment of royalties, and exerted extensive control over published editions of plays in the Russian empire. Thanks to the vigilance of the RTO and tsarist censorship, Eastern European Yiddish editions and Russian translations of Gordin's plays actually attest to a surprising degree of fidelity to authorized American texts. The pirated text of *Der yidisher kenig lir* published in Warsaw in 1907 is almost identical to an authorized Russian translation of 1912, suggesting that the pirated text was sufficiently "canonical" to warrant its serving as the basis for a legal translation.[5]

Despite concordances among pirated, authorized, and translated texts, the problem of their divergences in performance and from the manuscripts remains. As Sophie Glazer has scrupulously documented, the manuscript version of *Der yidisher kenig lir* was never performed.[6] I examine manuscript versions for divergences from more widely available texts, but my preference has been for published texts overseen either by Gordin himself or by his colleagues and the executors of his estate. When these editions are not available, I use texts that were published in the Russian empire which differ little from authorized versions published after 1909. All of these widely available editions enjoyed a theatrical authority that the manuscript texts did not. At some point, the play that is has to take precedence over the play that might have been.

Because there are many excellent studies of the Yiddish theatre but few of its dramatic literature, the focus of this study is on the dramatic text rather than its performance. While the study of stage art is ideally approached through analysis of both text and performance, Gordin's dramatic output alone is so prodigious as to necessitate some limitations even on its scholarly consideration. I am keenly aware that this study does not and cannot provide an account of Gordin's many spheres of interest and activities and that limiting discussion to his career in Russia and to three of his Yiddish plays constitutes a narrowing of focus that is at odds with the titanic nature of his energies and achievements. It is my hope that interested readers will turn to the works of scholars of the Yiddish theatre—in Yiddish and English—for a fuller account of Gordin's work as a journalist and producer in New York and of the theatrical realizations of the plays discussed here.

Gordin's plays are an important bridge between the old world and the new, and like all good bridges, they are utilitarian but have a real and symbolic beauty and integrity in their own right. While none would argue that Gordin's plays approach the level of the works he adapted, his dramas offer evidence of the complexity and sophistication of the early American Yiddish theatre, which looked as much to the literary traditions of the Russian past as it did to the hectic energies of the American future. In this his plays offer clear evidence of the genuinely transnational character not only of the Yiddish stage and its players but also of Yiddish plays themselves. Gordin's drama was part of a multiethnic and multilingual Jewish culture that cannot easily be reduced to its being "Russian," "Jewish," or "American." For Gordin, this was not a weakness but its greatest strength, as the Yiddish theatre itself became an essential medium for negotiating the forms and function of a modern Jewish identity.

   Historians of Russian-Jewish culture and politics have, in the past decades, increasingly demonstrated and argued for the necessity of viewing their subject not as a discrete entity but through the dense and complex connections that Russian-Jewish artists and activists forged with neighboring, non-Jewish cultures. Gordin's work both demonstrates and advances what Chone Shmeruk calls this "poly-systemic" sensibility.[7] Gordin's plays take as given that Jews might be citizens of more than one nation and that it is culture that forges the best links between them. Perhaps the interconnectedness of Russia, Russian literature, and Russian Jews that Gordin's plays insist on, and their belief that Russian culture is vital and essential for American Jews, will play some role in the evolving study of Yiddish drama and literature. And perhaps cognizance of the cultural union of Russia and her Jews will reach back to Russia and to Russian studies, which may yet see that Jewish art and letters are an indelible and native component of Russia and of Russian literature.

CHAPTER ONE

Amerika

Hamlet, the Yeshiva Boy. The Jewish Heart. Bar Kochba. Disaster on the Titanic. Shmendrik. Sabbatai Zevi, or The False Messiah. The Jewish King Lear. High and low, ancient and modern, comic and tragic, adapted and original—New York's Yiddish theatre had something for everyone. It offered nothing less than the Jewish experience itself, retold in popular art. For more than three decades, hundreds of thousands of immigrant Jews spent their earnings on theatre tickets, lionized Yiddish actors, formed vociferous claques, and avidly followed the furious polemics that Jewish intellectuals carried on in the press with playwrights and performers. Curious visitors from uptown peered through the gilded doors of the Yiddish theatre and were astonished at its vitality, its creativity, and the ferocity of the people's attachment to it. Both mirror and lamp, Yiddish theatre reflected immigrant experience, aspirations, and fears and held itself up as guide and mentor in the arduous process of adaptation to American life.

"Adaptation" was both abiding theme and working method to Jacob Gordin, whose works became a cornerstone of the Yiddish repertoire in its so-called Golden Age in the late nineteenth and the early twentieth centuries. Credited with the reform of the Yiddish stage in New York through his introduction of conspicuously literary dramas, Gordin was a pivotal figure in the evolution of the modern Jewish stage, and his plays permanently altered ideas about what the popular Yiddish stage should—and could—do as an artistic medium.

When Gordin began his career as a playwright, the professional Yiddish theatre had existed for scarcely two decades. Its comparatively late emergence in the otherwise long history of Jewish art has been attributed to a variety of factors, not the least of which was the prohibition in Deuteronomy 22:5 against a man's wearing a woman's garments. Generally interpreted as an interdiction against theatrical performance, the stage's cause was not aided by its pagan Greek origins, its association with sexuality and display, or its potential for sparking public disorder. The theatre's highly visible, communal nature, which ensured that participation in or attendance at a Jewish theatre was tantamount to a public declaration of one's membership in or sympathy for that community, did little to recommend the art to Jewish communities anxious to avoid any conflict with their gentile neighbors. Because of these hindrances, Jewish theatrical expression remained fragmentary and compartmentalized, limited to specific groups within a community, but rarely reaching all members of it.

The tradition of amateur Jewish theatrical performance that emerged in sixteenth-century Europe with the *purimshpil*, or Purim play, was a case in point.[1] The participatory nature of synagogue readings of the Book of Esther during the holiday of Purim had gradually evolved into full-blown, parodic enactments of the events recounted in the text. Productions grew elaborate (and ribald) and are still a feature of many Hasidic congregations today, but because *purimshpil* performances remained firmly anchored in the religious Jewish world and subject to its strictures—on who might perform a play or when and where it might be staged—they had little practical connection to the secular, professional theatre that evolved in the late nineteenth century.

Scripted Yiddish drama emerged from a milieu that was very different from that of the seasonal Purim play and dramatic texts actually preceded the existence of a Yiddish theatre in which it might be performed. The origin of Yiddish drama dates to the early nineteenth century, when *maskilim*—adherents of the Haskalah, or Jewish Enlightenment—used the dramatic form to argue for Jews' greater engagement with the non-Jewish world. The first Yiddish dramatists, Aaron Halle-Wolfssohn, Shloyme Etinger (1800–1856), and Yisroel Aksenfeld (1787–1866), used their plays to advocate the secular, integrationist agenda of the Haskalah.[2] Their use of the non-Jewish dramatic form as a vehicle for treating Jewish issues underlined the essential compatibility of "goyish" art forms with Jewish content. Lacking

a Jewish theatre, however, maskilic dramas were more likely to be
read than staged, and the roots of the professional Yiddish stage are
conventionally traced to Avrom Goldfaden's (1840–1908) productions of his own plays in Jassy, Romania, in 1876.

Goldfaden was a popular and well-regarded lyric poet who wrote
in both Hebrew and Yiddish, yet his public readings of his Yiddish
verse had proved distinctly underwhelming to a Romanian café audience, who vastly preferred the performer who followed him—a Broder
singer, or itinerant Jewish performer of songs and sketches.[3] Reportedly, as Goldfaden watched the Broder singer bring the house down,
the chastened poet was inspired to create his own dramatic scenes for
performance.[4] He quickly found an audience hungry for theatre in
the Jewish vernacular, and there followed a period of rapid development of the Yiddish stage in Eastern Europe, as Goldfaden and other
impresarios raced to satisfy audience demand. In less than a decade,
Goldfaden had turned out dozens of plays, among them *Shulamis, Di
kishefmakherin* (The Sorceress), and *Di tsvey kuni-lemls* (*The Two
Kuni-Lemls*), which were destined to become classics of the Yiddish
repertoire, and Goldfaden's company would tour with great success
to St. Petersburg's imperial Mariinsky theatre in 1879 and 1881–82.[5]
But as swiftly as the Yiddish theatre had risen, its expansion in the
Russian empire was abruptly curtailed. In 1883, partly in response
to the violence that followed in the years after the 1881 assassination
of Tsar Alexander II and partly to rid itself of the inconvenience of
having to vet plays for a people associated with the worst effects of
the public disorder, the Russian Ministry of Internal Affairs severely
restricted theatrical presentations in Yiddish.[6] It also established a
second level of local controls whose capricious enforcement made it
difficult for any but the most determined company to perform. The
net effect of the restrictions was to greatly retard the evolution of the
Yiddish theatre in the Russian empire.

The subsequent emigration of many of the first generation of Eastern European Yiddish playwrights—Joseph Lateiner (1853–1935),
Moyshe Hurwitz (1844–1910), and Nokhem Shaykevitsh (Shomer)
(1849–1905)—along with a huge portion of their audience, fueled the
growth of the American Yiddish theatre, especially in New York.[7] By
1883, when Lateiner arrived in the city, the Jewish immigrant population was able to support—just about—more than one permanent
Yiddish theatre. Lateiner's playwright-rival, the self-styled "Professor" Hurwitz, was attached to the company of the comic actor Sig-

mund Mogulesco (ca.1856–1914), and the two troupes engaged in fierce competition for audiences.

The practical necessity of turning out new plays as fast as possible to appeal to a limited audience that was unlikely to see any play more than once meant that the early Yiddish playwrights' works had few literary ambitions. Hurwitz's and Lateiner's plays were vehicles for spectacle, romance, high-flown language, and colorful sets and costumes—what Irving Howe called the "consolations of glamour," for an audience seeking respite from their jobs as laborers, garment workers, peddlers, and clerks.[8] The general financial instability of any theatrical enterprise was exacerbated by producers' attempts to increase their box-office revenue by leasing ever-larger houses. Any risks that a "literary" repertoire might also pose were unlikely to have been profitable and were therefore rarely attempted.[9] Yiddish theatres played what paid, and what still pays the world over: melodrama, musicals, comedies, and romances.

The theatre culture of the Lower East Side prized audience and actor interaction above all else. Direct address to the house, crowd-pleasing improvisation and clowning, and spontaneous encores of particularly pleasing musical numbers were the rule, not the exception. Audiences brought infants to the theatre and shelled out for fizzy drinks, peanuts, apples, and candy from the hawkers who circulated through the house. Neither actors nor audience approached the theatrical experience with the kind of politesse and reverence that would become the norm in the twentieth century. Spontaneity, inspiration, energy, cathartic emotion, and forceful expression were the hallmarks of the Yiddish stage, which Nahma Sandrow has called the last in the "grand nineteenth-century Romantic tradition."[10]

Tickets cost from a few cents in the gallery to up to a dollar for the best orchestra seats, a range that was varied enough to ensure that a broad cross-section of the Jewish immigrant community (except the very pious) made up the theatregoing public. The correlation between theatre audience and Jewish community would come to figure prominently in the culture wars that later surrounded the Yiddish stage, when its audience came to stand in for the immigrant population entire.

Writing in 1900, uptown visitor John H. James noted in the *New York Dramatic Mirror*, "The poor Jew toiling and sweating in his room in an East Side tenement looks forward beyond the monotony and grime of his surroundings to evening when, in the brilliantly lighted theatre, he can meet his friends, recognize on the stage the types with which he was familiar in the old country, and listen to the songs of his people."[11] Theatres were meeting places, secular temples, and a focal point for those who would influence the community that attended them. As Nina Warnke has documented, by the late 1880s the Yiddish press began to lament the commercial, populist character of the Yiddish stage and to berate its actors and playwrights for pandering to audiences' preference for entertainment, over the theatre's potentially enlightening influence.[12] The left-leaning press's campaign would not really gain momentum, though, until the arrival of the Russian writer and journalist Jacob Gordin in the summer of 1891.

New York's Lower East Side was a long way from where Gordin had begun. Born May 1, 1853, in Mirgorod, in the old Cossack lands of the Poltava province of central Ukraine, Gordin was the middle child and only son of a family whose sympathies reportedly extended both to the charismatic piety of Hasidism and to the upstart secularism of the Haskalah.[13] Educated at home by both Hebrew instructors and secular teachers, Gordin excelled in Russian, Ukrainian, and German.[14] The question of to what degree Yiddish could be considered his native language cannot be answered with certainty. Letters to Gordin from his two sisters—written in an ungrammatical Russian, by hired scribes—suggest that although the women of the family understood Russian, they communicated primarily in Yiddish.[15] Certainly, the evidence of Gordin's plays and his New York journalism points to a fluency in Yiddish, albeit one heavily influenced by Russian, the language that was undoubtedly Gordin's preferred tongue and in which he began his career as a writer.

Gordin reportedly began publishing in the 1870s in a number of Russian and Ukrainian newspapers, including the radical *Pravda* (Truth); the liberal, pro-Jewish *Odesskii vestnik* (Odessa Courier); the politically liberal but anti-Jewish *Golos* (The Voice); and even the vigorously Judeophobic *Novorossiiskii telegraf* (Novorossiysk Telegraph).[16] None of this can be substantiated, however, as Gordin's work in these early years was, in accordance with contemporary journalistic convention, unsigned.

Gordin married Anna Lazarevna Iskewitz (ca. 1859–1924), in 1872; the first of their eleven children, Sophia, was born in 1873, and a second, Lizzie, arrived in 1874.[17] From there, the picture of Gordin's life in Russia grows murky. A three-year gap between the births of his second and third children, from 1874 to 1877, coincides with a period in Gordin's life that is the most obscure in his history and, consequently, held up as the most formative.

By dint of his having—à la Sholem Aleichem's (1859–1916) feck-less *luftmentsh* hero Menachem Mendel—badly invested his wife's dowry, Gordin is said to have earned a living traveling southern Rus-sia and Ukraine, working as a teacher, an Odessa stevedore, an actor in a traveling Russian company, and a farm laborer.[18] Of these, only Gordin's occupation as a "teacher in a *talmud-toyre*" (a communally funded elementary religious school) can be confirmed, both by refer-ence to contemporary periodicals and by his police file.[19]

The only well-documented activity in Gordin's past, notice of which preceded his arrival in New York, was his establishment of the reform-minded Spiritual-Biblical Brotherhood (Dukhovno-bibleiskoe Bratstvo) in 1881. Reiterating a view that had circulated in maskilic circles since the eighteenth century, Gordin's group argued that per-secution of Russian Jewry would cease only when Jews themselves abandoned their "exploitative" professions (moneylending, tavern-keeping, and commerce) and took up productive agricultural labor. In tandem with its advocating productive physical labor for Russia's Jews, Gordin's group also proposed reforming Jewish worship by re-turning Judaism to its core biblical tenets and by denying the legal authority of the Talmud.

The rational, liberal emphases of Gordin's Brotherhood might have attracted more adherents than it did were it not for the outbreak of anti-Jewish pogroms in 1881. Not long after the pogroms that began in his own home city of Elisavetgrad, where the Brotherhood was based, Gordin heaped insult on injury by publishing a letter that ac-cused Russian Jews of provoking pogrom violence by their attach-ment to said exploitative professions. Gordin's letter was widely re-printed and roused a storm of controversy that nearly proved fatal to the Brotherhood.

When not antagonizing liberal and conservative Jews alike, Gor-din achieved considerable notoriety owing to his work as a journalist and editor in Elisavetgrad and Odessa. Specializing in satirical feuil-letons, comic sketches, and theatre reviews, Gordin wrote under a va-riety of pen names, among them "Yakov Mikhailovich," "Ivan Koly-uchii," "Yan," "Alfei," "Evpatii Kolovrot," and "N.N." According to Gordin's biographers, this proliferation of pseudonyms was part of an effort to mislead tsarist censors. Legends circulated by Gordin himself suggest a link between his journalism and a warning by friendly government contacts that he was in danger of imminent arrest. It was only then that Gordin is said to have decided to leave Russia. He allegedly fled the country with the help of friends, under cover of night, and arrived a few weeks later in New York City, in July of 1891.

FIRST STEPS

In the summer of 1891 Benjamin Harrison was serving out his single term in the White House, Thomas Alva Edison had applied for a patent on a camera that he called a "Kinetograph," and William Morrison's electric motorcar trundled down the streets of Des Moines, Iowa, on wooden wheels, at times reaching the terrifying speed of twenty miles per hour. Plans were already under way for the World's Columbian Exposition in Chicago, which would mark the four hundredth anniversary of European settlement of the Americas amid a dazzling display of technological marvels, bizarre curios, and a whole lot of lightbulbs. Indeed, European settlement continued apace in the western states and territories, abetted by the Dawes Act and the de facto end of armed Indian resistance on the banks of South Dakota's Wounded Knee Creek. Western settlers' ranks were bolstered by some of the millions emigrating to America, in numbers so great that a new processing facility off the New Jersey coast would be opened in January of 1892, on Ellis Island.

Jacob Gordin did not pass through its halls. Nor did he ever show much interest in life beyond the five boroughs of New York City, much less in people and events in Iowa or South Dakota. Although Gordin lived out his eighteen years in the United States in a volatile and often violent period broadly characterized as the "Progressive Era," the protracted and widespread efforts to reform electoral politics and parties, corporate trusts, city services, railways, and many other aspects of American government and society attracted Gordin's interest only fitfully, and only as they had a direct impact on immigrant Jewish New York.[20] Though occasionally moved to offer journalistic commentary on Eugene Debs or the exploits of robber barons, the tumultuous and contradictory tendencies of the period were not the subject of Gordin's sustained interest. What concerned Gordin were the mutually entwined worlds of Jewish cultural and political life in immigrant New York and in particular their noisy confluence in the Yiddish theatre.

Jewish immigrants' first contact with the heady nexus of art, politics, and progressivism in lower Manhattan often came through "settlement houses," aid and educational institutions that merged traditional Jewish philanthropy with Progressives' pursuit of "improvement." The Hebrew Sheltering House Association and the Hebrew Immigrant Aid Society were two of the first institutions to greet the Eastern European Jews who arrived in the United States during the period from the 1880s to the First World War. The settlement houses offered job training, English language classes, lectures, civics lessons, and more, as part of efforts by their more established Jewish-American founders to convert "the Yiddish-speaking immigrant into a self-respecting Jew and an American."[21] The assumption that "Yiddish-speaking immigrant" and "self-respecting Jew and American" were mutually exclusive conditions did not appeal, however, to the Russian-born Jewish intelligentsia that dominated political and cultural discourse on the Lower East Side.

Owing as much to a Russian tradition of social responsibility coupled with cultural activism as to the prevailing American passion for reform, Jewish radicals of socialist, anarchist, and less coherent political passions organized a variety of cultural and educational opportunities for the newly arrived immigrants. Jewish activists held forth in the press, in cafés, and in public lectures and rallies, in Yiddish and in Russian, and they had set their sights on the Yiddish theatre as well.[22]

Jacob Gordin's political sympathies were of the decidedly less well-articulated variety. Though never a socialist in the doctrinal sense, he did reserve a genuine revulsion for bourgeois gentility, mercantile striving, and the belief that success could be measured in dollars. Gordin's reverence for education and practical enlightenment, and his facilities in both Russian and Yiddish soon brought him into the orbit of the radical Russian-Jewish intelligentsia. His ties with the fledgling weekly *Di arbayter tsaytung* (The Workman's Paper), established in 1890 by a group of leftist intellectuals that included Abraham Cahan, Louis Miller (1866–1927), Morris Hillquit (1869–1933), and Bernard Vaynshteyn (1866–1946), soon returned Gordin to his old career in journalism—but in a new language, and for a new audience.

Di arbayter tsaytung offered its readers current events with a socialist slant, as well as novels translated into Yiddish (with a socialist slant), historical and cultural articles (with a socialist slant), and opinion pieces (ditto). Gordin's first article in Yiddish for *Di arbayter tsaytung* reflects house style accordingly; it was published on August

21, 1891, and signed "Yankev ben Mikhl," the Jewish version of his Russian pen name "Yakov Mikhailovich." The article describes a pogrom that broke out in Gordin's home city of Elisavetgrad on July 14, 1891, when Gordin himself was already in Scotland, awaiting passage to New York.

Reporting on the pogroms put *Di arbayter tsaytung* in something of a bind, as both poor and middle-class Jews were victims of mob violence, and ethnic Slavs' brutality against their Jewish neighbors had logically to be linked with their own disenfranchisement by the rapacious forces of capitalism and tsarist oppression. Gordin's article seeks to explain the conflict of a Russian soldier and a Jewish peddler, the incident that sparked the pogrom. The report shifts adroitly from the intimate interaction of thief and victim to the larger canvas of the destroyed market, from Russian to Jew, and from Yiddish to Russian. To describe word of the pogrom's spread, he employs a bitterly ironic Hebrew: "The glad tidings [*psure toyve*] that they were beating the 'zhidovkes' immediately spread over the entire city."[23] But for the language of the article, Gordin's "conversion" to the Yiddish cause is little marked, whereas his hostility to even the most humble of Jewish mercantile occupations is very marked.

That Gordin published his first article in Yiddish scarcely three weeks after arriving in New York must refute the legend that he was not fluent in the language before arriving in the United States. His confident command of Yiddish is also evident in his next piece for *Di arbayter tsaytung*, "Di oblave" (The Raid), advertised as a "heartbreaking tale of the ruined and oppressed lives of the Jews in Russia."[24] The writer Abraham Cahan, who had been in England when Gordin arrived in New York, recalls taking special note of this feuilleton.[25]

Gordin makes accomplished use of the tonal range of Yiddish in "Di oblave," which is set in the slums of Kiev and focuses on Reb Moyshe Levi and his family, who do not have residence permits for the "holy city." Against a backdrop of a peaceful, moonlit spring night, Gordin contrasts the restful world of nature with the restless anxiety of the quarter's Jews, who await a police raid. Gordin's style is terse:

> Whose footsteps do we hear at such a late hour? Whose copper buttons are illuminated by the moon's pale beams? Whose heels click across the cobblestones of the ghetto? Be still, little Jew! The patrol is coming . . . Get your last cent ready for a bribe. Get ready to be taken

away with murderers and criminals, because you are a Jew and also live and eat.[26]

Reducing the tsarist police patrol to disembodied copper buttons and clicking heels, Gordin employs a menacing onomatopoeia to suggest their approach: "Di kuperne kneplekh kumen tsu neenter un neenter" (The copper buttons come closer and closer). Moyshe Levi bribes the police regularly, but his elderly father and younger sister, Esterke, recently arrived from the country to see a doctor about her sudden blindness, must be hidden, for there is no money to bribe the officers to overlook the newcomers. The contrast of light and dark in the opening paragraph is echoed in Esterke's loss of sight and in the darkness within and without the apartment. Where is the lamp, cries Moyshe Levi, "Mir viln nit blaybn in der finster!" (We do not want to remain in the dark!). In Kiev, Moyshe Levi the "refined Hebraist and Talmud scholar, the *maskil* and clever man, has become simply 'Moshka the Yid,' forced to bow his head to every drunken peasant, take off his hat and bow to every policeman, and give a bribe to anyone who might expose him." Moyshe Levi—educated and refined—is "light," gleaming weakly against the enveloping "power of darkness" around him. The darkness wins: Esterke is accidentally smothered to death.

"Di oblave" is an atmospheric tale of terror, and Russia the monster outside the door. Its very real anger at the codification of antisemitism in tsarist law was a subject rarely addressed in Gordin's Russian writing, but new readers and new circumstances in New York required a reappraisal of established methods. This transformative process would find its most successful incarnation in Gordin's imminent emergence as a playwright and "reformer" of the Yiddish stage.

DER DRAMATURG

The story of how Jacob Gordin became a Yiddish playwright suggests that material, rather than aesthetic, needs propelled the creation of his first play for the Yiddish stage, *Sibirya* (Siberia), in November 1891. Stories like "Di oblave" did not pay enough to support life in Manhattan, much less leave something to send to Anna Gordin, who would remain for two more years in Elisavetgrad with their many children.

Gordin's new friend Philip Krantz (Jacob Rombro, 1858–1922), a prominent Russian-born socialist and a former editor of *Di arbayter tsaytung*, had many contacts in the Yiddish theatre, and he reasoned that it *couldn't be too hard* to write a Yiddish play. Journalists, even the haughty Cahan, were known to turn to the Yiddish stage, lured by the promise of substantial advances and box-office returns.[27] Most of the Russian-Jewish intelligentsia on the Lower East Side, including Krantz, held the opinion that the quality of the Yiddish theatre was not high. The popular stage's visual and visceral appeal seemed to come at the expense of its literary qualities, and they accused Hurwitz and Lateiner of doing little more than turning second-rate German plays into third-rate Yiddish plays. Surely, the erudite Gordin could produce something at least as passable for the Yiddish theatre. Gordin, feigning ignorance of the Yiddish stage, did not demur when it was suggested that he meet with the influential actors who were the real power in New York's Yiddish theatre.[28] He even admitted to being curious about the species of man a Yiddish actor resembled. Would he wipe his nose on his sleeve? Spout doggerel and dance on tabletops?[29]

In the autumn of 1891, Gordin met with Jacob P. Adler, David Kessler, Sigmund Mogulesco, and Sigmund Feinman.[30] Intelligent and dedicated to their craft, the actors left a favorable impression, and Gordin claimed that he came away from their meeting in a Lower East Side café thinking, "If Yiddish actors are men like other actors of the world theatre, why should the Yiddish theatre not be like other theatres?"[31]

On the basis of what Gordin saw during a visit to the Union Theatre in the autumn of 1891, though, the Yiddish theatre would have a long way to go before it could claim parity with any other. In appalled tones, Gordin describes a play in which a blind miller dances about speaking cod German, while someone sings an aria from an Italian opera, and people run around shouting and hitting one another. The audience whistled, children squirmed, and peddlers hawked soda water and apples. "Everything that I heard and saw was far from Jewish life, was vulgar, without aesthetic merit, false, vile, and rotten."[32] Gordin needed little prodding to craft a better drama, and while he may have abjured the fantastical sets, gold crowns, live horses, and stirring choruses of his predecessors and competitors, he was not above exploiting the old Yiddish theatre's capacity for thrills and high drama. Despite his avowed preference for "realism," Gordin's plays are a canny combination of the didactic and the diverting.

Alongside disquisitions on high culture, he offers homicides, adultery, illicit pregnancies, union skullduggery, and a generous selection of musical numbers. Where Gordin diverged from writers like Hurwitz or Lateiner, who also adapted works from non-Jewish writers, was in his own intense intellectual engagement with the source texts and in his desire not merely to copy non-Jewish literary models but to extend their reach and impact by remaking them as popular Yiddish drama.

SIBIRYA (SIBERIA, 1891)

Gordin's method of adapting non-Jewish literary texts for the Yiddish stage was not one he arrived at with his first dramatic effort. Nina Warnke's reconstruction of the plot of Gordin's first play, the no longer extant *Sibirya*, which premiered at the Union Theatre in November of 1891, suggests his limitations in developing original material:

> The play tells the story of Rubin Cohn who, charged with a crime, is sentenced to exile in Siberia. The prologue, opening with a Russian song, shows Cohn's escape from the transport that is taking him to Siberia. He changes his name to Rozentsvayg, and settles with his wife and their two children in a town, where nobody knows his identity. Many years later he has become a well-to-do merchant and respected member of the community. His son Samuel, a medical student, and Fanya, the daughter of his competitor Berl Taratutye, are in love. The cruel Taratutye, however, who hates Rozentsvayg, discovers his old secret and denounces him to the police, ignoring all pleas to spare him. Fanya, distraught that her father prohibits her marriage to Samuel, commits suicide. The play ends with the old Rozentsvayg leaving once again for Siberia.[33]

Sibirya prefigures several staple dramatic elements of Gordin's plays: a father of compromised integrity is helpless to protect a beloved child's suffering, the chief villain is not capricious tsarist might but venal merchants, and the setting is not actually Siberia but the Pale of Settlement. Another prominent theme, the potential for making oneself over, transforming one's identity, is also evident in the character of Cohn/Rozentsvayg, who undergoes a dramatic shift in his public identity. He is not absolved of his sins, however, because he becomes a merchant, rather than dedicate his second chance to an "honest" profession. Taratutye is the principal scoundrel because he is both traditionally observant and a merchant, but Rozentsvayg's failures compound the perfidy, which destroys the next generation.

The circumstances of *Sibirya*'s production have passed into legend: skeptical actors, horrified at Gordin's plainspoken Yiddish text, devoid of comic verses, ditties, and opportunities for stage business, reluctantly stage the bizarre new play. The opening night audience grows restless through the first two acts. Jacob P. Adler chides the philistines for their failing to recognize the aesthetic revolution taking place in their midst. Cowed, the audience remains till the end and is involuntarily drawn into the story. The playwright stays away from the theatre, fearing retribution and flying vegetable matter. The events validate the author's literary integrity, which the press promotes as a value for the Yiddish theatre as a whole.

Perhaps most noteworthy about Gordin's first full-length play for the Yiddish theatre is his attempting to take on a directorial role by insisting on the actors' fidelity to his text. Though often cited as evidence of the Russian influence on Gordin's writing and creative expectations, disciplined actors and respect for the text were by no means a given in the Russian theatre, either. There is no evidence that Gordin was aware of developments in the German Meiningen theatre or André Antoine's Théâtre Libre, frequently cited as precursors to the Moscow Art Theatre's much-touted insistence on scenic verisimilitude and the sacrosanct status of the text. Nor was Gordin likely to have been familiar with—or to admire—the work of the American director and impresario David Belasco (1853–1931).

Belasco's insistence on the preeminence of his unifying directorial vision and his focus on contemporary plays initially suggest parallels with Gordin's own approach.[34] But in his eighteen years in New York, Gordin never had a kind word for the American stage, which he dismissed as being overly interested in scenic effects, novelty, and empty diversions, and which had only a pernicious influence on the Yiddish theatre.[35] Neither did Gordin have Belasco's in-depth knowledge of stagecraft or Belasco's skill in the technical realization of his productions. Indeed, other than insisting on sets and costumes that did not patently contradict the milieus of his plays, Gordin's primary interest lay always in verisimilitude of character and language and not in the physical realization of the production. That Gordin, like Belasco, felt the urgent need for director-centered theatre, rather than the traditional, actor-centered approach, is evident from his complaints (as late as 1906) about the continuing lack of such an artistically unifying figure in the Yiddish theatre. Gordin lamented, "How long will an edifice that is built without an architect stand?"[36]

In the absence of a director to ensure the realization of a coherent, unified vision of the play, Gordin attempted to fill the role himself. In *Der pogrom in rusland oder Palestine in amerike* (The Pogrom in Russia or Palestine in America), his fourth play, Gordin insisted both on fidelity to his text and on linguistic verisimilitude that entailed that the character of the Russian policeman (played by Gordin himself—literally policing his recidivist actors) speak only Russian. Not surprisingly, his attempts to wrest control of the production from the actors provoked their equally emphatic resistance. Audiences also proved reluctant to embrace a theatre that demanded their submission to a single, directorial will. Had the cause of Gordin's "realist" theatre not been taken up by the radical intelligentsia and by *Di arbayter tsaytung* and the *Forverts*, his call to order would have had much less effect than it did.

Indeed, the failure of Gordin's next plays demonstrates how tenuous his hold on the audience really was. Rebellion against crowd-pleasing Yiddish theatrical tradition drew forth not so much a revolt in the house as it did a bored yawn. The short-lived *Der pogrom in rusland* and *Tsvey veltn, oder Der groyser sotsyalist* (Two Worlds, or The Great Socialist) were markedly less successful than *Sibirya*.[37] Neither text is extant.

Gordin blamed the failure of his latest plays on his audience's untutored tastes and the lack of critical attention paid by the press. Abraham Cahan had lavished many column inches on *Sibirya*, but Gordin's next plays attracted no such interest.[38] Gordin's address on the subject, "Vegn di [*sic*] drama *pogrom*" (On the Drama *The Pogrom*), adopts the wounded tone of an artist whose works have not garnered their due. In a process he was to repeat in later years, Gordin outlines the principles and hierarchies of his artistic credo.[39] Good plays do not engage in bombast and sensationalism or rely on outlandish effects and costumes or vulgar jokes; good plays portray real people in all their faults and dignities. Gordin urged the audience not to accept theatre that would be more appropriate to a circus or to put up with actors better suited to work as clowns.[40]

This disdain for popular Yiddish theatre is not surprising. In all his years in Russia as a theatre reviewer, Gordin had never shown the slightest interest in or appreciation of popular or folk theatre (*balagan*—its very name a pejorative in both Yiddish and Russian). In Russia, Gordin's rhapsodies were reserved for high art: for the German romantics, classical music, Aleksandr Pushkin, and Tolstoy. Yet there he had pleaded for a stage that released mankind from "customary vulgarity and coarseness," for a stage that let men "see noble images and marvelous visions," for there was "too much prose already in the lives of men."[41] This vaguely elevating, primarily romantic aesthetic would be tempered in the Yiddish theatre by Gordin's didactic tendencies, the economic imperatives of the box office, and critics' preference for a stage in the realist style. Gordin's approach combined high-art source material, provocative sociopolitical debate, and the strategic incorporation of old-style Yiddish theatre conventions. But Gordin's primary innovation was in his democratization of high art for the Yiddish-speaking immigrant community; the redemptive and transformative power of literature itself is the abiding principle of Gordin's creative work.

Gordin's best plays dispense with the overt sociopolitical focus of *Sibirya* and *Der pogrom in rusland* and tie their fortunes to another literary work. His plays do not introduce comic incongruity between themselves and their progenitors, but are linked to them by a range of characteristic devices: repetition, inversion, conflation, and direct reference. The marked gaps between Gordin's adaptations and their originals, their disjunctions and discrepancies, allow him to invoke the works and wisdom of Goethe, or Shakespeare, or Tolstoy, but also to reject the idea that the meanings of their texts are in any way fixed. Literary continuity between Yiddish drama and non-Jewish fiction is asserted even as the latter is upended and reconfigured for the Jewish stage.

The most sophisticated and enduring of Gordin's plays are those that draw either entirely or in part on works of Russian literature. His debt is not always obvious. Sometimes the link is a forceful element of the plot and the title, as in *Di kreytser sonata*. Sometimes it is evident in a seemingly throwaway line that reveals a deeper engagement with a source text, as in *Khasye di yesoyme*. In *Der yidisher kenig lir*, one source text, Shakespeare's, has almost entirely obscured another, Turgenev's *Stepnoi korol' Lir*, the dimensions of which are addressed below.

DER YIDISHER KENIG LIR

Der yidisher kenig lir is probably the most written-about play in Gordin's oeuvre, and not without good reason.[42] In terms of its impact and longevity it finds rivals only in the operas and comedies of Goldfaden. *Der yidisher kenig lir* was Gordin's breakthrough drama, the one he regarded as his first important play, and the one that established both his working method and the means by which he "reformed" the Yiddish theatre.[43]

For scholars, the play has manifold attractions, offering oblique commentary on the wrenching displacements of immigration, a representation of the eternal agon of generational discord, and a fascinating naturalization of Shakespeare's original. It proved equally enticing to Gordin's contemporaries: intellectuals were drawn to the theatre by the prospect—perhaps grisly—of Shakespeare in Yiddish. Both strange and familiar, it offered further proof of the theatre's utility as a force for acculturation and vital evidence of the flexibility, range, and depth of Yiddish as a literary language. Ordinary folk might be drawn by the title's promise of a king, suggesting as it did that the play was a colorful historical drama of the sort churned out by Lateiner and Hurwitz. The title's combination of chutzpah, homage, and bait and switch would remain a hallmark of Jacob Gordin's dramaturgy.

Gordin's attraction to Shakespeare's play, which he probably read in Russian translation, would be due in part to the centrality of two themes to which Gordin himself returned again and again in his own writing: the flawed father who is unable to save a beloved child, who perishes because of the father's sins, and the fatal force of hypocritical role-play, what Cordelia calls "that glib and oily art / To speak and purpose not" (I.i.226–27).[44] The latter theme lent itself particularly well in Gordin's adaptation to treating subjects such as religious hypocrisy, pretense, and critique of the Yiddish theatre, but the Yiddish drama pays particular attention to the question of the power and limitations of speech itself.

Speaking—its free exercise as well as its control—is closely related to what Leonard Prager has called Der yidisher kenig lir's "oral anxiety."[45] Prager finds in the recurring images of the abundance or withdrawal of food a metaphor for Jewish communal cohesion and its fracturing and reformation in American immigration, as generations renegotiated the traditional hierarchy of patriarchal authority amid the social upheaval of the new world. The transfer of power from old world fathers to new world children is further presented in Gordin's play as evolution from a tradition marked by clouded vision and atavistic prejudice to a modern age that values science, women's emancipation, and openness to change.

The marked prominence of food originates less in Shakespeare's play, though, than in Gordin's other source text, Turgenev's *Stepnoi korol' Lir*.[46] In Turgenev's novella, food's proffer and consumption is also a focus of conflict, and the Russian Lear is similarly neglected and deprived of food by his daughters. But Turgenev's "oral anxiety" is less gustatory than verbal, and food is really a correlate of the mouth, an analogue of language itself. The mouth that eats and speaks is the real agent of the Russian Lear's destruction.

Turgenev's novella recapitulates the contrast that Shakespeare draws between speech and silence, whose juxtaposition is evident in Cordelia's very first line, "What shall Cordelia speak? Love, and be silent" (I.i.62). Their tension in Shakespeare's *Lear* finds an echo in an abiding concern of Turgenev's work, a feeling that words are, as Elizabeth Cheresh Allen argues, "insubstantial at best, and deceptive at worst, as suspect as the figure they metonymously come to represent."[47] This suspicion and Turgenev's oft-noted regard for silence, both as an "aesthetic ideal and as an attribute of character," are inverted in *Stepnoi korol' Lir*.[48] If in Shakespeare's play silence proceeds from a fullness of love that need not speak to be, in Turgenev's novella silence is not so much a retreat "from the world of compromised speech" as it is a strategic move to capitalize on the glibness of others.[49] The Russian work's voluble, expansive protagonist stands in marked contrast to his daughters, whose taciturn circumspection suggests not reserved depths but stalking predators.

This reversal of Turgenevian norms echoes the inverted values of the world of Shakespeare's Lear, and their own textual relationship in turn becomes one of the focuses of Gordin's play. *Der yidisher kenig lir* is particularly interested in the relationship of literary texts to one another and the influence that one brings to bear on another. Gordin further complicates these intertextual relationships by contrasting the powers of the spoken word with the written one. Which wields greater force: text or performance, word or deed? Gordin's work joins the Russian novella and the English play in a Yiddish drama that offers a Jewish resolution to the conflicts its source works address.

STEPNOI KOROL' LIR (1870)

Turgenev's novella employs a framing narrative that opens on a winter night among a group of six old university friends, who are discussing the astonishing fidelity that Shakespeare's "types" bear to contemporary individuals. This emphatic statement of the relationship

of human character to literature—of literature's power both to describe human types and to shape perception of them in reality—is
paramount in Turgenev's transfer of Shakespeare's Lear to a Russian
milieu.[50] Shifting the action from ancient, pagan Britain to provincial
Russia in the 1830s and 1840s, Turgenev declares the field of literature to be unbounded by national, linguistic, or temporal limitations.
For a writer whose fiction was so closely identified with social causes,
Stepnoi korol' Lir is a declaration of aesthetic independence whose
central intertextuality looks to literature, rather than politics, as an
expository force of the ways of the world. This aesthetic focus becomes the basis for Gordin's adaptation of Turgenev, in which those
who know the texts that describe their world can shape their own in
accordance with or defiance of the "master" text.

Turgenev's narrator relates the history of a provincial gentry landowner, Martyn Petrovich Kharlov, whom he calls "a King Lear."[51] As
seen through the eyes of the then fifteen-year-old narrator, Martyn
Petrovich is a throwback to the epic heroes (*bogatyry*) of old Rus'.
Like a modern *bogatyr'* he dashes about his run-down estate on a
cart pulled by an improbably skinny nag (an analogue of the *bylina*
[epic folk song] hero Dobrynya Nikitich's scrawny but preternatural-
ly strong colt). Martyn Petrovich is almost twice the size of a mortal
man, is all but illiterate, and is unreasoningly proud of what he claims
as his ancient "Shweedish" (*vshedskii*) ancestry. Kharlov is regarded
with much affection by the narrator's mother, Natalya Nikolaevna,
a wealthy widow whose life he saved some twenty-five years before.
Nevertheless, King Lear of the steppes is never permitted farther than
the dining room of the widow's house, because he exudes a strong
smell of earth, and his table manners are like those of Polyphemus
(*PSS*, 10: 191).

Turgenev's invocations of Greek titans and Russia's pre-Christian
mythology make clear the spiritual valences of this world, which
though peopled by priests and dotted with churches and holy masses
is a world in which Christian power is limited and almost entirely restricted to merely formal expression. But though this is a world without God, it is not without gods, powers whose logic is inscrutable
and gifts unevenly distributed and whose whims only occasionally
coincide with our own desires. Evil is not punished, nor is good re-
warded, and humans can only wonder at its workings. "Everything
in the world," declares the narrator, "both good and bad—is given to
man not according to his deeds, but as a result of some kind of as yet

unknown but logical laws, which I will not take upon myself to spec-
ify, but which on occasion it seems to me that I dimly sense" (*PSS,*
10: 263). The "logical laws" that the narrator suspects underpin his
world, the pattern on which the events of the story unfold, are in fact
those of Shakespeare's Lear. The same ill portents, inversions of expected norms, intimate betrayals, and glimpses of the bestial aspect of
man shape the events of the narrator's tale and his narration of them.
But for the Russian Lear, there is no catharsis, no restoration of order, no Fool to comfort him in his destitution, and no Cordelia. The
narrator sees his neighbor's kinship with Shakespeare's pagan Briton,
but Turgenev's Lear himself has no such knowledge. Almost illiterate
and only partially domesticated, this elemental Russian Lear acts out
a drama whose outcome he is helpless to alter.

Martyn Petrovich has only two daughters, and although the
younger, Evlampiya, displays some latent similarities to Cordelia,
by and large she takes after Regan. Evlampiya is unmarried and
having an affair with the husband of her sister, Anna. The narrator's widowed mother acts as counsel, a female Gloucester or Kent,
but she is also an unwitting agent of the titular hero's doom. It is
she who provisions him with a wife, a brother-in-law, and an odious
son-in-law, Slyotkin.

The Russian Lear has fits of melancholy, assigns meaning to dreams
and omens, and is given to gloomy ruminations on the futility of existence. After a dream of a black colt, which Martyn Petrovich interprets as a sign of his imminent death, he decides to divide his estate
between his daughters. This is a point of pride with him: death may
take him on a whim of its own, but it will not determine the timing of
the disposition of his estate.

Things do not, of course, turn out well. Martyn Petrovich is at best
ignored and at worst abused by his daughters and is entirely subject
to the will of his petty tyrant son-in-law, Slyotkin. Kharlov goes hungry and unkempt and is ultimately turned out of the house, with the
explanation that his room is needed for "housekeeping." The old man
goes to his neighbor, the widow, and is so bedraggled and unshaven
that he is initially mistaken for a bear that has wandered into the
courtyard. The widow takes Martyn Petrovich in, but while he waits
for his room to be made up and for dry clothes to be given him, his
own brother-in-law, a ne'er-do-well and hanger-on known as "Souvenir," enters.

A malignant version of Lear's Fool, Souvenir had warned Martyn

Petrovich that his daughters would betray him, and now he laughs at the old man:

> He used to call me a leech, a parasite! He said, "You haven't got a roof of your own!" And now look who's become the leech, who's just as bad! Which one is Martyn Petrovich, which one is the rascal Souvenir—now it's all the same! You'll feed on handouts as well! They take any old crust of bread, one that the dog turned up its nose at . . . They say, here you go, eat this! Ha ha ha! (*PSS*, 10: 245)

It is this mockery, rife with the food and consumption imagery that Gordin transposes to his play, that finally propels Martyn Petrovich to act. Enraged by the reminder of his hunger and homelessness, Kharlov returns to his estate and begins tearing apart the roof of his manor house with his bare hands. Roaring, he flings the materials around the yard as an audience of serfs, neighbors, and family gather to watch the spectacle. Kharlov rages until a support beam sends him crashing to the ground, where he dies of his injuries.

Years later, the narrator meets the elder daughter, Anna, now a widow with two children and a prosperous landowner herself. It is rumored that she poisoned Slyotkin. The narrator also chances to see the younger daughter, Evlampiya, outside St. Petersburg, where she is installed as the prophet of a secretive group of religious dissenters. Driving by with her retinue, she casts at the narrator an imperious glance that speaks of a "long-accustomed, ingrained habit of encountering only adoring, unquestioning obedience" (*PSS*, 10: 265). She has inherited her father's royal prerogative but, unlike him, will suffer none of its consequences.

The feasibility of Gordin's adapting *Stepnoi korol' Lir* for his own dramatic work is suggested by a number of elements. Turgenev's transfer of Shakespeare to Russia offers a successful model of literary transplantation, making Gordin's shift to merchant-class Jewish Vilna part of an established process of naturalization. The character of Slyotkin, repeatedly described as a stereotypically Jewish "type," also suggests possibilities:

> My mother called him the little Yid, and, truly, with his crisp curls, black, eternally damp eyes, like stewed prunes, his hawk nose and full, red mouth, he did recall the Jewish type; only his skin was white and he was, altogether, rather good looking. He was obliging, as long as matters did not affect his personal profit. Then he immediately became frantic with greed, even to the point of tears; he was ready to beg all day for a rag, to recall a promise one hundred times, taking

offense and whimpering if it was not immediately carried out. (*PSS*, 10: 199–200)

Slyotkin reappears in Gordin's play as Harif, the husband of the Jewish King Lear's eldest daughter. The role played by Turgenev's narrator's mother, Natalya Nikolaevna, shifts to Khane-Leye, the wife of Gordin's Lear. Both women act as counselors, although their advice, like Kent's, is ignored and their murmurings of alarm are more chorus backdrop than they are influential voice. The Turgenev novella's focus on the purely domestic sphere, absent the international intrigues of the Shakespearean drama, is also retained in Gordin's transfer.

Gordin's most noticeable borrowing from Turgenev, though, is in his title character's dogmatic faith in the power of his "word." For Kharlov, it is his verbal promise to his daughters, rather than the legal act that documents it, that has the force of the Almighty behind it: "The Lord God knows (and here he raised his hand over his head) that this earthly sphere will crumble before I take back my words or . . . (and here he even snorted) become a coward, or repent what I have done!" (*PSS*, 10: 221). Turgenev invested considerable effort in researching the exact legal procedures for the title character's transfer of property and had pressed his estate steward, N. A. Kishinsky, for details and documents to establish the legality of Kharlov's passing all his goods on while yet living.[52] This is echoed in Kharlov's own detailed knowledge of the legal underpinning of his actions—"Don't you remember the law? If he who has received a gift makes an attempt on the life of the donor," said Kharlov, pausing between words, "then the donor has the power to demand everything be returned" (*PSS*, 10: 255). But Kharlov does not at any point retract his words, and the written word's subordination to this oral law is underlined by the ease with which what is written may be abrogated. The law is analogous to the solid-looking but shoddily constructed house that Kharlov dismantles by hand. Yet Kharlov's faith in the power of the spoken word proves just as misleading, for as he lies dying, the meaning of his own last words is uncertain: "Well, daugh . . . ter, I do not . . . " (Nu, doch . . . ka . . . Tebya ya ne pro . . .) (*PSS*, 10: 257). Does he refuse to forgive her (*proshchayu*)? Does he refuse to banish her (*progonyayu*)? Or does he refuse to curse her (*proklinayu*)? In the end, the instability of the spoken word, its vulnerability to time, the frailties of the body, and self-serving interpretation, is its undoing. The written word endures, and perpetuates injustice, as Kharlov's property remains with those who brought about his end.

Gordin's characters echo the credence that Turgenev's Lear lends the spoken word in their own heightened anxiety about what is said, what is unsaid, and who is accorded the powers of speaking. Their quarrels over who will talk and who will listen mark some of the play's tensest interactions, but they also point the way forward to the resolution of their differences. For it is not only speaking but also listening that effects the shift from blindness to vision and from hunger to plenitude.

Der yidisher kenig lir is set in the home of a wealthy Vilna merchant, Dovid Moysheles—the closest that Gordin can come to a modern Jewish king. But both traditional Jewish ambivalence toward monarchical power and Gordin's own anticapitalist values confer on the wealthy protagonist a less than sympathetic mien.[53] The challenge that kingly power presents to heavenly power and the wealth that is always, for Gordin, the coefficient of corruption are precursors to inevitable downfall. Yet Gordin's deviations from his textual models are immediately evident, and it is in this gap between model and improvisation that *Der yidisher kenig lir*'s claim to being both adapted and original lies.

At rise, Dovid Moysheles's wife, youngest daughter, and servant bustle about preparing the table for a festive Purim meal. The Jewish Lear's wife upsets the careful balances of Shakespeare's original and shifts the weight of the plot away from the English play's tragic denouement. Joel Berkowitz and Leonard Prager have noted that the Purim setting further underlines the Yiddish play's potential for reversals, which are closely associated with this holiday and the narrative trajectory of the Book of Esther that is its basis.[54]

Veering from slapstick to threats of genocide, Esther chronicles the rise of a Jewish orphan to the royal palace of Persia, where as queen she intercedes to prevent her people's annihilation. The massacre planned by the king's minister Haman fails, and Haman himself is hanged on a gallows of his own making. Marked in Western and Eastern Europe with the *purimshpil*, parodic inversions and theatrical performance became synonymous with the holiday. With its yearly reenactment of the fall of the mighty and the elevation of the humble, Purim's cyclical nature hints at both the downfall of Dovid Moysheles and his restoration.

The audience's first glimpse of the patriarch is through the nervous preparations made for his arrival. The youngest of the three daughters, Taybele, begs an invitation to the celebration for her tutor, the *maskil* Yaffe. Khane-Leye, Taybele's mother, gives nervous assent, as the modern "German" opinions of the pompous Yaffe run the risk of angering the temperamental, traditional patriarch.

Yaffe expresses Gordin's cherished views on education, his rejection of religious "fanaticism," and the utility of the natural sciences. The others call him *der daytsh*, as he is a modern Germanized Jew, who speaks a Germanized Yiddish that marks him as a linguistic as well as a spiritual alien among his more traditional employers. Yet for Yiddish theatregoers long accustomed to this elevated dialect of the Yiddish stage, Yaffe's *daytshmerish* formulations might lend him a certain noblesse, one that tempered his portentous pronouncements when spoken in the cadences of the old Yiddish theatre. It is vouchsafed to Yaffe to explain the salutary aspects of the eternal return of Purim:

> *Yaffe*: *Guten Abend!* Ah, you are still celebrating Haman's downfall—it serves him right. He saw what happened the previous Purim, what a bad end he made of it, but he paid no heed and once again came after the little Jew—and once again the Jews have hanged him, long live the old story [*geshikhte*] with its hamantaschen and noisemakers![55]

Here "repetition" has several meanings and implications. Repetition proceeds from a failure to learn; Haman is doomed to repeat his attacks and be repulsed and hanged year after year. Repetition is at the heart of Jewish custom, which ritually transforms threats to Jewish survival into party food, a literal consuming of the enemy that neutralizes his threat. That threat is further transformed in the *purimshpil*, theatre that brings Jewish history—and the story itself—to life. Repetition is the basis of theatrical reification, from which the *purimshpil* crafts a narrative of survival and triumph, a yearly return of victory.

The necessity of avoiding the mistakes of Haman is explicit in Yaffe's enjoining the family to think less of the "old *megile*" (the Book of Esther) and "more of something new" (4). Repetition, as in the case of Gordin's own adaptive method, must include difference, must incorporate modern variation in order to ensure its renewal. This echo of Gordin's Spiritual-Biblical Brotherhood's call, too, to base Jewish worship on traditional texts, interpreted and adhered to in "the spirit of the times," finds querulous expression in the doctrinal divisions represented in the household of Dovid Moysheles.

The eldest daughter, Etele, has wed Harif—he is a *misnaged*, or adherent of traditional Orthodox Judaism, noted for its fierce antagonism of the charismatic, mystical Hasidic movement. Etele and Harif are forever at the throats of the middle daughter, Gitele, and her husband, Moyshe, a habitually intoxicated Hasid given to kabbalistic mutterings and reflexive reiteration of his rebbe's sayings. Along with Yaffe the maskilic interloper, Gordin has assembled the leading movements in Eastern European Judaism and grouped them round the table as quarrelsome brothers and sisters, whose animosities are barely checked by the Tito-like powers of the mighty Dovid Moysheles. The patriarch's arrival prompts anxious calls for "quiet!" (6).

Gordin's Lear, like Shakespeare's, demonstrates his power through verbal control: he calls for speech, for silence; he summons choruses of unanimous assent and performances of songs, even from the reluctant Yaffe. But it is only Taybele's silence that commands Dovid Moysheles's attention. When she rejects her expensive Purim gift, the wounded patriarch accuses Yaffe of putting words into her mouth. Yaffe in turn balks at the idea that he has been force-fed maskilic ideas that are not his own, protesting, "Even in your own home I will not permit you to dictate what I must and must not say!" (12).

The characters' apprehensions about repeating the words of others, of being forced to express views contrary to their own, reflect the Yiddish play's own potentially uneasy borrowing of non-Jewish texts for its plot. The source texts—Shakespeare's and Turgenev's—provide a structure, but also imply a predetermined outcome, of which Gordin's most articulate characters are very aware. But if the borrowed plot imposes its own order, the happy ending to Gordin's Lear play argues that it is not an order that is impervious to revision. Repetition need not doom one, like Haman, to making the mistakes of the past. Gordin's play itself represents the "new word" that ensures its survival through incorporation of the old texts of Shakespeare and Turgenev, but with a modern, Jewish difference. Cognizance of the plots that structure the world of *Der yidisher kenig lir* is the means of liberation from it.

As Joel Berkowitz notes, "It is Dovid's recognition of the characteristics he shares with Shakespeare's King Lear—a parallel repeatedly pointed out to him by the *maskil* Yaffe—that makes him see that his older daughters were false and the youngest one true."[56] Armed with knowledge of the master plot, Gordin's characters can alter their own. Borrowed plots become not a cause for repeating the mistakes of one's literary progenitors but a means of release from them. Through repetition—of history and stories (which are one and the same, *geshikhte*, in Gordin's play)—the enlightened individual can revise and rewrite existing narratives. This internal recognition of the master plot is what distinguishes Gordin's play from other treatments of the Shakespeare tragedy, such as Nahum Tate's *King Lear*. Tate's characters do not know that they are in a Shakespeare adaptation, but thanks to Yaffe, Gordin's do.

The theatre itself, an art of repetition that simulates spontaneity and puts words in mouths, is the means of shifting from ignorance to recognition. Gordin is at pains, too, to emphasize that it is the Jewishness of this rewriting of Shakespeare and Turgenev that enables the tragic plot to resolve happily. Setting the play at Purim, the nexus of the Jewish and the theatrical, underlines the way in which the theatre, like Dovid Moysheles, licenses particular varieties of speech and performance, makes of repetition a creative strength rather than a weakness, and can act as a force of enlightenment and renewal.[57] Yiddish theatre that assimilates non-Jewish models and learns from them becomes the means of eluding the mistakes of its progenitors.

At the Purim meal, Dovid distributes his estate among his daughters so that he may leave for Palestine to devote the rest of his life to study of sacred Jewish texts. For Gordin, return to the Jewish homeland is unalloyed folly that is compounded by Dovid Moysheles's decision to retreat further into religious study. In Gordin's world, the Talmudic word has always exerted a tyrannical hold on modern Jewish life, and devotion to it and return to Palestine are an abandonment of the lives Jews have struggled to make in the Diaspora, a renunciation of Jewish belonging to a world shared with gentiles, a world of which *King Lear* is itself a part.

Khane-Leye is alarmed at the prospect of having nothing to live on but their children's remittances. Taybele, upset at her parents' departure and her own committal to the care of Harif, speaks her mind:

> I know, father, that you're going to be very angry with me again, but I must tell you the truth—I do not like your plan at all. What is there in it for me to like? What can there be in it to make me happy? That

you're leaving us?! Or that you're handing me over to that hypocrite, Avrom Harif? Papa! Don't permit yourself this happiness. Listen to me, don't do it! I beg you! (15)[58]

Taybele's plea ends with her asking Dovid Moysheles's blessing for her plan to study medicine in St. Petersburg with Yaffe. Predictably, the patriarch is infuriated; he had expected to hear "sweet words of gratitude" and a blessing for his journey, but now she is stealing his thunder. As Taybele is cast out, Yaffe, trailing like faithful France in her wake, pauses to ask the patriarch if he knows of a play called *King Lear* by the "world-famous writer Shakespeare" (16). Yaffe draws parallels between Dovid Moysheles's treatment of Taybele and Lear's of Cordelia and notes, "May God protect you from the end King Lear meets" (16). The act ends with Dovid Moysheles's calling for more songs and merriment from the now rather glum party around the table.

The second act restates the theme of reversals by opening with a parodic inversion of the previous act, as a haggard servant, Shammai (called Trytel in the manuscript)—Dovid Moysheles's own comic double—pleads for silence from a disobedient child. He, Dovid, and Khane-Leye have returned from the Holy Land to the house that now belongs to Etele and Harif. Food is scarce and filial respect even scarcer, and act 1's festive party table has given way to a locked larder guarded by Etele. Also reversing his early injunctions, Dovid Moysheles cries, "No, no, do not be silent! Remind me every minute of what I have done!" (20).

The entrance of Taybele, shortly to depart for medical school, is met by Dovid's stony silence and refusal to even look her in the eye. Eventually, he reproaches Taybele for betraying the Jewish people by her rejection of the traditional role of a Jewish wife. Yaffe notes that still he plays the part of King Lear, a power he tries to exercise by demanding silence of the quarreling Harif and Yaffe:

> Dovid Moysheles: I will tell you who is the master of the house . . . I have seen what goes on in this house and I have been silent, I have not interfered. I have seen how you robbed and stole from my children and me, and I have been silent. I have seen how within three months of my leaving for Eretz Israel you stopped sending money, and I have been silent. Do you think that I am a broken clay pot that you can trample underfoot? Thief! Hypocrite! Do you want to know who the master of the house is? I am! Dovid Moysheles! Stand on your feet when I'm talking to you! Give me the key to the cupboards and larder and cash box, give me the key! (27)[59]

Dovid Moysheles's breaking his penitential vow of silence is spurred not just by hunger but by outrage at financial malfeasance. His money was once the metaphoric key that granted him power to command speech and silence, but his impoverishment, commensurate with his malnourishment, now extends also to his verbal powers. His rebellion is short-lived.

Dovid Moysheles's initially puzzling refusal to retract what he bestowed on his children is preserved as the last evidence of his dwindling powers of speech. He declares that his word is all, dearer to him than the estate itself. He would rather suffer than retract that word, which must take the place of nourishment itself. As in the case of Turgenev's Kharlov, the imaginative hold that this "word" has is such that the legal document ensuring its enforcement is an afterthought. Like Kharlov, Dovid Moysheles points out to Harif: "Russian law allows anyone to take back what they have given away! Do you know this?" (27). When at another crisis point Yaffe pleads with him to call in the police to settle matters, Dovid Moysheles again refuses (38).

Dovid Moysheles's thrall to his own spoken word is exacerbated in the play's second half by his blindness from cataracts, which forces the patriarch to make a crucial shift from seeing to hearing, as his knowledge of the world is reduced to physical sensation and vocal language. His limited vision forces him to look to his "own inner world," because, as he states, "the world outside has vanished for me forever" (33). Echoing the mad Lear's counsel to the blind Gloucester—"A man may see how this world goes with no eyes. Look with thine ears" (IV.vi.146–47)—the shift to hearing forces Dovid Moysheles to listen not simply to what is said but to how it is said.

Hearing forces Dovid Moysheles to reevaluate language unbiased by appearances in a crucial scene in act 3, when Taybele, who has had no contact with her parents for five years, returns with her medical degree. She hides herself in order to listen to and to watch the exchanges between Shammai and the blind Dovid Moysheles. She hears that he misses and loves her, but when she reveals her presence, he grows alarmed: "Taybele! You were there the whole time, you heard what I said? You heard everything?" (33). Angry, Dovid Moysheles recants in a desperate attempt to assert his authority over a performance he cannot control, because he cannot see his audience and gauge his own words accordingly.

Act 3 ends with a nightmarish scene of Moyshe the Hasid's drunken brethren mocking and manhandling the blind old man, who decides, with Shammai, to try his luck with strangers. "Yaffe the teacher calls me the Jewish King Lear. Ha ha! Honor to the king! Make way for the king! Long live the new, blind beggar! Alms for the Jewish King Lear! Alms for the poor! Alms! Alms!" (39).

Act 4, like the Book of Esther, ends where it began, with a feast: the curtain rises on a prosperous interior, a table laden with food, and Khane-Leye announcing again that "all is in the best order" (39). But there are differences: the home belongs to the newlyweds, Taybele and Yaffe, who come by their money not through commerce but through their medical practice. While Etele and Harif continue in their nefarious ways, Gitele and Moyshe are reconciled with Taybele and Yaffe, who pursue legal means of wresting the contested estate from Harif. The law, indeed, is the only thing that truly frightens Harif and Etele—but it is the *zakon,* the *gezetst,* the *gerikht*—the rule of tsar and state, not God, that ensures their surrender (29, 41-42, 46-47).

A storm rages outside and Dovid Moysheles, as in act 1, is as yet absent. His return is signaled by Taybele's thanking her guests for a wedding song and sighing, "I don't know why, but your song reminded me of my childhood and my good father. The memory is sad, but very sweet" (43). The sudden reappearance of Dovid Moysheles and Shammai, announced that very moment by a knock on the window, looks at first like dramatic ineptitude on Gordin's part. But in a world that invests speaking with the force of law, with sustenance, with power and wealth itself, that language should have magical summoning abilities is not out of keeping with the play's general preference for performative speech. To speak of Dovid Moysheles *is* to summon him back from the wintry streets of Vilna.

After an emotional reunion, at which Shammai assures Taybele that all during his wanderings with Dovid Moysheles, her name "never left his pure lips" (44), the patriarch begs Taybele to "let an old, blind beggar die near you. Let me hear the sweet voice of my child, let me hear the steps of my child's little feet" (45). Dovid Moysheles pleads with God to open his eyes so that he might see his child for one minute, which summons Yaffe to his side. The doctor announces that a simple operation on the old man's cataracts will restore his sight, but, in fact, it has already been symbolically restored by his expressions of love and forgiveness. As Dovid Moysheles is led offstage for his operation, Etele and Harif run in with the letter that Yaffe has written to the procurator, detailing their withholding of the estate. Only their fear of arrest prompts a reconciliation with the family and a promise to return the money that they have withheld. But the patriarch declines:

> Have no fear, I will cause no one harm, and that which I once gave
> to you will be returned once more to you. I am already old, and sick,
> and weak. I cannot speak for long, but one thing I will say: be satis-
> fied with what you have, do not strive to seize the whole world in
> your hands . . . Be pious, be good and heed the lesson of my example,
> of Dovid Moysheles, or as Yaffe calls me, the Jewish King Lear. (47)[60]

Dovid Moysheles's speech reiterates the possibility of happy escape
from sorrowful repetition; it acknowledges the reality of his present
state, a recognition that returns to him the powers of the word. He
does not demand his audience's silence, or claim the sole power of
speaking, because he "cannot speak for long." He urges moderation
and the lessons of literature, amid visual reassurances of prosperity,
familial unity, and reconciliation. The written word in Gordin is the
peacemaker; it is the rule of law that forces Etele and Harif to repent
their evil, whether or not their confession is sincere. Capitalizing on
traditional Jewish reverence for the text, Gordin shifts that accustomed awe to a different source, the demonstrable power of the rule
of secular law. But though the written law acts as *Der yidisher kenig
lir*'s deus ex machina, it is channeled through the spoken word of performance, a medium that cannot but acknowledge the essential balance of the written and the spoken in the theatre.

Yiddish theatre lore holds that Jewish immigrant audiences had
little conception that plays were performed from written texts and
not invented by actors themselves. While Gordin's play itself might
appear to disappear from view, seeming to be the spontaneous outpourings of its actors—which is, after all, the goal of modern theatre—he carefully foregrounds Shakespeare's text. It rarely fades
from notice, thanks to the constant reminders of its prophetic powers voiced by Yaffe and Dovid Moysheles. It is *Stepnoi korol' Lir*
that retreats to the background, to be recovered only through recourse to the written text. The eternal irony of the theatre, that it
is only half finished as text and yet only the text remains, applies
with special force to Gordin's works, whose greatest successes, as
Zalmen Zylbercweig observed, were themselves always in adapted
works, not in original ones.[61] Gordin's works link themselves forever with their source texts, fading as they fade, enduring as they
endure. Dovid Moysheles's fealty to the "word" is really Gordin's
own, as the writer indentures himself to another's work and is liber-
ated only by reading, only by the text that remains as proof of the
debt owed.

Public and critical response to *Der yidisher kenig lir* validated Gordin's working method and lent strength and luster to further efforts by Yiddish writers and actors to adapt Shakespeare for the Yiddish stage. Gordin himself would write one more *Lear* play six years later, when *Di yidishe kenigin lir, oder Mirele efros* (The Jewish Queen Lear, or Mirele Efros) had its premiere in 1898. Turgenev, too, would have another outing on the Yiddish stage in Gordin's reworking of *Asya* (1858) in *Khasye di yesoyme*, staged in 1903.

But even after the premiere of the play that established his career as a Yiddish playwright, Gordin seems not to have entirely made his peace with his new occupation. He had not, apparently, given up an old dream cherished by the Spiritual-Biblical Brotherhood—that of establishing a Jewish agrarian commune in America. Gordin made a trip to the Woodbine Colony in New Jersey in 1893, to investigate the possibility of his settling there with some of his old friends from the Brotherhood. The plan came to naught, but Gordin's very interest in the colony, even as he established a successful career as a playwright, suggests a lingering longing to realize the agrarian dreams of his years in Russia.[62]

That same year Gordin also met the famed Russian populist and writer Vladimir Korolenko (1853–1921), who was on his way to the World's Columbian Exposition in Chicago. Gordin recounted their meeting in a revealing lecture in 1897 to the Society of Russian Students.[63] Approaching Korolenko and presenting himself as a politically engaged Russian émigré writer, Gordin seems to have gone on at some length about "our Russian people," "our zemstvo," and "our Ministry for Public Education." Korolenko listened patiently and expressed some surprise at Gordin's continuing preoccupation with the Russian people. When he asked what Gordin was doing now in America, the latter sheepishly admitted to being "merely" the author of Jewish dramas. Korolenko asked, "Are the Jews who visit your theatre not a people? Is not your serving them, advancing their interests, helping them, enlightening them, the very same great and holy mission that you pursued in Russia, but were unable to accomplish?" As Gordin tells it, on hearing Korolenko's words he grew "somewhat ashamed" of his inability to see the Jews as a people in their own right, and he confessed to finding it "even painful" to recall this encounter now.

And yet recall it Gordin did, before a Russian-speaking audience composed of Russian Jews like himself. This capsule version of the wayward Jewish intellectual's awakening and "return" to the Jewish fold, fleshed out with stirring remarks about the utility of the theatre as a weapon of enlightenment, puts an impeccable political imprimatur on an undertaking that was in truth largely aesthetic. Gordin would maintain this posture—with some notable lapses—until his death. His plays usually passed muster with the guardians of political culture in the left-wing Yiddish press, ensuring the support of the influential arbiters of secular Jewish culture, while the plays themselves enacted a more lasting and far-reaching artistic revolution on the stage itself.

As the years passed, Gordin's status as the most prestigious Yiddish playwright in New York solidified, despite the fierce opposition of more conservative elements in the immigrant community. In his adaptations of Ibsen (*Nora, oder Nes bitokh nes* [Nora, or Miracle upon Miracle, 1895]; *Der folks faynt* [Enemy of the People, 1896]), Schiller (*Reyzele, oder Zelig itsik der klezmer* [Reyzele, or Zelik Itsik the Musician, 1897]), Goethe (*Got, mentsh, un tayvl* [*God, Man, and Devil*, 1900), and Hauptmann (*Di shvue* [The Oath, 1900]), he would continue to advance the cause of non-Jewish art. Gordin's forays into topical political subjects were always much less successful, and works like *Der rusisher yid in amerika* (The Russian Jew in America, 1895), famous for impugning labor officials, were not long in the repertoire. Neither did Gordin's attempts at historical subjects, like *Galilei, der martirer fun visnshaft* (Galileo, Martyr for Science, 1895) or *Der mamzer, oder Lucretsia bordshia* (The Bastard, or Lucrezia Borgia, 1901) bear fruit. Many plays had only a few performances, and their texts are no longer extant. Works that did endure were adapted from first-rate writers, especially those of Russian writers.

Gordin's adaptive process and his choice of source texts and subject matter were a way of recovering a distant Russia that could not be reached by any means other than through her texts. Gordin presents European and especially Russian literature as vital and necessary to his Jewish audiences, but the larger idea that his plays advance—that literature is a model for a life that can be comprehended and rewritten according to one's own desire and needs—is one that chimes with a particularly American mythology of immigration as redemption and renewal and with a Jewish faith in the inevitability of deliverance that follows flight from oppression. It might even be said that in setting out to valorize the values and culture of the old world, Gordin ended by validating the foundational narratives of the new.

CHAPTER TWO

In the Old Country

The Reformer

A man stands aboard a ship bound for New York, gazing at the wintry, gray Atlantic. Sea winds whip the blackening clouds; waves crash against the hull of the old steamer and flood its decks with sheets of icy water. But the man grips the railings, eyes fixed on the horizon. The persecution he has suffered, the silencing he has endured, the sacrifices he has made for his ideals will not have been in vain. His eyes are alight with hope for the possibilities that await him on the other side of the sea, far from his Russian homeland.

This man is not Jacob Gordin. But he would like you to think that he is.

The hero of "Der shvimender orn" (The Floating Casket) is a Russian Jew bound for New York on the steamship *Devonia*.[1] But there the similarities end. This literary creation of Gordin's has devoted his life to the cause of Russian revolution; he has suffered exile, hard labor, censorship, and the distrust of both his own people and those whose liberation he serves. His health broken but his spirit unbowed, Gordin's hero sets off for America, but he dies en route.

This story appeared in 1892 in the inaugural issue of *Di tsukunft* (The Future) as "Di shvimende trune (a fantazye)" (The Floating Coffin [A Fantasy]).[2] Despite the parenthetical title, the tale draws deliberate parallels between the life of its hero and that of Yakov Gordin—a Russian writer with rumored revolutionary connections, lately become Jacob Gordin—a Yiddish writer with rumored revolutionary connections. The story is one of the earliest articulations of Gordin's fictive biography, and while it veers widely from the historical record, in one respect the tale remains true to the circumstances of the writer's leaving his homeland. The passage from Russia, a journey across water that is rich with mythic connotations of transformation and rebirth, did mark the death of one Jacob Gordin and the birth of another.

Who was Yakov Gordin before he became Jacob Gordin? The latter's elision of the former was so successful that the specifics of his life and work in Russia have largely eluded three biographers. Soviet-era restrictions on Jewish research prevented clarification for much of the twentieth century, but the mystery of the first thirty-eight years of Gordin's life also reflects his own efforts to shape his Russian past into both a story of origins and a blueprint for the future. That future, as a radical intellectual and reformer of the Yiddish theatre, derived its authority in part from the reputation Gordin had earned as an activist and writer in his native Russia. Yet accounts of this career are both strikingly uniform and surprisingly sketchy and offer little beyond the naming of a few newspapers and some dark mutterings about Russian censorship.

Before he became the Yiddish theatre's most vocal and prolific advocate, critic, and author, Gordin was a Russian writer and religious reformer, the author of fiery jeremiads against his fellow Russian Jews, and a public figure who was regularly accused of being a Christian convert. Gordin's notice as a reformer of the Yiddish theatre and the controversy he stirred as a result represented a continuation of a program and pattern of behavior begun long before he arrived in New York.

Yet Gordin rarely offered specifics regarding his work as a religious reformer and on occasion circulated outright falsehoods about it. Because so much existing Yiddish scholarship is predicated on Gordin's own highly suspect report of events, this chapter separates historical facts from Gordin's historical fictions. Prerevolutionary Russian accounts of the Spiritual-Biblical Brotherhood and recent English-language scholarship are compared with contemporary accounts of Gordin's activities, his own statements in the press, and reports from a large dossier compiled on the sect by the tsarist secret police. The account offered here of Gordin's early years as a "reformer" suggests that between his public and creative work in Russia and New York there were more continuities than breaks and that the shift from "Yakov Gordin" to "Jacob Gordin" was only one of many transformations in his creative life.

THE ERA OF THE GREAT REFORMS

Gordin came of age in the Reform Era, a period of political and social change that was of a rapidity and sweep almost without precedent in modern Russian history. In just under thirty years, serfdom was abolished, judicial reform established legal rights for all imperial subjects, and limited forms of popular, local government (the zemstvo) were instituted. Higher education was made more accessible to women and ethnic minorities, and censorship was relaxed to enable a measure of public debate on politics and the state. And a growing political subculture gave rise to an anti-tsarist movement that turned to terrorism in the 1870s and 1880s, with cataclysmic results.

The Russian empire's Jewish subjects contended both with these changes from without and with other turbulent forces from within; adherents of the Haskalah, or Jewish Enlightenment, argued for a modernized Judaism and greater participation by Jews in the political and cultural life of their homelands. While less far-reaching in its effects on the broader Jewish populace in Eastern Europe than it had been in Western Europe, the Haskalah was critical in animating the modernizing efforts of the emerging Russian-Jewish intelligentsia. The development of a sophisticated Yiddish literature and nascent professional dramatic theatre, the revival of Hebrew as a vernacular and modern literary language, and the rise of a secular Jewish culture in the Russian language and of a Jewish press were all, in some measure, products of the Jewish Enlightenment.

The majority of Orthodox and Hasidic Jews, however, remained distant from these modernizing currents. Hemmed in economically and socially, the putative isolation and backwardness of Jewish communities in the Russian empire convinced both liberal Jews and the tsarist government of the need for change.[3] Yet they differed strongly as to how reforms should be undertaken and why.

THE JEWISH QUESTION

Russia's annexation of former Polish territories made the empire home to half a million Jews by the end of the eighteenth century.[4] It is estimated that by 1881 they numbered 2,835,000.[5] For a state that measured its subjects' loyalty in terms of their ethnic and religious congruence with that of the Russian Orthodox tsar himself, Poland's Jews presented unique problems and provoked special anxieties.

The Russian government's policies toward its Jewish subjects os-
cillated between conciliation and repulsion, but both tendencies were
motivated by a perception that Jews constituted a threat to Christians. Medieval ideas of Jews as "Christ killers" and seekers of Christian blood for imaginary Jewish rituals (the blood libel) had shifted to a fear of Jews as economic exploiters. The new paranoia took
its cues from Jews' traditional concentration in finance and service
economies, giving rise to a belief that Jewish moneylenders charged
ruinous interest rates, that Jewish tavern-keepers facilitated peasant
alcoholism, and that Jewish merchants cheated their illiterate peasant customers. The alleged source of this Jewish malevolence was the
Talmud, the vast body of rabbinic exegesis whose rulings became the
basis for Jewish religious law. Reportedly, the Talmud enjoined Jews
to feel no solidarity with their non-Jewish neighbors, who could be
exploited with impunity. Because of the centrality of the Talmud to
Jewish life, worship, and education, its alleged bias was perpetuated
through the generations. Repudiation of the Talmud was essential, in
the view of the Russian state, to Jews' becoming trustworthy members of Russian society, and no civil liberties could be extended before
Jews foreswore it. In the meantime, the Russian government reasoned
that Jewish menace could be contained by confining them to designated areas of the Pale of Settlement, thus limiting Jews' economic
and geographic mobility.

Under Alexander I (r. 1801–25) and Alexander II (r. 1855–81), leg-
islation was passed that sought to assimilate Jews into Russian society
through education and rural settlement.[6] A Russian education, it was
reasoned, would encourage Jewish participation in secular culture
and society and loyalty to the tsar who had furnished that education.
Rural resettlement of town-dwelling Jews would defuse tensions by
thinning populations in volatile areas, provide settlers for newly an-
nexed Russian territories in the south, and turn Jews away from professions as merchants and tavern owners. None of the tsars, however,
dissolved the Pale of Settlement or provided consistent application of
their assimilationist and resettlement policies.

Russian-Jewish leaders and intellectuals themselves acknowledged
that Jewish concentration in a very small number of professions was
neither desirable nor sustainable. They argued that discriminato-
ry laws that limited professional and educational opportunities for
Jews were largely to blame for the poor state of Christian-Jewish relations. While there was nothing innate to Judaism that predisposed it

to condone economic exploitation, *maskilim* themselves could not defend Talmudic study because it came at the expense of secular learning—which itself was thought to thwart the retreat of the masses into "superstition" and "fanaticism." Integration could be facilitated by greater access to secular education, but also through religious reform that shifted focus to Judaism's rational and philosophical traditions, rather than to its ritual observance. *Maskilim* also promoted a return to the land and to what they felt was the inherent dignity and utility of agrarian labor, which could also combat accusations that Jews were only suited for "parasitic" professions.[7]

The problem was how to introduce these reforms, which were designed to emancipate the Jewish community from within, when the Russian state itself resisted emancipation of its Jews from without. The state argued that emancipation could not be initiated from above before the Jews themselves had shown a willingness to abandon their much-discussed exploitative professions, fanaticism, and isolation. And so the debate raged: where did the solution to the Jewish Question lie? Was emancipation contingent on reform of Jewish economic life or religious life, or both? How were they connected? Did Christian hostility stem from Jewish "exploitation," or was Jewish "exploitation" a result of Christian hostility? What was essential to Jewish faith and tradition, and what could be jettisoned in the drive to modernity and its beguiling promises of liberation and equality?

Jacob Gordin was sure he had the answers.

THE SPIRITUAL-BIBLICAL BROTHERHOOD (DUKHOVNO-BIBLEISKOE BRATSTVO)

The goal of Gordin's Spiritual-Biblical Brotherhood, according to one of its earliest admirers, Venyamin Portugalov (1835–96), was nothing less than "moral perfection."[8] The Brotherhood professed an Enlightenment reverence for reason, brotherhood, and a desire to involve Jews in the culture of its host nations. Yet almost from its earliest days the group earned the sustained and virulent ire of the public and the liberal Russian-Jewish press. Far from finding supporters among the editors and opinion makers of *Russkii evrei* (The Russian Jew), *Razsvet* (The Dawn), and *Voskhod* (The Rising), the Brotherhood was the object of their unrelenting criticism.

Was this because the Brotherhood had found support at the opposite end of the political spectrum, in the Russian state? Not exactly; within six months of its establishment in the spring of 1881, the Brotherhood was under police surveillance.[9] Even after obtaining official government recognition in 1885, the group remained under observation by tsarist spies. Six years later, in September of 1891, the tsarist state would shut the Brotherhood down and continue to keep watch over Gordin in New York, to make certain that he did not return to Russia.[10]

Neither could it be said that the Brotherhood enjoyed popular support. Among the Jews of Elisavetgrad, Gordin's group was so widely disliked that in June of 1884 a long-simmering discontent with their sectarian proselytizing boiled over. The Brotherhood's meetinghouse was besieged for six hours by a five hundred–strong Jewish mob that roared, threw rocks, and tried to break into the building.[11] For several months afterward the Brotherhood's meetings were conducted under police guard.[12]

Nor did controversies in connection with the Spiritual-Biblical Brotherhood cease with Gordin's emigration. The Russian-born rabbi and popular East Side lecturer Zvi Masliansky (1856–1943) called the group a "plague" and referred to them in his memoirs as a "new Christian sect," a rumor that was echoed in the conservative New York press.[13]

How did a group devoted to Jewish spiritual and social renewal, egalitarian communal life, and healthy agrarian labor arouse such furious opposition from every corner? The opposition that the group engendered had little to do with their program of reform and a lot to do with Gordin himself, whose actions both raised the Brotherhood's public profile and invited widespread opprobrium. As Gordin was the organization's founder and galvanizing force, the Brotherhood's views are principally his. Moreover, the Spiritual-Biblical Brotherhood was not just Gordin's public declaration of his plan for the reform of Jewish life and faith; it was his model of the ideal community and spiritual life. Long after Gordin left Russia, its values and methods continued to exert a profound influence on his writing, and for that reason they bear closer examination.

THE SPIRITUAL-BIBLICAL BROTHERHOOD CREED

The Brotherhood's earliest articulation of its tenets appeared in an 1881 article in *Odesskii vestnik*. The article is cited verbatim by Yakov Priluker (1860–1935), the founder of New Israel (Novyi Izrail'), a religious reform movement inspired by the Brotherhood.[14] Priluker's pamphlet suggests that the Brotherhood first appeared early in 1881 but that it attracted no notice whatsoever, a judgment confirmed by the complete absence of evidence for its existence until March of 1881.[15]

The article begins by noting the Brotherhood's dissatisfaction with "Jewish fanaticism" (*evreiskii fanatizm*), a maskilic characterization of pious Jews that had become part of the tsarist government's own vocabulary. Fanaticism was the alleged source of Jewish insularity, alienation, and perceived superiority, and it provided justification for exploitation of non-Jews. But the author of the *Odesskii vestnik* article (i.e., Gordin) announces that the most debilitating effect of fanaticism is on religion itself.

The writer defines religion as conscience, justice, and truth and argues that all of the great religions—Buddhism, Judaism, Christianity, and Islam—insist on the primacy of deeds and conscientious conduct. None, he claims, has specific directions for the ritual observance of its teachings, but because ritual is easier to perform and regulate, ruling castes and priesthoods promote ritual observance. Organized religion substitutes the mechanical worship of a higher being for the more difficult striving for a higher truth. Instead of "serving good," religion devolves into merely "serving God," when in fact "these are two separate concepts."[16]

This misguided conflation of religion, God, and ritual gives rise to an entire school of philosophical thought that prefers rarefied debate to the true, real-world bases of religion. Under sophistic Talmudic influence, Jews have come to see the essence of their faith and its only duties in the performance of daily rituals. The Brotherhood feels otherwise:

We think that God is the sum of the highest reason, the purest truth, and the holiest justice, and demands of us no external or unnecessary forms and rituals. In the same way, it cannot be pleasing to Him if our prayers are written in a language that is incomprehensible to the majority. We firmly believe that one can be a useful and honest person even without formulaic prayers. If it suits one to pray, to confess before one's own conscience, to pour out accumulated grief before one's soul, then one may do this according to one's own inspiration, and, moreover, in a language one understands, because prayer like this is natural, and, it follows, useful.[17]

The Brotherhood rejects what is not useful and in accordance with

reason and the "spirit of the times": traditional Jewish dress is an unnecessary marker of difference, and dietary laws are wasteful superstition. Work that is not useful is exploitative, and the Brotherhood calls
on all Jews to elevate their physical, mental, and moral level through
physical labor, particularly of the agrarian variety. Once Jews have
proven their willingness to work, no nation will scorn them, and Jews
will take their place as equals among their neighbors.

There is little that is new in the article's bland recitation of the
standard diagnostic criteria of the Jewish "problem" or in their prescriptions for its cure: reason, brotherhood, economic and religious
reform, agrarian labor. There is little to offend die-hard *maskilim*,
Christians, or the government, and that may explain the Brotherhood's failing to attract the attention of any one of these. Only one
aspect of the Brotherhood's program—its humanist theology—stands
out as in any way different from other proposals for Jewish reform.

By declaring that "God" and "good" are two separate entities, the
Brotherhood focuses entirely on human action, creativity, and potential.[18] Like religious humanist movements such as the early Unitar-
ians, who regarded "God" as a paternalistic concept that encouraged
passivity, the Brotherhood's eschewing a supernatural divinity is emphasized in the remarks with which the article concludes, "We are
all children of one great family and our mother earth."[19] Though the
Brotherhood does invoke a divine figure when referring to prayer that
"cannot be pleasing to Him" if in a language incomprehensible to the
one who utters it, the focus of the discussion remains less on a divine
object of prayer than on the utility of prayer itself. Prayer has cathartic powers; no mention is made of communion with or intercession of
the divine. Religion remains "the sum of all that is good and elevated
in mankind."[20]

The Spiritual-Biblical Brotherhood's classically maskilic emphasis
on utility, and its hostility to isolationism and superstition, retains
only the barest connection with traditional Jewish religious observance. It is not even clear from this article that it has a Judaic basis for
its creed. The Brotherhood would clarify its status as a Jewish organization in later press announcements, but despite regular restatements
of its core Judaic principles, its status as a purely Jewish organization
was always in some doubt.

After the pogroms of 1881, the liberal Jewish press accused the
Brotherhood of couching its program in religious terms solely to
win privileges for the group from the government. Comparisons of

the Brotherhood to the separatist Karaites were rife.[21] Years later, Gordin's perpetual antagonist Moyshe Leib Lilienblum (1843–1910) would deny that Gordin had any real interest in religion at all, arguing, "To the authorities and the Russian press he presented himself as a reformer, and to the Jews he presented himself as a socialist, or a Tolstoyan."[22] Gordin's old friend, colleague at the Educational League, and anarchist journalist Hillel Zolotarov (1865-1921) defended this strategy, alleging that Gordin could not openly promote the Brotherhood's main cause, which was socialism.[23] Years later, in the United States, Gordin himself went so far as to claim that the sect was a front for subversive activities and even denied being its founder, a claim that is patently untrue.[24]

Years of debate on the Brotherhood have failed to establish whether it was indeed a religious organization or whether its spirituality was merely a cover for its social (or socialist) activities. But neither function is contradicted by the view advanced in the *Odesskii vestnik* article, in which religious reform is not separate from social reform but a fundamental element of it. Whereas debate in Russian-Jewish intellectual circles and in the tsarist government tended to distinguish between religious and economic reform as related, but not identical, problems, Gordin's Brotherhood saw no difference between them. If the purpose of rational, humanistic religion is to institute justice on earth, then religion and social action cannot but be essential components of each other.

The religious humanism of the Brotherhood sheds light on a puzzling aspect of Gordin's career in New York, when his pugnacious secularism, his sympathy for atheist socialism, and his plays' hostility to any but the poorest of the pious stood in strange contrast to his history of religious activism. The Brotherhood's rejection of a divine figure suggests that Gordin's resistance to conventional religious piety was less an expression of distaste for Judaism per se than a general impatience with theism of any stripe. The Spiritual-Biblical Brotherhood rejected a supernatural God, supplanting a divine figure with a positivist, materialist, and rational description of the world; reason was Gordin's faith and conflicted neither with his maskilic social sympathies nor with his spiritual convictions.

But as *Razsvet* itself would note in Gordin's obituary many years later, "Preaching a religion without God, among a Jewish intelligentsia that was fundamentally secular and entirely indifferent to the soul's need for religion, could not but end in failure."[25] *Razsvet* had wondered even at the sect's founding in 1881 if the Brotherhood would have any success in inspiring the masses.[26] That it did not is suggested by Priluker's noting that "society truly paid no attention whatsoever to the revelations of the 'brotherhood,' and did not even make an effort to take interest in its teachings, successes, or the number of its followers."[27]

One of the few discussions of the Brotherhood that was reported in the Jewish press was by A. Firer, who filed a story from Elisavetgrad dated April 3, 1881, on remarks made by the founder of the Spiritual-Biblical Brotherhood. Gordin's thundering declaration has all the hallmarks of the writer-activist at his most adamantine, and its heightened rhetoric suggests a more concerted effort to attract public notice:

> The religious indifference of our Jewish intelligentsia, the Pharisaism and hypocrisy of our lowest social classes, the cynical expressions of atheism by the various rogues and ignoramuses who conceal their intellectual mediocrity and moral nakedness with European costumes and broken Russian, the excessive purism of the rabbinate, the blatant pseudo-prophesying of the tsadiks and the mass of religious ceremonialism should have called forth a religious movement of people seeking moral and religious renewal, people whose religious needs cannot be satisfied by the putrefying carcass of our rabbinical ritualism and its spirit of restrictive formalism. No![28]

Any potential interest in the Brotherhood that these articles may have generated was swiftly overtaken by much larger events. The Brotherhood's next appearance in the press would be very different, and it was not one that anyone would ignore.

THE POGROMS OF 1881

On March 1, 1881, the terrorist group Narodnaya Volya (People's Will) finally succeeded in their attempts to assassinate Tsar Alexander II. The murder in St. Petersburg sparked public unrest, but it was not until six weeks later that the worst violence occurred.

Rumors had been building for some time before Easter week of 1881 that actions would be taken against the Jews for their perceived role in the assassination.[29] The governor of Kherson *guberniya* (province), Aleksandr S. Erdeli, was sufficiently alarmed at the possibility of violence in Gordin's home city of Elisavetgrad that he ordered a heightened police presence on its streets. Mounted squadrons patrolled the city, and taverns, shops, and market stalls were closed in the interests of preventing interethnic clashes. Efforts at averting conflict proved so successful that after three days, the chief of police, I. P. Bogdanovich, allowed shops and taverns to reopen. And that is when the trouble began.

According to most reports, around four o'clock in the afternoon on April 15 a fight broke out in a Jewish-owned tavern. Some accounts involve a Russian patron's breaking a drinking glass, whereupon the Jewish innkeeper began hitting him.[30] Another report asserted that the innkeeper was aware that he was being goaded and that when he attempted to expel the provocateur, a cry went up that "ours" were being beaten; a fight soon broke out between the Jews and the Christians in the pub.[31] Police arrived, but the crowd dispersed outside and began breaking windows and looting Jewish shops and homes. The cavalry proved all but useless in subduing the crowds, which included many curious onlookers. The noise of breaking glass and the drifting feathers from torn quilts and pillows, which coated the streets like a strange snow, agitated the soldiers' horses to such a degree that they spent as much time calming the animals as they did discouraging the looters. Policemen, preoccupied with processing the initial group of looters, were not on the streets to prevent further abuses, and the violence escalated.

It continued on April 16 and 17, when the numbers of *pogromshchiki* (perpetrators of pogroms) were swelled by peasants who came into the city from the countryside. The violence abated in Elisavetgrad only on April 18, with the deployment of still more troops.[32] Violence continued in surrounding areas and extended to Jewish agricultural settlements outside the city. Pogroms broke out in Kiev and Kishinev and reached Odessa in May. By the end of the year, it is estimated that pogrom violence had occurred in more than two hundred towns and villages and had left some forty people dead, with many more raped, robbed, or wounded.[33]

The pogroms of 1881 are commonly regarded as a watershed event that forced many Jews into a fundamental reassessment of their prospects in Russia. The mob violence and its aftermath have been cited as the impetus for accelerated Jewish emigration, for the discrediting of liberal claims as to the possibility of Jewish emancipation in Russia, and for the rise of proto-Zionist and Jewish socialist organizations. For Jacob Gordin, however, the pogroms appeared only to confirm views that he already held—that Jewish suffering was a direct result of Jewish "exploitation" and that the former could not be alleviated without eliminating the latter. He said as much in an open letter to Russian Jewry that was published in early June in the Kharkov newspaper, *Yuzhnyi krai* (Southern Border). In the ensuing weeks, both the Jewish and the anti-Jewish press reprinted and commented upon Gordin's letter.

It is really only at this point that Gordin establishes a public persona, that of the combative leader of a crusading group of reformers, intent on the religious and social reconstruction of Russian Jewry. Though an ill-judged and poorly timed offensive, the fact remains that it was only this letter that catapulted Gordin and his fledgling movement into broad public notice, and he, at least, would scarcely ever leave it again for his remaining years in Russia.

The text of Gordin's letter is reproduced in its entirety here:

> Brother Jews!
>
> Each of us probably knows that in order to rid oneself of a hellishly painful toothache the most appropriate course of action is to pull the ailing tooth out by its roots. In order to deaden this harsh pain, doctors destroy the nerves . . .
>
> We Jews have a moral sickness that causes us more pain, torment, and suffering than the very worst physical ailments: our evil habits, which are deeply ingrained in our life.
>
> You have seen, my brothers, what kind of horrifying dramas have played out in recent days before your very eyes; how mercilessly and vilely they have mocked your property, and more importantly, your human dignity. You have seen how defenseless, isolated, helpless, and despised by all you are: no one took pity on you; no one extended a hand of friendship . . . Unfortunate brothers, do not think that I have the ill intention of rubbing salt in your wounds *only* in order to summon new agonies; do not think that this is not painful for me as well. Woe is me! I am pained for you, and because of you . . . Did not my heart bleed when I saw you—insulted, degraded, beaten, robbed, expelled from your homes? Could I remain calm when you, my brothers, blood of my blood and flesh of my flesh—were in boundless grief? But what happened has passed, and you, my brothers, should think about the future. Consider: why does no one respect you, or love you, or pity you. The lowest levels of Russian society wait only for an opportunity to fall upon you; the merchants would like to see you torn to pieces; and the aristocracy looks upon your fall with indifference. Why do these different segments of Russian society, which have no obvious common interests, hate you with such unanimity and like-mindedness? Can it really be only religious hatred? Our greed for money, our insatiability, cupidity, pursuit of profit, our importunacy, abrasiveness, our inordinate strutting and extravagance, our slavish and stupid imitation of the arrogant and unbridled Russian

gentry, our usury, tavern-keeping, middle-man dealings and all our other misdeeds cause the Russian people to take up arms against us; they rouse the envy of the merchants and the contempt of the ruling classes. Certainly, there are among you people who are honest, hard-working, and modest in their desires, but they are lost amid the mass of swindlers who day and night think of nothing but money and profit and have no other interests or needs in life.

The sad events of recent days give me the right to remind you, brothers, that now is the time to extract the rotten teeth with which you have bitten others, and which have again and again caused you unbearable pain and suffering. My dear brothers, your nerves, the nerves of your everyday affairs and occupations have been destroyed for a time; gather your courage and pull these rotten teeth—usury, bootlegging, middle-man dealings and all other exceedingly dishonest and immoral pursuits—from your mouth once and for all, and make of yourselves honest, industrious people, who live their lives in such a way as to render the least harm to others. Remember the words of our great singer of Psalms: "a man who is wealthy but not wise is like a beast that asks for forgiveness." I know that now you are in despair, bitter, pained; that you suffer . . . Come to us, beloved brothers, come! Impatiently awaiting you is a spiritual family of good, tender, and receptive people. Come, our arms are outstretched and words of comfort await you from God's own sacred Torah (holy texts). We love you passionately and sincerely, although sometimes we speak the bitterest truth, because you are our brothers and we wish with all our heart and soul to comfort, calm, and soothe you. Believe that in our brotherly bosom you will find ease! Because where—where else, can you hear words of comfort and edification?

You will say that *we*, the spiritual biblists, are few in number, that we are unknown, without wealth or power. Yes, now there are few of us, but we are rich in spirit, strong in our striving toward better things, powerful in our feelings and known for our good aspirations. We wish to serve not Moloch, but God's truth and the brightest, highest reason. Brothers, can it really be that this God comforts you not, and will not reward you a hundredfold with spiritual and moral wealth?

I call to all of the noble and vital forces of Jewry with this entreaty: brothers, awaken! Take up the good cause! Serve your people! With a brave hand throw off the accretion of centuries! Enough of pale tradition's gleaming, enough boasting of your senile solidity; better we draw from the fresh and life-giving source of modern life; better we be fresh, healthy, morally flourishing people! Renewal, renewal! Give your people what life, time, science, and mankind's duty demand! Give them firm moral convictions and rational beliefs, and with these you will return to them spiritual peace, and elevate them in the eyes of those closest to them . . .

A Biblical Brother[34]

A mixture of lamentation, paternalistic chiding, high-flown rhetoric, excruciating dental metaphors, and bizarre self-promotion, the letter's style is characteristically Gordin's. The welter of adjectives ("defenseless, isolated, helpless, and despised"; "insulted, degraded, beaten, robbed, expelled") remains a hallmark of his publicistic style in both Yiddish and Russian. There is an uneasy oscillation between exterior and interior viewpoints and first- and second-person narration, as the speaker initially aligns himself with his "brothers" and speaks of "we Jews" and "our prophets," only to retreat from this allegiance by speaking of "your" sins and "your" nerves and the need for "you" to renounce "your" exploitative ways. Acutely conscious of his own status as reluctant insider and self-constructed outsider, the "Biblical Brother" remains on the periphery of Jewish suffering, decrying his own pain ("Woe is me!") while nevertheless insisting on his remove from it ("Did not my heart bleed when I saw you—insulted, degraded, beaten, robbed, expelled from your homes?"). The letter's attempt to turn Jewish suffering to the advantage of the Brotherhood's membership rolls falls offensively flat, the more so as Gordin's rhetoric apparently strives to echo Judah Leib Gordon's (1831–92) rallying cry for Jewish integration, "Hakiza ami!" (Awake My People! 1866).

The letter's parenthetical explanations ("God's own sacred Torah [holy texts]") and appearance in a liberal, Russian-language newspaper indicate that its targeted readers were ethnic Russians and assimilated Jews. Gordin cannot have been unaware that the antisemitic press would pick up on his letter, as indeed they did, swiftly proclaiming that the letter was proof that Jews recognized their complicity in their own suffering.[35]

When the editors of *Voskhod* and *Russkii evrei* noted the gleeful Judeophobe response to Gordin's letter, they declared it incumbent upon themselves to reprint and comment on the offending piece, thereby ensuring its even broader dissemination. *Voskhod*'s editor, A. E. Landau, likened the Brotherhood's leader to Yakov Brafman, the apostate author of the poisonous *Kniga kagala* (*Book of the Kahal*, 1869), and condemned the "Elisavetgrad prophets" for playing into the hands of antisemites.[36]

Yet Gordin's letter repeated old arguments on Jewish reform. In 1876 the socialist *maskil* Aaron Liberman (ca.1845–80) had also accused Jews of bringing on their own persecution by their exploitation of non-Jews.[37] Morris Winchevsky (1856–1932) said much the same in 1878. Callousness toward the Jewish victims of the pogrom was marked among radical socialist factions of the Jewish intelligentsia, many of whom were keen to read signs of nascent social revolution in the brutal mob violence. Abraham Cahan, then a student in Vilna, declared, "We regarded ourselves as 'men,' not as 'Jews.' Jewish concerns had no appeal to us. There was one cure for all the ills of the world—socialism. That was the fundamental law of laws for us. To say that the pogroms did not interest us is an understatement."[38] Radicals reasoned that as "exploiters," Jews were rightful targets of peasant mobs, whose rage would certainly be turned on the next level of oppressors: the police and the tsarist state. Where radicals saw the beginnings of a peasant overthrow of economic and political oppression, Gordin saw the beginnings of Jewish overthrow of economic and spiritual stagnation.

Nor was the Spiritual-Biblical Brotherhood's post-pogrom call for Jewish reform an isolated one. Simon Dubnow repeated these arguments about Jewish reform in *Voskhod* itself in 1883:

> In its everyday religious form there is much in Jewish life that does (being lethal and undesirable *in and of itself*) and can impede the success of legal reforms, or can render the latter of less utility than they are capable. It follows that these elements that are lethal in social relationships and impede beneficial elements—insofar as this depends on Jews alone or on only some of them—must be eliminated.[39]

As a way of gaining notice for the Brotherhood, the letter was a spectacular success. As a way of gaining converts, it was an equally spectacular failure, as the backlash from the letter forced the group into a perpetually defensive position, particularly with regard to the Russian-Jewish press, which never tired of imputing the worst motives to the Brotherhood. In the years to come, the sect would clarify its aims and positions though periodic statements through the Russian press, as if still attempting damage-limitation for the anger generated by its "Biblical Brother."

Gordin himself was the first to try to explain his position in less inflammatory terms. Three weeks after the editors of *Russkii evrei* characterized members of the Brotherhood as ignorant, half-baked Karaites, whose organization was scarcely three months old and was headed by a vagrant who tried to use the trauma of the pogroms for publicity purposes, Gordin issued a statement through the *Elisavetgradskii vestnik*.[40]

Gordin repudiated accusations made against him and the Brotherhood, noting that "almost all" the members of the Elisavetgrad sect had themselves been robbed and beaten in the pogroms. Rumors that he himself had participated in a government committee to aid those arrested as looters were, Gordin declared, absolutely false.[41] Also lacking any foundation was the belief that the Brotherhood was merely trying to curry favor with Russian society and the state by condemning Jewish "exploitation." As to the accusation that the Brotherhood talked a lot about agricultural labor but did not actually engage in any, Gordin hotly protested that he and his group had been trying for at least half a year to acquire land.[42]

In an article printed a few weeks later in *Russkii evrei*, Gordin again attempted to set the record straight regarding his own status (not a vagrant), his group (not three months old), their beliefs (not as *Russkii evrei* represents them), and their advocating but not engaging in farming (not their fault, and someone was trying to help them acquire land).[43]

Gordin's indignation was understandable but impolitic in view of the storm that he himself had roused by his original letter. Signs that Gordin understood this situation are evident in an interview in St. Petersburg's *Nedelya* (The Week):

> We spoke with him about his conduct, and he himself admitted to us that he had made a rude and unfortunately irremediable error. The remaining "brothers" insisted on the moral purity of their leader with all their strength. But thanks to his error, he was decidedly unpopular among the majority of the population, and this, to a significant degree, hindered the development and expansion of the tenets of the new faith.[44]

A number of Gordin's biographers and researchers on the Brotherhood assert that after the letter debacle, the movement fell apart and Gordin retired to the countryside until 1883, when the Brotherhood reconvened.[45] There is no evidence, however, that any of these events happened.

Pronouncements by the Brotherhood in the Russian press in 1881 and 1882 point to its continuing survival throughout this period, and the initiation of a police watch of the group in the autumn of 1881 suggests that the Brotherhood very much remained in active service. A defunct organization would scarcely merit the attentions that the secret police allotted to it—surveillance, the interception and copying of letters, and the hiring of informants to infiltrate the Brotherhood's ranks.

Thanks to the unstinting efforts of the Okhrana (tsarist political police), preserved in Gordin's police file is a letter of October 1881 in which he remarks that he has sent his wife and children to stay with his parents, while he remains in Elisavetgrad. As something of an aside, Gordin says that he will "probably" head to the countryside in the spring to farm (*zanimat'sya zemledeliem*).[46]

It is not clear where Gordin intended to farm. The Spiritual-Biblical Brotherhood owned no land, and given the May Laws' proscriptions on Jews' mobility and purchase of land and the beginnings of a long economic depression in Kherson province, it is unlikely that Gordin bought land himself in this period. It is probable that the only land he would or could have worked belonged to his parents; as a town-dwelling small businessman (*meshchanin*), Gordin's father's land was probably on the order of a kitchen garden, rather than the grand Tolstoyan scene that Gordin's biographers imply.[47] Given the Brotherhood's continued activities between 1881 and 1883, it is unlikely that Gordin spent much time out of Elisavetgrad or other cities in Kherson or neighboring provinces, where the Brotherhood opened branches in Kremenchug, Odessa, Nikolaev, and Uman.

It is also difficult to find any basis for dividing the Brotherhood's existence into two distinct periods—1880–81 and 1883–91, as previous research argues.[48] Because there is no evidence that the group ceased to exist between 1881 and 1883, there are no grounds for claiming that Gordin spent "several years" in this period working as an agricultural laborer.[49] Indeed, it is more likely that the myth of Gordin's retreat to the countryside to engage in redemptive agrarian work owes more to the story's retelling in the United States, when an inaccurate label of Tolstoyanism had been attached the Brotherhood's early days.

Moreover, at this juncture a new group of Jewish reformers, Yakov Priluker's New Israel, appeared in Odessa to proclaim a similar set of objectives. Far from being defunct, the Brotherhood had gained imitators.

YAKOV PRILUKER, "NEW ISRAEL," AND THE CHRISTIAN QUESTION

In January of 1882, an Odessa schoolteacher named Yakov Priluker announced to the world the foundation of New Israel. Like Gordin's Brotherhood, New Israel desired to turn Jews into productive participants in the affairs of their Russian home. They too rejected the

Talmud, circumcision, kosher dietary laws, and "exploitative" Jewish professions. Priluker acknowledged the groups' similarities:

> I must here mention, that about a year before I began my work a similar movement had sprung up in Elizabethgrad, in the government of Kherson. [. . .] a teacher in a private Jewish school, Jaakoff Gordin, a man of great energy and oratorical power, became the leader of a circle of men and women aspiring towards a higher and nobler spiritual life. Rejecting the Talmud and accepting the Bible only, they accordingly called themselves "Bibleizi," or confessors of the Bible. Gordin, too, cherished the idea of an amalgamation of the reformed Synagogue with a purified Protestant Christianity, as represented to a certain extent by the Stundists and other Russian sects; but under the existing political regime the slightest allusion to such an aim would have been fatal to work among the Jews. I reviewed in my book the aspirations of the "Bibleizi," and encouraged them in their work; Mr. Gordin came to Odessa to consult with me, and we decided to continue the work with renewed zeal, hand in hand, our ideas and principles being essentially identical.[50]

By stating that the aims of the Brotherhood were "essentially identical" to those of New Israel, Priluker ascribes some of the more peculiar of his own tenets to Gordin's sect. Yet never did the Spiritual-Biblical Brotherhood demand, as Priluker's group did, that its members call their synagogues "churches." Nor did it require that firstborn children of members be named "Alexander" or "Alexandra" in honor of the tsar. Nor did it request that its members be allowed to wear distinguishing clothing, so as not to be mistaken for rabbinical Jews.[51] Priluker later revised these tenets, but some were mistakenly ascribed to Gordin's sect, an error that Gordin himself tried to correct.[52]

There were other differences between the two groups. Priluker's principles are laid out in a more scholarly argument than those of the Brotherhood. Unlike Gordin, who rarely makes reference to a single tractate of the Talmud in his rejection of it, Priluker cites specific texts in his argument with rabbinic Judaism. His book, Evrei-reformatory, is an elegantly written and eloquent diagnosis of the problems afflicting Russian-Jewish society, which makes the later turn of Priluker's reforming zeal so troubling.

Yakov Priluker converted to Christianity within a few years of leaving Russia, and his memoirs appear to justify his conversion with respect to his activities as a Jewish reformer. The logical outcome of Priluker's brand of reform—a conclusion that he encourages—is conversion to Christianity. Priluker was by no means alone in this tendency, as the high-profile conversion of another Jewish reformer, Yosef Rabinovich, and the parallel phenomenon of messianic or "New Testament Jews" and "Jewish Baptist Christians" in Russia and Ukraine of this period bear witness.[53] Indeed, that Gordin did *not* convert to Christianity puts him in the minority among Jewish activists who desired closer relations between Jews and Christians.

The most serious question that Priluker's group raises with regard to the Spiritual-Biblical Brotherhood is the extent to which the latter can be regarded as desiring the "amalgamation of the reformed Synagogue with a purified Protestant Christianity." Both Kalmen Marmor and Zalmen Zylbercweig devote significant space in their biographies of Gordin to his links with the Ukrainian Stundists, a dissident Protestant evangelical sect that Gordin sincerely admired. There is much in Gordin's Russian writing that does suggest a profound sympathy for Christianity, particularly Protestantism. Priluker's conversion and Gordin's sympathetic literary treatment of Stundism and his own well-documented friendships with leading Stundist dissidents also bolster the impression that the Brotherhood was Christian. Further reinforcing this idea was the Brotherhood's insistence on the "biblical" basis of the group's faith, which often appeared to extend to the New Testament as well.

Typical of this tendency was a January 1884 report on the Brotherhood's anniversary celebration that included a sermon by Gordin on "the lives of Moses and Jesus Christ." The sermon "pointed out the significance of their teachings and those of other moral people in general, and the members of the new-formed brotherhood in particular."[54] Further remarks by Venyamin Portugalov only appear to deepen the conviction that the Brotherhood was a Jewish organization with heavily Christian leanings. Referring to Gordin's sermon on Moses and Jesus, Portugalov noted:

> This speech raises the idea of an amalgamation, a reconciliation between Jewry and Christendom. With great talent, the speaker was able to point to the solidarity that connects the two religions, and the few things that divide them. It is precisely and principally for this that the Spiritual-Biblical Brotherhood, having renounced the decrepit and criminal tendencies of the Talmud, is completely and sincerely assimilating the moral teaching of Christ.[55]

Use of the term "amalgamation" or "merger" (*sliyanie*) with regard to the Jewish Question was customary in discussion of the circumstances under which full civil rights should be extended to Jews in

Russia. "Merger," which is frequently and inaccurately translated in the twentieth century as "assimilation," was viewed as a means of improving Jews' economic position and weaning them from "fanaticism." "Merging" Jews more closely with Christians did not necessarily imply the elimination of Jewish religious difference or their conversion to Christianity, although doubtless in some corners that would have been seen as an ideal resolution. Portugalov, however, refers to the "merger" not of Judaism with Christianity but of "Jewry" (*iudeistvo*) with *khristianstvo*, meaning both "Christianity" and "Christendom." In keeping with Portugalov's discussion of "Jewry," the latter usage is more likely and suggests that he is speaking principally of economic and social integration.

More troubling, though, is the last line of Portugalov's letter, in which he refers to the Brotherhood's "completely and sincerely assimilating the moral teaching of Christ" (vsetsele i iskrenno usvoivaet nravstvennoe uchenie Khrista). What at first glance appears to confirm the group as proselytes for Christianity looks, on closer examination, to be less certain. Is "sincerely assimilating the moral teaching of Christ" really the same thing as conversion? Or does this phrasing leave room for what seems to have been the actual practice of the Brotherhood—treating the New Testament as a continuation of the Hebrew Bible? Later statements by the Brotherhood present Jesus as a Jewish prophet, a radical rabbi whose followers represented the most successful Jewish sect of all time.[56] This practice was itself an inflammatory one for a state and church that upheld Christianity's ahistorical independence from Judaism. Readings of the Gospels as Jewish texts, by a group advocating the merger of Christendom and Jewry, might have appeared to the authorities less an attempt to Christianize Jews than an effort to Judaize Christians. "Judaizing" sects, which observed Jewish customs but were nominally Christian, were strictly outlawed by the Russian state.[57]

Did Portugalov (himself an unconverted Jew and Brotherhood member) intend to leave readers with the impression that the Brotherhood was a messianic Jewish sect? The ambiguity of Portugalov's phrasing is a feature of many of the Brotherhood's decidedly nebulous attempts to define its creed, which may owe to theological vagueness or self-preservation. If readers—who included the Russian police—were unable to determine whether the Brotherhood's members were Jews preaching Christianity to Jews, Jews preaching social and religious reform to Jews and Christians alike, or religious humanists preaching a radical reimagining of religion itself, one potentially more troubling than either of the first two, then so much the better. The success of the cat-and-mouse game that the Brotherhood played with the Russian police for ten years suggests that the policy worked remarkably well. The police themselves evidence confusion regarding the constituency and ideological orientation of the group, which in 1881 they noted was "joined by several Jews," suggesting that officials regarded the group as not Jewish but Christian.[58]

The Brotherhood's own communications with the authorities are very adept at avoiding reference to the group's actual religious confession. This tendency is evidenced in a petition for legalization of the Brotherhood that Gordin and two leading members of the sect, Anna Pokrasova and Grigorii Bernshtein, submitted on July 30, 1884, to Governor Aleksandr S. Erdeli. The petition requests leave for the group to gather, proselytize, select their own rabbi, maintain vital statistics records (*metricheskie knigi*—"metrical books"), and acquire land for an agrarian colony. The Brotherhood received official recognition from the Ministry of Internal Affairs on January 12, 1885.[59] Erdeli is quoted as favoring the Brotherhood's requests, "in view of the fact that the Brotherhood's beliefs and aspirations contain nothing contradictory to existing resolutions, and that it strives toward the eradication of the crude fanaticism and religious delusions of the Jewish masses."[60]

Clearly, the Spiritual-Biblical Brotherhood was engaged in an intricate dance with the tsarist authorities, some of whom appeared sympathetic to the Brotherhood, whether or not they were entirely sure of its motivations. The ambiguities of Gordin's representation of the Brotherhood suggest that Lilienblum's characterization of him as having "two faces" should be revised. Gordin presented at least three public faces: for the authorities, he was a reformer of unspecific confession but no demonstrated disloyalty to the state. For the Jewish press, he offered himself as a Jewish reformer along traditionally maskilic lines. For the Russian press, he was the founder of a Jewish sect that held Christianity in high regard but proposed its own religious humanist tenets. Yet none of these identities was in serious contradiction with any other. The fusion of the spiritual and the practical, of religious reform with economic restructuring, of Jewish and Christian integration, had always been the group's platform, and it would remain so to the end of its days.

By January 2, 1883, at the Brotherhood's annual anniversary celebration in Elisavetgrad, members heard a report on the proposed amalgamation with New Israel.[61] It was a bit of good news after a difficult year, in which the members of the group were forced to admit that their efforts were proceeding at snail's pace. A leading "brother" offered some cheer in his report on the sect's gaining members in Petersburg, Vosnesensk, Odessa, and Kremenchug. And, in the realm of pure fantasy, it was reported that the Brotherhood had "many" followers in America, thanks to the efforts of members who had emigrated after the pogroms.[62]

The Brotherhood's dogged optimism, despite evidence that its cause was an unpopular one, is typical of Gordin's own fierce and reckless confidence. Though characteristic of the era of the Great Reforms, by 1883 this optimism was sorely out of joint with the times. The pogroms of 1881–82 and the fallout from Gordin's public pronouncements combined to turn what might have been a genuinely radical social and religious movement into an isolated and embattled sect. That the Brotherhood survived as long as it did speaks both of Gordin's tenacious commitment and its members' cohesion and sense of purpose. The Brotherhood's members had a strong attachment to one another and especially to Gordin, and it was a bond that weathered years of public controversy, internal divisions, and even Gordin's immigration to the United States. More than twenty years after leaving Russia, Gordin corresponded more regularly and more intimately with the Brotherhood's former members than with his own sisters.

The ideal that the Spiritual-Biblical Brotherhood represented—of a community of like-minded individuals who swam against the tide of custom and public opinion, in search of a more just and engaged life—was one that Gordin would replicate in his life as a Yiddish dramatist and journalist. Far from being the unwanted result of his running afoul of conservative religious leaders, Abraham Cahan, or lowbrow audiences, the controversies that Jacob Gordin stirred at every juncture were actively courted. Anger and outrage were proof of life itself, without which no creative endeavor was possible.

CHAPTER THREE

A Russian Writer

When Jacob P. Adler made his appeal to the disgruntled opening-night audience of *Sibirya* in 1891, he pleaded for their patience and openness to the strange new play in part because its author was, he declared, a "famous Russian writer."[1] Similar assurances of rigorous quality control were applied by *Di arbayter tsaytung* to Gordin's first story in Yiddish, "Di oblave," which was promoted as the work of a "famous Russian-Jewish writer."[2] Reverence for Russian literature was a given among immigrant New York's leftist Jewish intelligentsia, for whom Russian writers enjoyed a close association with radical political activism.[3] Russian literature was widely perceived as taking an oppositional stance to the oppressive tsarist state—even if in reality many of Russian writers held positions at the imperial court or spent much of their working lives in the tsar's civil and armed services. The sterling example of Turgenev, Tolstoy, Nikolai Chernyshevsky (1828–99), and Vissarion Belinsky (1811–48) was paradigmatic; apparent anomalies like Mikhail Saltykov-Shchedrin's (1826–89) successful civil service career, Ivan Goncharov's (1812–91) sideline as a censor, or Nikolai Gogol's (1809–52) frequent, craven appeals to autocratic might did little to blot the radical prestige of Russia's writers.

It was natural for Jacob Gordin to be promoted as a Russian writer as well, although he was hardly famous, and his colleagues at *Di arbayter tsaytung* and the Union Theatre had no actual acquaintance with his Russian fiction or journalism. Its exact nature, as well as its relationship

to his Yiddish dramaturgy, remained, like most of Gordin's life in Russia, a mystery. Nor do the garbled summaries of the stories that Gordin
was supposed to have published in Russia offer convincing proof that his
biographers had any familiarity with them either.[4] This very unknown
quality meant that Gordin's career as a Russian writer might be sum-
moned as evidence of his revolutionary sympathies or decried as proof
of his monstrous hostility to his fellow Jews. Neither assertion, however,
had any basis in actual knowledge of Gordin's Russian writing.

Gordin's fiction appeared regularly in St. Petersburg's prestigious
Nedelya in the 1880s and early 1890s, and he enjoyed great popularity as a columnist in Odessa and Elisavetgrad. Gordin's Russian writing reveals many connections with his dramas, which draw on the
"types," settings, and conflicts of his earlier work. Characters familiar from his plays—bluff, tyrannical patriarchs; noble, self-sacrificing
daughters; and coquettish, hypocritical matrons—have their genesis
in a story cycle called *Evreiskie siluety* (Jewish Silhouettes, 1885–
91), set in the Pale of Settlement. Its poor and middle-class Jews differ little from those of his Yiddish plays; family dynamics, business
schemes, and sudden, violent resolutions are all in evidence. But the
stories of *Evreiskie siluety*, unlike their theatrical descendants, remain, as the title indicates, two-dimensional outlines in the starkest
black and white.

Gordin is at his best in his reviews and feuilletons, which antici-
pate the topical, controversial aspects of his Yiddish playwriting, while
largely avoiding the leadenly programmatic tendencies of his longer
prose works. Of particular interest, too, is Gordin's development of a
multiplicity of narratorial personae, who are deployed as roving cor-
respondents, theatre reviewers, and satirists. Their fractured and contradictory perspectives present a startling contrast to the Jacob Gordin
who is familiar from the Lower East Side newspaper world, from which
he advocated realism and antibourgeois values in tones that ranged
from the magisterial to the irascibly magisterial to the witheringly magisterial. Yakov Gordin is unpredictable, contrary, and very funny and
frequently offers radically opposing positions to the views espoused by
Jacob Gordin. Taken more with romanticism than with realism, concerned more with elevating fictions than with edifying examples, and
more aesthete than ideologue, Gordin in his Russian journalistic writing reveals a restless and compartmentalized creativity.

This chapter addresses Gordin's Russian writing as a precursor to
ideas and techniques that were developed in the Yiddish plays. It sug-

gests that the deficiencies of Gordin's Russian fiction, which suffers from its author's willingness to subjugate aesthetic values to political ones, were modulated in his Yiddish drama by their intertextual character. Gordin's didactic, moralizing tendencies were subdued in his plays by the double-voiced nature of his adaptive method. Where his Russian fiction struggles to convey the complexity and depth required of third-person omniscient narration and his Russian journalism charms by its kaleidoscope of varied and competing voices, Gordin's Yiddish drama became the ideal medium for their combination. In drama, Gordin's faculty for ventriloquism and parody was married to a practical method based on citation and textual interpretation. While Gordin's ethical imperatives were by no means displaced in his plays, which continued to advance his cherished views on issues like women's emancipation and the sins of capitalism, his moralizing was tempered by the dramatic form's own multiple voices and viewpoints. Gordin's transformation from a not-so-famous Russian writer into the leading Yiddish playwright was a matter not only of linguistic change but of the merging of intertextual dramatic form and journalistic practice.

EVREISKIE SILUETY (JEWISH SILHOUETTES, 1885–91)

Published in *Knizhki nedeli* (Booklets of the Week), the literary supplement to St. Petersburg's *Nedelya*, *Evreiskie siluety* varies greatly in quality. In addition to lyrical and sensitive portraits of Russian Jews caught between Slavic and Jewish worlds, the cycle also includes wearingly tendentious caricatures of Jews as exploiters and scheming social climbers. The stories' chief interest lies in their representation of highly theatricalized processes of positive and negative self-transformation, which find form in depictions of spiritual awakenings, conversions, *embourgeoisement*, and immigration. Gordin is intensely interested in human beings' attempts to exceed their origins and limitations, but he is concerned even more with their failure to do so. Defeat typically befalls those who attempt to conceal the irremediable fact of Jewishness. Gordin's characters are invariably undone in abrupt and public turns of events: a humble Jewish mother's appearance at a society party, a schoolyard taunt that reveals a hidden ethnic identity, a murderous pogrom mob that finds a convert not quite Christian enough. Jewish "gentility" is insubstantial and impermanent, an illusory performance that frequently yields fatal results.

While piety is never advocated, neither is conversion an option, and apostates in particular meet nasty ends. Those who manage to elude the long hand of Jewish fate treat their identity as a performance, manipulated to suit prevailing conditions.

The title character of "Avramele Shloper" (1885) is successful in terms of both the performance that he maintains and the effortlessness with which he eludes its consequences. His story opens with a description of a gloomy scene: "On one of the most remote streets of the city of N. stands an old, gloomy, unplastered building. Instead of a fence, adorning the building are large heaps of rubbish and cinders, covered with feathers and clotted blood."[5] The narrator then proceeds to dismantle this squalid scene, a narrative device that prefigures the dismantling of the title character's own deceptive appearance: "'Remote streets,' 'a gloomy building,' 'clotted blood'—all this offers the reader's fantasy a broad expanse. Perhaps he is already imagining a scene of villains, robbers, terrible crimes, and murders" (11). These Gothic trappings are merely the result of poverty and the neighboring butcher's dumping his trash in this forgotten corner. The building is really a prayer house for a quorum of tailors, headed by Rebbe Avramele Shloper. His piety, knowledge, and talents as a calligrapher and scribe have earned him the respect and love of the entire town. There are even whispers that he is a *lamed-vovnik*—one of the thirty-six saints who live concealed in each generation.

Such is Avramele's repute that not even his profane habit of drawing figurative representations of biblical patriarchs can damn him in the eyes of his neighbors.

> From a distance it appeared as if the portraits were created of tiny lines and points, but on closer inspection, the butcher noticed that the points and lines were microscopic Hebrew letters. Moses was composed entirely of the words of Deuteronomy, and David from the text of his own psalms. All this was the work of the hands of the rebbe Avramele. (15)

This beguiling illustration of the word's power to conjure images from itself and of itself provides a clue to the character of Avramele. He uses his knowledge of the Torah, Talmud, and kabbalistic writings to conjure his own image as the saintly rebbe—one that is equally profane, given his true nature. Thus disguised, Avramele gains the trust of the townsfolk. When he confides that he has invented a machine that will turn gold and silver into worthless metals, they are entirely credulous. He plans to devalue all precious metals in the world, putting the rich on a par with the poor. However, before unleashing the powers of this device, Avramele promises to safeguard his friends' meager holdings of gold and silver. All they need do is bring their precious goods to him for safekeeping. When the tide turns, *they* will be the rich ones. A week before Rosh Hashanah, however, Avramele vanishes with all of the villagers' valuables.

"Avramele Shloper" submerges its distaste for Hasidic "fanaticism" in a classically satirical portrait of piety as charade. Like all successful conmen, the Tartuffian Avramele is a consummate actor, gauging his audience's desires and shaping his performance accordingly. Unlike Tartuffe, however, he manages to conceal his true nature even from the reader, until the mask is pulled off in the story's final page. While Molière's audience enjoys the luxury of dramatic irony, no such advantage is conferred on Gordin's reader.

The association of performance with deception is treated with less brio in the stories that follow, in which doctors and lawyers and wily businessmen use education and eloquence to disguise their Jewish origins. Their Jewishness will eventually be revealed, either by fate or family members, who often amount to one and the same thing.

The title character of "Doktor-vykrest" (The Converted Doctor, 1885) is an army physician named "Tsimes," a nasty Sganarelle who is baptized for professional reasons. Merchants, patients, and the military find him useful, but they call him "Yid" behind his back. He jokes and laughs and ingratiates himself with them, but during a pogrom, his disguise is stripped from him in a cruel turn of events:

> He inserted himself among a pogrom mob, joking with them and doling out advice. At the height of the pogroms Tsimes ran into a mob in a narrow side street. Despite his uniform and ribbons, they surrounded him on all sides, and demanded fifty rubles for vodka.
>
> "What do you mean, what do you mean?" began Tsimes, in a feigned, joking tone. "Are you really going to insult an Orthodox Christian this way?"
>
> "If you're Orthodox—cross yourself!" cried someone. Tsimes bared his head and crossed himself with great religious feeling.
>
> "That's nothing! Now any Yid is ready to cross himself. Show us you're wearing a cross."
>
> "Why do you need a cross if I'm standing right here?" said Tsimes, jesting.
>
> "Show us a cross!" barked someone menacingly, and a powerful hand tore his waistcoat and shirt from him. His chest was bared, and no cross was found upon it. The sound of clubs rang out. Tsimes remained prone on the sidewalk.[6]

If the Jews of Gordin's tales are duplicitous and faithless, the non-Jewish world to which they seek entry is capricious, violent, and unforgiving, because the chief merits it holds for those who seek its acceptance are financial. Yet even Jews who court that world for idealistic reasons—a daughter who wishes to attend medical school, a businessman who tries to give his family financial security—usually end up taking their own lives.

Gordin's "happy" endings, though, are almost more disturbing than his tragic ones. "Syupriz" (The Surprise, 1885), a precursor to *Got, mentsh, un tayvl* (*God, Man, and Devil*, 1900), omits the suicide that is the moral climax of the Yiddish play and offers a happy—and disturbing—resolution of its central incestuous triangle. The hero of the tale is Barukh-Moishe, a handsome, muscular fifty-year-old with black eyes "full of life and fire," who enjoys a mean line in traditional Jewish scholarship.[7] But no etiolated, otherworldly Talmudic scholar is he—Barukh-Moishe also works his own small farm and is kind to his peasant helper, Ivan (who, in a saccharine touch, calls Barukh-Moishe "Daddy"). So well versed is Barukh-Moishe in matters of kosher dietary law that townsfolk seek his advice, and he has even shown his superior knowledge of Jewish law when wrangling with the local rabbis. Well versed in French, German, natural sciences, and mathematics, Barukh-Moishe is also a musician, and like Hershele Dubrovner of *Got, mentsh, un tayvl*, he can often be found playing soulful melodies on his violin.

The only blot on Barukh-Moishe's happiness—given his brilliance, sobriety, sterling work ethic, good looks, and superlative mastery of productive interfaith dialogues—is his barren, "sickly, slovenly, and slow-witted" wife (60). Barukh-Moishe is within his rights to divorce her, and his ardent gaze falls on her niece, Rivekka. She declares her love for her uncle in a speech that resolves the classical conflict of love and duty by uniting them in incestuous marriage. Barukh-Moishe summons the two local rabbis, who look on, open-mouthed, as he puts a ring on Rivekka's finger and declares her his wife in a wedding ceremony uncannily like that of the Spiritual-Biblical Brotherhood. The story ends with a happy scene of Barukh-Moishe singing a lullaby to his baby son while Rivekka pores over philosophical tracts.

Barukh-Moishe is as wooden and unconvincing as his twentieth-century cousins, the flinty-eyed, stern-jawed, and ideologically imperturbable heroes of Soviet socialist realism. The grating report of

Barukh-Moishe's qualities reaches an ecstatic high when the narrator describes the hero's musical performance:

> He permits himself this joy only once a week—on the Sabbath. But with what passion does he surrender himself to it! Carried away by various fantasies of his own devising, he forgets everyone and his whole soul drifts far away, transported to the blue distance, to the east, immersed in the hoary legends of long ago. He soars over the magnificent Jordan, is carried over the cedars of the majestic Levant . . . (59)

Musical performance, unlike performance that may be little more than dissembling, offers imaginative access both to history and to its transcendence. Zion may be rubble in reality, but its ancient magnificence is restored through Barukh-Moishe's musical transports.

Barukh-Moishe is nothing less than the reconciliation of all oppositions—Jew and Russian, *maskil* and Hasid, scholar and farmer, scientist and artist, lover and patriarch. An utterly improbable figure, he is Gordin's own golem. Gordin is at his best in chronicling the intricate processes of deception, and Barukh-Moishe fails as a character because he has nothing to hide; Hershele Dubrovner succeeds as a character because he deceives himself, if no one else. The success of *Got, mentsh, un tayvl* is due not only to Gordin's adding *Faust* and the Book of Job to the play's mix but also to the play's transposition to the stage. The actor literally fleshes out Gordin's two-dimensional characters, and the distance between actor, character, and mask and between truth and illusion becomes the inescapable coefficient of all action.

The next installment of *Evreiskie siluety* suffers an even more precipitous decline in the story of "Shmuil' Kurelapnik" (1885). Not content with being merely a tavern-owner, vintner, bootlegger, and arsonist, Kurelapnik has a taste for the theatrical as well. Rather than suffer a pogrom, he stages his own: under cover of night, Kurelapnik drags out his own furniture and goods onto the street before his house; he breaks a few panes of his windows and scatters feathers from a pillow on the whole mess. Then he leaves for a neighboring town. He deceives the *pogromshchiki*, but he charges his Russian creditors for the damages he has allegedly suffered.

That *Evreiskie siluety* includes stories in which a pogrom is an illusion, or in which pogrom marauders repent their evil, or where Jews who are "really" guilty of "exploitation" and opportunistic conversions are at the blunt end of mob justice, suggests a lingering need to rewrite the events of 1881 into a more manageable narrative. Gordin returned to the pogrom theme in his last stories for *Knizhki nedeli* in 1891, in his first article in Yiddish for *Di arbayter tsaytung*, and in *Der pogrom in rusland*. Only then does he seem to have exorcised the demons of 1881, in the manner in which his plays would also conquer the past: by rewriting its events and its texts to suit present needs.

Performance and the processes of deception emerge as dominant themes in *Evreiskie siluety* by Gordin's returning again and again to the alleged Jewish faculty for "passing." When he shifts away from this vein of inquiry, Gordin's stories diminish severely in quality, a problem exacerbated by his inability to create a psychologically convincing character using third-person narration.

"Aptekar' na vse ruki" (An Apothecary of All Trades, 1886) avoids interior characterization entirely by focusing on ornately itemized surfaces:

> A luxuriously appointed apothecary on a main street; a double-headed eagle hovers over the apothecary; in the windows are aquariums with little golden fish; exotic plants in the corners; walls and ceiling decorated with murals painted in oils; on the shelves and étagères are plaster figurines and statuettes, busts of great men, and appropriate military insignia. There are courtly pharmacists and apprentices with curled hair; all are Polish gentry and their manner of address is pretentious, sweet, Polish, of Olympian pomposity, conceited, precise and neat. Pan Lyashchinsky himself presides from behind his writing desk, giving out orders and instructions right and left, always in Polish.[8]

As in Gordin's plays, in which a beautiful sitting room always coincides with a rotten, heartless, materialistic family's inhabiting it, so too does the outward glitter of Pan Lyashchinsky's pharmacy mask its owner's inner corruption. It is an elaborate masquerade by one Velvel Barukhovich from Zhitomir, who supplies the rich with abortifacients, the poor with substandard medicines, and himself with a stream of non-Jewish mistresses. Only once, when his daughter dies suddenly of diphtheria and he is unhinged by grief, does Lyashchinsky briefly "revert" to Judaism. His conviction that he is being punished for his charade of a life lasts only a month, and soon Lyashchinsky is careering about town with an unidentified blonde.

Gordin's construction of Jewishness is contradictory, implying both that it is a permanent and inescapable condition, which cannot be eluded through conversion, assimilation, or subterfuge, and that it is a performance, endlessly open to revision. The Spiritual-Biblical Brotherhood argued something similar: Judaism possesses an inviolable and unchanging core—the Torah—which is itself nevertheless always open to reinterpretation. This same ideal underlies Gordin's approach to adaptation for the Yiddish stage: the source text continues to exist in its original language and form but is always available for revision for the Yiddish stage. Performance expands but does not alter a text's essential nature, nor does it compromise the original's integrity, which is presented in a form more accessible to a new audience.

Paradoxically, what is a strength for the Yiddish stage and for the Brotherhood—the core text's potential for revision and modernization—represents only hazard when expressed as a character trait. Thus Gordin's villains use their "Jewish" pliability to become almost indistinguishable from the Russian majority, while others simulate piety as cover for nefarious deeds. Gordin's heroes, by contrast, are singularly lacking in dissembling skills and express no contradictions between being and seeming. They present a unified personality to the reader, riven by no internal contradictions.

In "Evrei-shtundist" (The Jewish Stundist, 1886), Gordin presents another variation on his contradictory model of Jewish character. In it, the Stundists come to the depressed town of Svetlozarovka, and under their sober, hardworking influence, the peasants convert to the dissenters' faith and give up drinking. Their sobriety and much-improved work ethic leaves the (exploitative, money-obsessed) Jews of the town in a bad way. But the Stundists have pity on the Jews as well, and they show their generosity to Menasiya Traub, a widowed tailor with three children. In the manner of shoemakers' elves, the Stundists clean Menasiya's house and feed his children. They also read aloud from their Russian-language Bible. When Menasiya expresses surprise at some elements of the Book of Isaiah, the leading Stundist, Chernobril, replies:

> Why, this is your Bible, only in Russian translation. These are your prophets, but you did not listen to them. These are your teachers, but you have rejected them. The Jews are the source, the root of everything, and we have only grafted ourselves to the root: we offer the fruits, but the source withers.[9]

Menasiya has a spiritual awakening, but his happiness is brief, as the disgruntled local Jews inform on the tailor, and he is conscripted. Discharged from the army two years later, he finds that the Stundists have looked after his children while he—beaten, mocked, and tormented—served his term. Chernobril declares, "Our brother Menasiya has borne his cross like a warrior for Christ, and we must rejoice and celebrate and praise the Lord our Maker" (142). Today, we are told, Menasiya is a married man and a farmer and one of the most honored of Stundist brothers.

Though stridently didactic in tone, "The Jewish Stundist" is opaque in the lessons it teaches. Melodramatic turns, such as the cabal of local Jews conspiring to turn Menasiya over to the authorities, stretch credulity, as do the protagonists invested with a surfeit of good qualities and the villains with an oversupply of negative ones. Yet Gordin works very hard not only to demonstrate the essential decency of his Jewish hero but also to emphasize the essential Jewishness of Jesus of Nazareth. The Jewish community organization's turning Menasiya over to the tsarist police in the manner of a latter-day Sanhedrin and Menasiya's disappearance and miraculous return in *imitatio Dei* strive to underline the parallels between Jewish suffering in nineteenth-century Russia and one particular Jew's suffering in ancient Judea.

While not without artistic interest, the *Evreiskie siluety* cycle suffers for its author's willingness to sacrifice artistic quality to social ideals. The goals to which Gordin dedicated his public life—the reform of Jewish faith and life, the rapprochement of Jew and Christian that would follow the elimination of Jewish "exploitation"—were higher goals in the attainment of which he set all of his talents and energies. In the great Russian tradition of social protest and philosophical debate through literary art, Gordin strives to join the ranks of his literary heroes, Tolstoy and Turgenev, but ends up with something closer to Chernyshevsky. It was only when the Spiritual-Biblical Brotherhood was in decline that the artistic level of Gordin's fiction would rise.

JOURNALISM

The majority of Gordin's Russian writing was for the regional *Elisavetgradskii vestnik* and *Odesskie novosti*; a consistent feature of his journalism for these papers is the use of varied authorial personae. The earliest is "Yakov Mikhailovich," who retains Gordin's given name, patronymic, and stentorian tones. But Yakov Mikhailovich's touch is lighter, his observations incline to the absurd, and he is often very funny. Gordin's only explicitly Jewish character, Yakov Mikhailovich made his first appearance on a train bound for the unlovely Ukrainian town of Golta.

"PUTYOVAYA ZAMETKA" (NOTES ON THE ROAD, 1885)

Golta was to have been just a stopping point on Yakov Mikhailovich's journey to the city of Voznesensk, as detailed in the story "Putyovaya zametka." The city's name alludes to transcendent, heavenly heights (*voznesenie* means "ascent" and "Ascension"), and the journey's symbolic, vertical dimension is emphasized by the impossibility of its narrator's actually reaching this desired end along the horizontal road that he travels by train, by wagon, and on foot. Golta is a provincial Gehenna, sister city to Sholem Aleichem's destitute Kasrilevke of *Dos naye kasrilevke* (*The New Kasrilevke*, 1901). While Gordin's town lacks the imaginative force and depth of Sholem Aleichem's, there are nevertheless numerous parallels between the two.

Kasrilevke is a Jewish world cut loose from its traditional moorings, and its inhabitants fight their entropic decline with the only means of generating heat at their disposal—talk. Talk is the only proof of life in Kasrilevke, but no one is actually listening. Meaningless repetitions, unanswered questions, unheeded cries of alarm retard rather than advance the plot, providing a verbal echo of the story's opening scene, in which a tram travels halfway to its destination, only to reverse the length of the track it has already covered. The conflagration with which Sholem Aleichem's masterpiece of comic horror concludes illuminates a Jewish underworld that is the more disturbing for the laughter it provokes.

Gordin's journey to the Ukrainian underworld of Golta has a similar focus on breakdowns of transportation and communication, and like Sholem Aleichem's narrator, Yakov Mikhailovich only comes to town in order to leave it—albeit with some difficulty. Yet where Sholem Aleichem's netherworld is entirely Jewish, Gordin's Golta is the locus of interethnic conflict. These are not the violent confrontations of the pogroms but verbal exchanges, and the Jews of Yakov Mikhailovich's story more than hold their own with their Ukrainian and Russian provocateurs. Talk—the inflated currency of Kasrilevke—has real value here.

"Putyovaya zametka" opens with that quintessential symbol of technological progress—the train. Yakov Mikhailovich boards a third-class carriage filled with tradesmen and brokers, Jews and gentiles. A fat priest, followed by a lackey laden with food and alcohol, sits opposite and asks impertinently, "Are you a Jew?"

> "And if I am a Jew?"
> "How dare you travel? Today's Saturday . . . the Sabbath."
> "You, it seems, are a priest?"
> "Yes. So what?"
> "How dare you drink so much? It's unseemly."
> "It's none of your business!"
> "It's none of your business."
> A pause. I take out a cigarette and light it.
> "Listen here, you're smoking on a Saturday?"
> "Listen here, do you always drink vodka?"
> "It's none of your business!"
> "It's none of your business."[10]

The priest's protesting the narrator's violation of Sabbath restrictions on travel and the kindling of flame reveals a familiarity with Jewish tradition and a defense of it against secular transgressors. The priest acts as an irritating substitute rabbi, reminding the defiantly secular Yakov Mikhailovich of who he is beneath his modern suit, clipped beard, and burning cigarette.

The priest's impertinent questions contrast with the polite language in which they are couched, as the priest addresses Yakov Mikhailovich using the formal "you" and the neutral "Jew" (*evrei*), rather than the offensive "Yid" (*zhid*). The parallelism and repetition of their exchanges suggest that the interlocutors are more alike than different. The other exchanges in the railcar, while hardly polite, are also marked by an unexpected intimacy, and each group has license to speak. The train equalizes their situations, literally putting them all in the same class, and reduces all to the status of subordinates at the arrival of the conductor.

In Golta, Yakov Mikhailovich faces the same dilemma that Sholem Aleichem's narrator encounters at Kasrilevke's station—namely, it's very hard to leave it. Eventually the narrator is taken to a wretched, filthy hotel, where he declines the services of a prostitute. When the cab fails to appear the next morning, the narrator is cheerfully informed that he cannot get a train for Voznesensk anyway, because there is no train to Voznesensk. Yakov Mikhailovich is stuffed into a broken-down wagon with seven others, who by variously pushing and pulling the rickety vehicle and its pathetic nag finally reach the station. His failure to reach Voznesensk prompts a tirade and an admonition to the zemstvo to look into the matter of Golta's disconnection from the wider world.

The void that yawns behind Sholem Aleichem's Kasrilevke is only briefly glimpsed in Yakov Mikhailovich's Golta. Gordin envisions practical solutions to contemporary problems, whereas for Kasrilevke there is no way out of its existential crisis, no solution that zemstvo or tsar could enact, for there is no place for rational action in Kasrilevke. In Gordin's Golta the interplay of Jews and non-Jews holds out some possibility of exchange, even if fraught with hostility. The motley group of multiethnic travelers plodding to the station behind a worn-out horse is Yakov Mikhailovich's Pale of Settlement version of Gogol's troika, but there is no need to stand aside, no danger of being dazzled by jingling bells and thundering traces. But Yakov Mikhailovich's poor wagon is still in motion, and escape is possible.

Friction and volatile exchange are the animating forces behind all of Gordin's writing, and motion itself constitutes an ideal. Drama, as Gordin observed, is the art of action, above all.[11] On the Yiddish stage, it finds expression in the tension of centripetal and centrifugal forces, exemplified by the pull of tradition and rebellion, family and the individual, duty and desire. None of these can be resolved, because the tension that sustains their opposition is life itself. The end to their conflict invariably comes when the individual decides to tip the balance in favor of one, rather than continue the agonizing balancing act of existence. Resolution is death itself, and it frequently takes literal form in Gordin's dramas.

For Yakov Mikhailovich, action is the practical social action advocated by his crusading columns, but it is also embodied in the character himself. His creation dates to 1885–86, a period when Gordin spent much time on the road, proselytizing for the Spiritual-Biblical Brotherhood while gathering and editing material on regional events for *Odesskie novosti*.[12] Yakov Mikhailovich's role as traveler and observer is in many ways the quintessential narrative persona of Gordin's Russian writing.

As Dan Miron and Leah Garrett have argued, the Jewish traveler as a recurring motif in Eastern European Yiddish writing is particularly useful for exploring the Jewish experience of exile and modernization.[13] But unlike the wayfarers of Abramovitsh or Sholem Aleichem, Gordin's travelers' destinations are not an extraterritorial or a reconstituted Eretz Israel. They do not wander in search of home because they are already there. What remains to be found is a meaningful life amid the myriad problems that Gordin's narrator encounters.

If Yakov Gordin celebrates the utility and dignity of agrarian labor and rural life, Yakov Mikhailovich details the darker dimensions of the life the Brotherhood valorized. His is a sober, critical voice, given to occasional lyrical flights and depressing summations, and his traveler pose ensures both his safe distance from events and individuals and the certainty of his escape. The traveler's remove is paralleled by the distancing device of the authorial persona itself, enabling Gordin to be at once removed and personal.

This distancing device was successful enough to warrant the creation of a variety of other authorial voices, each keyed to particular journalistic forms. "Ivan Kolyuchii" (Ivan the Sting) and his shadow twin, "Alfei," were credited with theatre reviews, satirical feuilletons, humorous editorials, parodies, and the occasional travelogue. The classically anonymous Latin letters "N.N." and "N." are pseudonyms used for Gordin's stories for *Knizhki nedeli*, but after 1889 they were also credited with a motley variety of local news articles and opinion pieces for the *Elisavetgradskii vestnik*.[14] "Yan," whose name, "I am N.," alludes to these other literary identities, is a rigorous theatre critic with an encyclopedic knowledge of European and Russian drama. He is sharply and often hilariously disapproving of actors, writers, and entrepreneurs who forget that they serve the muses first and mammon second. The last of Gordin's pseudonyms, "Evpatii Kolovrot," appeared first in August 1889 and had his last outing in February 1890. A philistine who cares only for food, drink, money, and parties, Kolovrot's moronic reports on his meals, business scams, and Elisavetgrad social events are some of the bitterest columns Gordin crafted and testify to a darkening tone in his writing in the early 1890s.

While Gordin's Yiddish biographers have stressed the role that censorship played in the multiplication of these personae, there is little in their work that would have invited censure. There are no covert denunciations of tsarist autocracy, sympathetic shout-outs to revolutionary brothers-in-arms, or even veiled criticisms of the state or church. Gordin's police file makes no mention of his ever having tested official patience with his journalism. While this arguably demonstrates his faculty for avoiding official entanglements, the most controversial aspect of Gordin's life in Russia was his role as head of the Spiritual-Biblical Brotherhood. Gordin's journalism singularly fails to divulge clues to his putative revolutionary sympathies.

If Gordin's journalism fails to add to his radical pedigree, it does suggest both a natural gift for dramaturgy and a fluid means of negotiating the fraught borders between the many worlds that he inhabited. His ethnic Russian personae discuss Jews and Jewish issues from the perspective of ostensibly objective outsiders; Ukrainian peasant narrators offer stark contrasts to the crass commercialism and callous indifference of the city, while Yakov Mikhailovich travels about the Pale to offer sober diagnoses of the ills that plague peasant communities. The distance these personae afford is of greatest utility in addressing the divide and overlap between Russian and Jewish worlds. When a reader complained that the *Odesskie novosti* spent entirely too much time discussing issues that "can be of concern only to the Jews," Ivan Kolyuchii responded:

> It is unthinkable that in our part of the world one could keep up with public life and public interests and not concern oneself with the Jews, who are organically connected to this society and its interests, and who are active and passive participants in all aspects of public activities that affect the fate of this region—economic, social, and political. To take an interest in the outstanding events of Jewish life means to take an interest in society.[15]

The mask permits Gordin to express measured opinions on Russian Jewry in terms that his statements on behalf of the Spiritual-Biblical Brotherhood, or even the tendentious *Evreiskie siluety*, would not permit. What necessitated the creation of authorial alter egos was not the suspicious tsarist state but the hostility that Gordin had engendered as leader of the Brotherhood. Where Yakov Gordin grew gradually more sclerotic and narrowly focused on the sect, Ivan Kolyuchii, Alfei, and Yan remained flexible and unbounded. This freedom to digress from the public Gordin performance is nowhere more strikingly apparent than in the theatre reviews credited to these characters.

THEATRE CRITICISM

The advancement of realism is a campaign with which Jacob Gordin is most famously and fractiously identified in the Yiddish theatre. It was Gordin who declared that under proper tutelage American audiences would come to "expect from the drama not a gilded falsehood but the real, bare truth of life."[16] It was Gordin who declared, "Realism is the only power that forces us to think of a better future,

because it shows us, without ceremony, all the undesirable aspects of
the present."[17] But not long before emigrating, Gordin's alter ego Ivan
Kolyuchii sighed wistfully:

> Realism has already conquered one region of the arts—it holds near-
> absolute sway in creative literature—and we have already more or
> less made our peace with this. But to allow it to enter the lofty realm
> of the plastic arts, into the realm of wondrous sounds and harmony,
> would be just too much. Give mankind a chance every now and then
> to remove himself from this vulgar and senseless life. Let him escape
> with the poet to the cloudless heights, to a world of fantasy and imag-
> ination. Just for a moment, let him glimpse a life poetic, colorful and
> luxurious. Instead of customary vulgarity and coarseness let him see
> noble images and marvelous visions. There is too much prose already
> in the lives of men.[18]

These remarks were made a little more than two years before Jacob
Gordin launched his "reform" of the New York Yiddish stage under
the banner of realism. The same writer who characterized romanticism as striving to "kill all matter, all nature in man,"[19] was the
very one who found realism in the Russian theatre to be "low" and
"common."

Ivan Kolyuchii's skepticism found outlet in a parodic imagining of
realist elements as applied to the florid operatic stage. Under the aegis
of realism, opera would abandon the supernatural and fantastical to
offer quotidian scenes of domestic life:

> — Aksinya! Go to the market! (*The mistress of the house sings.*)
> — Give me some money! (*The cook—a contralto.*)
> — Here are two rubles and fifty kopecks for you!
> — Shall I get a boneless cutlet?
> — Yes, yes, of course!
> *Duet*: Go, go on now! I'm going, I'm going!
> And come right back! I'll be right back![20]

Alfei, too, heaped scorn on realism in his version of a "naturalistic"
novel, which opened with intensely detailed scenes of nose blowing,
descriptions of room furnishings, and more nose blowing.[21]

Both Yan and Ivan Kolyuchii's theatre reviews indicate a preference
for heightened, emotional dramas, particularly when allied with
music.[22] Gordin's reviewers reserved particularly ecstatic approval for
melodeklamatsiya, a performance genre somewhere between a poetry recitation and a musical concert, which acquired popularity as well
in Yiddish theatre circles of the twentieth century.[23] Ivan Kolyuchii

hoped that *melodeklamatsiya* represented a new performance art that could avoid the afflictions plaguing contemporary opera, which suffered from "mendacious content and stilted musical devices," and dramatic theatre, which relied overmuch on "scenic effects" and "physiological realism." When the theatre was able to overcome both of these defects, it would truly become a force for "artistic truth," one whose aim would be to "ennoble the human soul, awaken noble feelings in it and call forth a striving for elevated things."[24]

Gordin's Russian reviewers' romantic preferences extended to the dramatic repertoire. An 1888 review of *Die Räuber* (*The Robbers*) praised Schiller's unification of "poetry and philosophy." The German poet was credited with "embodying the most abstract ideas in images full of poetry and beauty."[25] A similarly enthusiastic reaction was elicited by Byron's verse drama *Manfred*, performed by the celebrated German actor-manager Ernst von Possart (1841–1921).[26] Even in performances by weaker actors, Schiller's plays, like *Marie Stuart*, elevated the entire theatrical enterprise.[27] And every possible permutation of Goethe's *Faust*—as opera, text, or theatrical production—was held up as a paragon, whose characters and situations were as alive, contemporary, and "real" as any work of modern, naturalistic drama.

In contrast to the praise lavished on German romantic literature, the French variety left Ivan Kolyuchii and Yan cold. A performance of *La dame aux camélias* (1852), by Alexandre Dumas, fils (1824–95), prompted a sniffing comparison of French preferences for a stage that embellished life to Russian audiences' preference for "real truth" in its art. Skipping blithely through an ontological minefield, Yan explained that he did not mean real "in the material sense, but in the emotional one, in the sense of artistic fidelity and veracity."[28]

Thus begins a tortured exercise in defining realism by means of its national characteristics, a process initiated by the need to reconcile the achievements of Russian realist writers like Tolstoy and Turgenev with the odious realist theatre then sullying the Russian stage. Ivan opines:

> Russian realism is a healthy realism. It has nothing in common with that French zoological realism that so shocks the earnest admirers of pure art. Our novel, our drama, and our opera will no doubt serve true artists and those who value all that is beautiful, truthful and worthy of notice in all manifestations of the life around us.[29]

Where Gordin's critics on the Lower East Side associated realism with alien, "Russian" values and low, vulgar topics that corrupted "family purity," Ivan Kolyuchii associates realism with alien, "French" values and low, vulgar topics that corrupted the purity of high art. Russian realism, by his measure, is less interested in the squalid, sordid milieus of Zola or Balzac because Russian realism describes "reality, but not a vulgar, animalistic, completely ugly side of reality." Russian realism is "beautiful," "truthful," and "worthy of notice." It is "instructive and interesting, something that can provoke thought and force the heart to beat faster, and forces one to think about the meaning of life and the fate of man."[30]

While the impassioned but vague opposition of Gordin's reviewers to stage realism may suggest a pose adopted for the sake of entertaining readers, particularly in view of the parodic form much of the criticism takes, the fact remains that all of Gordin's theatre reviews exhibit a consistent preference for art that is romantic rather than realist. Gordin's Yiddish plays, for all that they were received as realist drama, also reflect a fundamental tension between the realist and the romantic. The contemporary settings, topical social issues, and modern, conversational language of Gordin's Yiddish dramas are never entirely subordinate to the mechanics of melodrama. Dramatic peripeteia, scenes of recognition and confrontation, musical interludes, and, in plays like *Der unbekanter* (The Unknown, 1904) and *Oyf di berg* (On the Mountains, 1906), verse dialogue, all argue for Gordin's continuing enthusiasm for romanticism, even as his supporters proclaimed the ascendancy of realism.[31]

At the same time that Gordin's theatre reviewers decried realism as an aesthetic, the highest praise they offered an actor was to call his or her performance "real." The prima donna of the Imperial Aleksandrinsky theatre, Maria Savina (1854–1915), is pronounced "truthful and real in the highest degree," and her "simple and natural acting" is almost shocking to audiences more accustomed to the gesticulations and shouting of provincial actors.[32] Savina "*lives* on the stage, while all of the others *perform*." Possart's performances are "alive" (*kak zhivoi*).[33] Conversely, bad actors are shamed for their creating characters resembling nothing so much as "decomposing corpses, disinterred from the graves of some long-forgotten cemetery."[34] Yan's advice to these offenders is to "be real, natural, and true to life."[35]

What emerges from Gordin's discussion of what is "real" and "realistic" in the theatre is a quality of performance, rather than scenic verisimilitude or contemporary subject matter. The actor is the anchor of the real who permits the playwright's free exercise of imagination. The flesh-and-blood performer allows the playwright to recombine *Faust*, the Bible, Shakespeare, and Beethoven in plays that strive for realism of character, rather than to simply eradicate the supernatural and unlikely. The "elevated" and "romantic" elements of Gordin's plays balance his later preference for a Yiddish theatre that ostensibly deals "only with what is on earth, with what is in man's nature, in his life, and in his relations with society."[36] Even Gordin's old enemies at *Voskhod* would concede in 1902 that his plays "depict real life, draw living characters, and express genuine feeling."[37] Certainly, a large proportion of Gordin's success can be attributed to the talents of the many remarkable actors with whom he worked; yet a revolution in the theatre rarely occurs independent of radical shifts in dramatic writing itself.

The sheer scope of the shifts that Gordin initiated in Yiddish dramatic and theatrical practice begs the question: how did he do it? How did Gordin go from being a Russian prose writer utterly incapable of creating a psychologically convincing character to being proclaimed "the greatest Yiddish dramatist," who "reformed the Yiddish stage" and "delighted, enlivened, and stirred so many Jewish hearts with his mighty pen"?[38]

Like the actors who lent their palpable reality to Gordin's dramas, he modeled his first fully realized characters on himself. The journalistic "I" obviated the more technically challenging third-person narration of Gordin's prose and gave rise to "Yakov Mikhailovich," "Ivan Kolyuchii," "Yan," "Alfei," "N.N.," and "Kolovrot." They jockeyed for position with a range of minor characters and occasional narrators—"Dyadushka Yakov," "Pita," "Okhrem Karpenko"—who surfaced briefly and vanished again. The half-dozen personae inhabited by Yakov Gordin, Russian writer, were reborn in plays that relentlessly try to resolve fractures in families, customs, languages, and cultures through recourse to the accelerated action of plot and the corrective forces of an idiosyncratic version of romantic realism. Jacob Gordin's becoming a Yiddish playwright was the logical outlet for the literary style that he developed as a Russian writer. For it was only there, on the Yiddish stage, that the many divided identities and loyalties that Gordin created and explored might be reconciled—if not in fact, then in fiction.

LEAVING RUSSIA

For more than a century, accounts of Gordin's leaving Russia have emphasized his departure under cover of night, threat of arrest, and conditions of great haste and distress.[39] The impression they leave is of his barely eluding a squadron of tsarist police with an arrest warrant and leg irons. The reality is rather different, but a story of creative stagnation, economic recession, and bureaucratic ineptitude lacks the mythic power of the story told in New York.

The legend of Gordin's flight was a necessary one in its own right. It captured the pathos of the unwilling exile who was expelled from paradise and could only recapture it in Yiddish dramas that cast a longing, backward glance at the lost land. But it also proved prescient. Seven months after Gordin decamped to New York, his fictive exile became an actual one, as the tsarist police circulated an order for Gordin's arrest should he try to return to Russia.[40] The police were only too happy to have Jacob Gordin leave Russia; their only fear was that he would return.

It was the Spiritual-Biblical Brotherhood that was most influential in Gordin's decision to emigrate. Since its legalization in 1885, the group proselytized, underwrote apprenticeships of young Jews as artisans and smiths, and funded medical treatment for Elisavetgrad's poor.[41] But the sect's failure to acquire land remained a demoralizing setback, leading Gordin in 1887 to ask his followers at another dolorous anniversary celebration:

> What have we accomplished of significance in this period of time? Our local society is small in number. Although there are followers of our teachings in other cities, there are no organized societies as such anywhere. Does the "Brotherhood" have any financial means? None whatsoever. Are there prosperous brothers among us who can come to our timely aid? No. The majority of followers of our teachings are poor, or craftsmen, or people of no fixed profession. Has the "Brotherhood" managed in this time period to establish an agricultural colony? No, the time for its foundation has not yet come. Has a professional school of any type been established? No. Do we have any kind of property, or any kind of a concrete achievement?[42]

Efforts to acquire land for an agricultural colony, with the help of Mark Lukich Kropivnitsky (1840–1910), the Ukrainian playwright and theatrical entrepreneur, and the philanthropist Aleksandr Sibiryakov (1849–1933), were ongoing. But if these attempts to acquire land and their petitions to the government failed, there was a sad conclusion to be drawn:

> If no hope remains, then we will be forced, against our will, to collect our things and leave our homeland, to set out across the ocean for America, where there are no obstacles to our being honest people and engaging in productive labor.[43]

This is a startling admission from one who had always rejected immigration as a solution to Russian Jewry's problems. Yet there was precedent for his thinking that where Jewish agrarian colonies had failed in Russia they might succeed in the United States.

The Russian-born Hebrew novelist and early Zionist Peretz Smolenskin's (ca. 1842–85) essay *Am olam* (*The Eternal People*, 1872) had provided the name for a movement that was established in Odessa in 1881 and which advocated the settlement of Jews in agrarian communes in the United States. The Am Olam movement established settlements in the United States in 1882 in Kansas, South Dakota, Oregon and other states, but these disbanded within a few years. Slightly more success would be had by the Baron de Hirsch Fund, established by Maurice de Hirsch (1831–96) in New York City in 1891. The fund's most successful endeavor was the creation of the Woodbine Colony in New Jersey in 1892.[44] Gordin himself applied unsuccessfully to the fund almost immediately after his arrival in New York in 1891 and would also pay a visit to Woodbine in 1893, even after he was established as a Yiddish playwright.[45]

The vexing issue of the sect's failure to secure government permission to acquire land eventually sent Gordin to St. Petersburg to seek audiences with ministers who might be sympathetic to the Brotherhood's ambitions. He had good reason to think that the authorities might show the group favor. The Brotherhood had by all appearances successfully distanced itself from rabbinical Judaism and had obtained official legal status in 1885 as an independent religious organization. It would seem reasonable that the May Laws' restrictions on Jewish settlement, purchase, or even rent of land outside of designated towns and shtetls would not apply to the Spiritual-Biblical Brotherhood.

In February of 1887, Gordin made his first trip to the imperial capital. *Nedelya* reported that initially Gordin's mission had been very successful, and he made ready to proceed with a formal application. Gordin had forgotten only one thing.

Mr. Gordin overlooked the fact that officially he is not a sectarian, not a Jewish Protestant, *but just a Jew*, whose stay in Petersburg is forbidden. The Petersburg police do not know, or at the very least, can be forgiven for not knowing, about the "Biblical Society" and its goals, even if they are approved by the highest governmental author-ity, and may slight Mr. Gordin like any old Srul or Gershka staying illegally in St. Petersburg.[46]

In fact, Gordin was officially a sectarian, yet when he ventured to avail himself of some of the Brotherhood's hard-won privileges, he was swiftly shown that for all practical purposes he was *"just a Jew."* When Gordin's failure to acquire a temporary residence permit was brought to his attention, and the danger of arrest made clear to him, he hurriedly quit the capital.[47]

Not only would the Spiritual-Biblical Brotherhood be unable to acquire any land in the foreseeable future, but Gordin's treatment in the capital made it clear that in practical terms he and his followers were no different from rabbinical Jews. However much members of the Spiritual-Biblical Brotherhood desired a rapprochement of Chris-tians and Jews, however antagonistic their relations with Orthodox Jewry, however they might insist on practicing their own form of wor-ship and their own rites, they were, in the end, Jews like any other. The limitations of religious reform as envisioned and practiced by the Spiritual-Biblical Brotherhood were painfully clear.

NEW FRIENDS, NEW PROBLEMS

Tolstoyans are the most unbearable people.[48]

—LEV TOLSTOY

Despite the setbacks of 1887, the Brotherhood persisted, and the police, as ever, maintained dutiful vigil. A long report by the local po-lice captain noted that while the sect's activities were not marked by any "particular infractions," its sermons featured increasingly promi-nent discussion of Lev Tolstoy.[49]

Tolstoy's agrarian and antiestablishment views had always had a place in the teachings of the Spiritual-Biblical Brotherhood, but it was never, as has often been stated, a Tolstoyan sect. Nor could it have been; Tolstoy's emergence as a religious thinker and advocate of agrarian redemption dates only to the post-1880 period, and the Spiritual-Biblical Brotherhood was established in 1881. While a particularly close and instrumental reading of the hay-mowing scene in *Anna Karenina* may have inspired an idealization of agricultural labor in Tolstoy's readers, the earliest colonies that professed "Tolstoyan" principles dated only to 1889. The increasing vigor with which Tolstoy advocated agrarian life and work in the late 1880s and 1890s certainly linked him strongly with this movement, especially among American Jewish immigrants, for whom Tolstoy came to be regarded as the "spiritual father of agricultural sectarians in tsarist Russia."[50] While Tolstoy's views were certainly appealing to the Brotherhood, and Gordin himself was an admirer of Tolstoy's fiction, it cannot be said that the Brotherhood was ever a Tolstoyan sect.

Indeed, Tolstoy's increasing prominence in the Brotherhood's proselytizing in this period was a source of intense and divisive conflicts within the sect and pitted Gordin against two new members of the group, Isaak Borisovich Fainerman (1863–1925) and Anatolii Stepanovich Butkevich (1859–1942).[51] Fainerman, who wrote under the pen name "Teneromo" in the early twentieth century, had made a pilgrimage to Tolstoy's estate at Yasnaya Polyana in 1885 and remained there until 1887, living among the local peasants with his second wife, Anna.[52] Fainerman was baptized into the Orthodox Church so that he might teach at Yasnaya Polyana's school for peasant children.[53] Butkevich characterized Fainerman's Christianity as less spiritual than sociopolitical, and Tolstoy himself regarded Fainerman as "not religious enough."[54] Indeed, Fainerman's Christianity proved to be less divisive than his Tolstoyanism.

Fainerman's time at Yasnaya Polyana coincided with visits by William Frey (1839–88) (Vladimir Konstantinovich Geins), a Russian-born non-Jew who was the leader of Jewish agricultural settlements in the United States. Through Tolstoy, Fainerman also made the acquaintance of Prince Dmitrii Khilkov (1858–1914), who, in turn, was acquainted with the Spiritual-Biblical Brotherhood.[55]

As it emerges in a letter to Butkevich in 1889, Fainerman's attitude toward the Brotherhood was opportunistic. Almost offhandedly, Fainerman urges Butkevich and his Jewish common-law wife, Elizaveta Shtykina, then in Tula being harrassed by police, to join him in Elisavetgrad, where Fainerman had joined forces with the "Brothers":

> If you make up your mind to come down, please do so. The Brothers
> haven't yet settled themselves on the land. We'll sort ourselves out

somewhere and take a few of the Brothers with us. Our old ladies
[*baby nashi*] will be midwives (my wife also studied in Petersburg,
she only needs to take the exam). You can bone up on some carpentry
from me. We'll do some carpentry. Summer, we'll work on the land.
You can come right now if you want. We'll spend some time in the
city, then head out for the countryside.[56]

Butkevich had spent five years in political exile in Siberia (1881–86)
for taking part in student demonstrations and had been arrested again
in 1887 for his passing involvement in a covert publishing endeavor.
He joined the Brotherhood in Elisavetgrad in the autumn of 1889, and
with Fainerman he brought much-needed cash to the Brotherhood.
Whether the half-thought-out plan to establish a colony ever had any
chance of success is doubtful.

Tolstoy himself did not finance any of the communes, colonies, or so-
cieties that were established either in his name or on the basis of his ideas.
Nor did he even support their establishment in principle. Too aware of
the financial, practical, and personal problems that such colonies presented, Tolstoy in no way encouraged their establishment. His followers,
particularly those with means, did not have as many reservations.

Arkadii Vasil'evich Alekhin (1854–1918) organized one of the first
Tolstoyan agrarian colonies, on his estate of Shevelovo, in Smolensk
province in 1889, and gave Fainerman, Butkevich, and the Spiritual-Biblical Brotherhood financial support.[57] In 1889, with Alekhin's monetary
assistance, the Brotherhood was at long last able to open a workshop for
Jewish artisans. This undertaking immediately attracted the notice of
the local police, who, after a lax few years of observing the Brotherhood,
stepped up their surveillance. Keeping watch on the workshop, the police
asserted that it was "founded on communist principles."[58] The workshop
produced goods that the Brotherhood offered for sale at the local bazaar,
providing a much-needed source of revenue. The workshop also did
double duty as an auditorium, where, the police reported, regular public
readings of Tolstoy's *Ispoved'* (*Confession*, 1882) and *V chem moya
vera?* (*What I Believe*, 1884) were held.

These meetings were the object of controversy among the
Brotherhood's members. Fainerman was reported to have publicly
referred to the tsarist government as "tyrannical" in one meeting, a
statement that Gordin, who had years of experience in playing cat and
mouse with local law enforcement, found distressing. Gordin asked
Fainerman to be more circumspect. Fainerman grudgingly agreed,
but he continued to make seditious remarks about the state, leading

Gordin and some of his allies to stop attending meetings for several weeks.[59] According to the police, Gordin also felt that Fainerman erred in urging the sects' members to antigovernment action not only because it was impolitic but because the most pressing need was to encourage people to change their way of life, only after which changes to the government might be undertaken.

Much of the conflict between Gordin and Fainerman also involved a personal element. Butkevich described Fainerman as one who naturally assumed the role of leader in any group. Tall and striking, Fainerman was charismatic, passionate, opinionated, and very charming when in a good mood, but very erratic otherwise.[60] Fainerman's conflict with Gordin (who was equally charismatic, passionate, and opinionated) was probably inevitable. At every juncture, the police report that Gordin urged moderation. Certainly, some of this restraint was enacted for the benefit of the police spies who he well knew to be in the Brotherhood's midst, but Gordin's conflicts with Fainerman were real and serious and led to the first divisions within the group.

Partly as a result of Fainerman's rhetoric and his contacts with Tolstoy, the police became increasingly convinced that the sect's real goal was the "overturning of the existing state order in Russia."[61] But as John Klier notes, in the years after the assassination of Alexander II, "the police were obsessed with revolutionary activity, and alert to its appearance anywhere."[62] Such was the hysteria that even a report that in 1888 Gordin had once attended a meeting of Elisavetgrad People's Will sympathizers, and had picked up some pamphlets, was enough to brand the entire organization as "politically unreliable" for a time.[63] After seven years of good to guarded relations with the police, and in light of the government's own granting of legal status to the Brotherhood, it is unlikely that the sudden, putative revolution being fomented in the sect's midst was an expression of its deeply held antigovernment convictions. It was Fainerman's intemperate rhetoric that led the police to step up their surveillance of the group, but it is notable that even after gathering their intelligence, the police made no effort to shut down the Brotherhood.

GLODOSSY

In October of 1889, Fainerman and Butkevich paid a visit to Glodossy, a town of about one thousand residents, many of them Stundists.

Officially classed as a shtetl (*mestechko*), Glodossy was not closed to Jewish settlement by the 1882 May Laws. In Glodossy, Fainerman hoped to establish an agrarian colony for those Brotherhood members who wished to take its teachings in a more actively Tolstoyan direction. Funding from Alekhin enabled Fainerman to purchase twenty *desyatina* (fifty-four acres) of land and several houses, which would form the basis of the Brotherhood's agricultural colony. In early December 1889, Fainerman, Butkevich, their respective families, and a number of members of the Spiritual-Biblical Brotherhood left for Glodossy to begin life as agrarian workers and artisans.[64] Gordin remained in Elisavetgrad.[65]

Gordin's writings for the entire period of the Glodossy exodus betray nothing of the division in the sect's ranks. There are no reports in the *Elisavetgradskii vestnik* of the Brotherhood's settlement there, despite the paper's regular coverage of events in Glodossy. Police reports indicate that the group of about a dozen were warmly greeted in Glodossy by the village's Stundist peasants. The Brotherhood's members set themselves up as carpenters, smiths, and shoemakers, while Anna Fainerman dispensed free medical aid to the peasants. Members lived and dressed simply and held their prayer meetings according to their own rites. But the experiment did not last.

The first evidence of trouble came in March 1890, when Fainerman left to visit Tolstoy at Yasnaya Polyana. A few weeks later, Butkevich wrote to Alexei Pastukhov, a mutual friend of his and Tolstoy's, of "disagreements" in Glodossy. On April 30, Tolstoy addressed a letter to Butkevich, Fainerman, and the members of the Brotherhood in Glodossy, counseling them to conquer their individual feelings of pride and expressing his hope that they would not abandon the colony at the first sign of conflict.[66] Tolstoy's encouragement could not save the colony. In mid-May, 1890, Fainerman left Kherson province with his wife and children and moved to Alekhin's colony at Shevelovo. Butkevich eventually returned to his family's estate at Rusanovo.

The Glodossy failure resulted in bitter feelings all around, but Gordin, at least, was validated in his original disapproval of both Fainerman and the colony. Anna Dobrowolski-Sherman, a member of the Brotherhood, related in her memoirs that "when the group returned three months later empty-handed, Gordin said smilingly that it was a very good experiment."[67] By September 1890, the land and houses in Glodossy were leased to someone else.

The police report admits to ignorance regarding the exact reasons for the failure of the Glodossy colony, and Fainerman and Butkevich would only ever admit to "disagreements" within its ranks.[68] That the harvest for 1889 was a poor one in the region, and with bankruptcies, hardship, and record numbers of people turning to charity organizations for aid, as reported in the news, cannot have made a difficult and poorly planned endeavor any more likely to prosper.[69] The sect survived the split, and some of those who had left returned to the Elisavetgrad group, but the Glodossy experiment prompted the police to take a more energetic interest in the Brotherhood's activities.

For those who cherish theories about the deadly reach and chilling efficiency of the tsarist secret police, or who would like to believe that Fainerman's imprecations against the state sealed Jacob Gordin's doom, or even that Gordin himself was a firebrand revolutionary who presented an incalculable risk to the tsarist autocracy, his file offers an enlightening corrective. While the story it tells is duller than the lively narrative of threat and flight that Gordin fabricated for his American colleagues and audiences, it offers a telling illustration of how slowly and inefficiently the mechanisms of the tsarist administration actually worked. In the end, Gordin's pseudo-socialism and Fainerman's rash words had less to do with the closing of the Spiritual-Biblical Brotherhood than did tedious bureaucratic irregularities and bad record-keeping.

THE END OF THE BROTHERHOOD

The beginning of the Brotherhood's end began simply enough, with its second request, in 1888, to be allowed to maintain its own vital statistics. This request was again met with a firm no. While the sect's legalization as a separate religious entity gave it the right to appoint its own rabbi (Gordin) and to hold its own services, vital statistics— from which tax records and conscription lists were compiled— remained the province of the official, "state" rabbi. A new "state" rabbi, Mordkhe Shapsovich—who had very little to do with the day-to-day function of the sect, and nothing at all to do with their spiritual guidance—was appointed in May 1889 to record the Brotherhood's vital statistics.[70]

As it later emerged, Shapsovich was not even living in Elisavetgrad, and as a result, the Brotherhood maintained no records of births, deaths, marriages, or even how many people counted themselves members. These matters went unnoticed, however, until a remark in

Gordin's police file in September 1890 noted that "the Brotherhood does not maintain a list of its members."[71] This report prompted a fuller investigation of the disarray into which the sect's records had fallen. Yet even though this report noted that the sect's wish to appoint Jacob Gordin as its official rabbi could not be supported because "confirmation of his political reliability cannot be given," almost another year passed before any action was taken.[72] Finally, on July 20, 1891, Shapsovich asked to be relieved of his duties to the Spiritual-Biblical Brotherhood. This prompted the tsarist police to make a decision regarding the sect . . . three months later. On October 7, 1891, the Ministry of Internal Affairs rescinded the 1885 order that had legalized the Brotherhood. By then, though, the Brotherhood was already in disarray, and Gordin had been in New York for more than two months.[73]

Far from being a relentlessly vigilant hydra, ever ready to strike down feisty upstarts who dared defy its might, the state was lumbering and inefficient. Memos were missed, letters crossed, and confusion reigned as to who actually had jurisdiction over the Brotherhood—the local police, the Kherson governor's office, the Ministry of Internal Affairs, or the Ministry for Foreign Confessions. Not only did the tsarist police never get around to issuing an arrest warrant for Jacob Gordin, but it took them six months to even notice that he had left the country.

The lack of an official arrest order does not mean that Gordin might not eventually have run afoul of the police. But the absence of any evidence that Gordin was under threat, coupled with the fact that members of the Brotherhood who actually *had* violated tsarist law were never arrested either, suggests that neither Gordin nor his followers were ever under any threat whatsoever.[74] Nor was Fainerman, who had a lengthy police file, or Butkevich, who actually had served time in prison on two separate occasions, threatened either. Well after Gordin's immigration, the former members of the Spiritual-Biblical Brotherhood continued to live in Ukraine, where some of them formed a successful dairy collective.[75]

The stories of Gordin's "escape" from Russia in a hayrick, under cover of night, after being tipped off by well-wishers that he was under imminent threat of arrest, is a colorful fiction. There was no arrest order, no squadron of soldiers coming with manacles, no threat of banishment or imprisonment. No one in the tsarist administration even noticed that Gordin had left Russia.

Why did he leave? Gordin's writing of the time suggests a profound feeling of frustration with the intransigence of Russian provincial life, the slow pace of change, and the indifference of the world to his most ardently held beliefs. The divisions and disagreements within the Spiritual-Biblical Brotherhood that led to a schism in its ranks also took their toll. Perhaps because of these complications the fault line between the many professional roles that Gordin played—as religious activist, editor, journalist, and creative writer—began to emerge. The theatre is the locus in which these fissures manifest themselves.

THEATRUM MUNDI

A two-part article by Ivan Kolyuchii in June of 1889, titled "Dovol'no! Dovol'no!" (Enough! Enough!), finds the reporter at the circus. Despite his distaste for its "repulsive" exploitation of animals and child performers, Ivan is inexplicably drawn to the "disgusting, appalling" show.[76] It's like alcohol, muses Ivan: something to deaden the senses, help you escape from the pressures of work. Because for public figures like Ivan, who "give everything to what they believe in," he has little to show for it:

> This is our misfortune, that every avenue of social action is blocked to us. No matter what the measure of your vitality, what kind of overwhelming strengths you sense in yourself, no matter how wonderful and lofty your strivings, however honest and noble your convictions—you will not overcome the apathy that surrounds you. You will not inspire the confidence of others, those who believe only in a life of force, the power of the whip, the sincerity of fools and cretins, and the capacities of mediocrity.[77]

Ivan's work, too, has begun to lose some of its charms, judging from the circus metaphor he employs to describe it:

> What are the duties of a clown? He presents our reality in somewhat exaggerated form, he offers an occasionally successful parody; he bravely shades and underlines our own weaknesses and the ridiculous aspects of our lives. Society forgives him his rude mockery because it is for their pleasure that he turns somersaults, falls to the ground, gets slapped, rubs his nose in the dirt, takes kicks and blows.[78]

But even clowns weary of pratfalls. Ivan Kolyuchii's feuilletons grow increasingly opaque, as he makes veiled complaints about life in Elisavetgrad and the futility of action. In "Letter to Readers," (Pis'mo k chitatelyam) in December of 1889, he effectively describes Gordin's own literary personae and offers a clue to the strategy behind their multiplication:

> In order to please you, to make you hear us out, to pique your inter-
> est, attract your attention, our literary fraternity employs various
> ways and means. Some of us appear before you dressed as jesters;
> some clown and play the fool for you, others drape themselves in
> the togas of moralists, a third will appear in the garb of a prophet, a
> fourth in the role of a popular trendsetter . . . They all have but one
> goal—to please you, to gain your approval.[79]

But now Ivan wonders if the efforts of his "literary fraternity" have had any effect. "Tomorrow I will depart the stage, to be replaced by another, and you won't even notice my absence—it makes no differ- ence to you whether I've fallen ill, or died, or succumbed to some misfortune, whether I am silent for a short time or forever." Per- haps his writing only temporarily disturbs the "stagnant and fetid swamp" of his surroundings, and all the frantic energies of his and these other "representatives of the printed word" are doomed merely to create eddies that dissolve into nothingness. Ivan cannot recon- cile himself to a life of passivity: "There is no intelligent human life outside of ideas, outside of progress, outside of hope for a better and brighter future."

In the ensuing months, Gordin's articles appeared with less fre- quency in the *Elisavetgradskii vestnik* and vanished altogether by mid-1890. Gordin's diminished public presence at the newspaper that had been his main source of income may well be connected with larger changes in the region. The retirement of the Kherson province's governor, Aleksandr S. Erdeli, in early June 1890, was cause for much anxiety on the part of Elisavetgraders.[80] In 1891 the *Vestnik* itself ceased publication; its demise may well have figured in Gordin's decision to immigrate to the United States in June of that year. Perhaps for Gordin as well, "labor, rather than liberty, re- mained the overriding concern in the decision to move to the United States, especially in the peak immigration years of the industrial era."[81]

LAST WORDS

There is perhaps a final clue to the reasons for Gordin's immigra- tion in his last story for *Knizhki nedeli*. Published in June of 1891,

"Vykrest" (The Convert) is qualitatively superior to Gordin's earlier work. Although still reluctant to explore his characters' interior perspectives, Gordin has grown more adept at suggesting their dimensions and conflicts. Although the path of Jewish fate in these stories leads, as always, but to the grave, the roads by which his characters travel and the worlds that they inhabit are rendered in elegiac tones, with great sensitivity to the many natural beauties of Ukraine. The melancholy strain that had always been a feature of Gordin's best writing took center stage in a series of stories that exhibit a depth of sympathy for Russian Jews that would scarcely have been possible a decade before. In a development that prefigures his evolution as a dramatist, Gordin grew as a prose writer at the very time he was preparing to leave his native land and native language forever.

"VYKREST" (THE CONVERT)

Gordin's last published Russian story appeared in *Knizhki nedeli* in the very month that he left his homeland. It too ends with a departure that eloquently suggests its author's own extended leave-taking, as well as the potential consequences of not breaking free. While not without the telegraphed symbolism familiar from both Gordin's plays and his *Evreiskie siluety*, "Vykrest" is concerned with a hero who wants to exceed the boundaries of a world defined by religion, ethnicity, and historical memory. What is in earlier stories construed as a fault, as inconstancy and deception, is here configured as a tragic affinity for two very different cultural sensibilities. The impossibility of their reconciliation or amalgamation leads to a multiplication of identities that is a result of the individual's ostracism by both Slavic and Jewish worlds.

The story's hero is eleven-year-old Berko, a poor tailor's son who resists all efforts to give him an elementary Jewish religious education in *kheyder*. Bored by lessons and prayers, Berko prefers playing out of doors with the peasant children. His frustrated father bursts out, "I'm going to kick you out of this house for good, just like God chased his disobedient children—Adam and Eve—out of their Garden of Eden."[82] The comparison is deeply ironic, for Berko's shtetl is a miserable town, "where money is so dear, and labor so cheap," and exile from it doesn't look like a bad deal. But home grows in nostalgic significance the farther you are from it. With the literal-mindedness of the child that he is, Berko takes his father at his word and leaves home.

> He set out along the road that runs beside the mills and pastures, toward the hills, where the sky joins the earth. He knows very well from *kheyder* that if you walk in one direction you will reach the river Sambation, which for six days in the week spits out fiery rocks, allowing none to approach its banks. But on the Sabbath day it quiets down, and lets you cross to the other side, where the ten tribes of Israel, banished from the holy land by Saul Manasseh, impatiently await the coming Messiah . . . (34)

The topography of Berko's Ukrainian homeland is overlaid with the imaginative landscape of Jewish folk legend, where the straight path of Jewish tradition will inevitably lead the wanderer to his long-lost brothers. The shadow of Zion, the Jewish past and future, is everywhere apparent in Eastern Europe. It is a trope frequently employed by Yiddish writers from Sholem Abramovitsh to Der Nister (Pinhas Kahanovitsh, 1884–1950), whose Slavic landscapes are sanctified by their connection, through their Jews, to an ancient past and faith. But never has this Judaized landscape been evoked by Gordin in his Russian prose, whose landmarks, language, and living folk tradition are, until this point, Slavic. Berko's vision of home is suffused with Jewish legend, but that legend is manifest in a Russian and Ukrainian reality. Far from being inimical and alien to Jewish folk belief, a poor substitute for the Zion of memory, Gordin's Slavic landscape is its inheritor, its modern-day incarnation. Jewish legend coexists and evolves in concert with its Slavic home, not in contrast to it. Thus Berko finds his lost tribe of brothers when a friendly Ukrainian farmer on a cart comes upon the boy as night falls.

Berko tells his story to the peasant, who assures the boy that there's nothing to fear: "'I'll take you home to my village. I've got five daughters, but God has given me no sons. You can be my son,' said the peasant, half-jokingly, half-seriously" (36). A little more than fifty kilometers from his shtetl, Berko begins a new life, as his *peyes* are shorn and he is given peasant clothing, and he is quickly absorbed into village life. In the spring, he is baptized into the informal, near-pagan Christianity of his adoptive family and is renamed Yegor. From then on, he is indistinguishable from the other peasant children. He tends animals, works in the fields, never spends a day in school, and grows strong and sturdy.

As the years pass, Berko/Yegor remains dimly conscious of his Jewish origins and family, but he thinks of them only during the High Holidays, when he recalls the dolorous grandeur of the Yom Kippur service. But with childish inconstancy, the mood and memories pass: "The past grew more distant, became less and less clear, and disappeared as if in a fog" (40). He grows up to be a model citizen of the village, marked out from the others only by his beautiful and distinctive singing:

> He sang with his soul and with feeling, giving every song a particular and entirely new kind of shading. To the quiet, pensive, and dreamy sadness of Ukrainian songs he added a moan of incomprehensible grief, a cry of despair, and a murmur of righteous anger. It was as if the long ago past was being mourned in this song; it reminded one of something people had long since forgotten, something precious, and lost to the ages. By this song, any Jew would have recognized in Yegor one of his own tribe. (40–41)

As with all of Gordin's heroes, Berko/Yegor's singing voice expresses his truest self, and it is only in music that Berko exhibits any depth of attachment to his Jewish kin and ancestors. Yet it is Ukrainian folksongs that are the vehicle for expression of a half-remembered Jewish identity. Their interpretation by a Jewish artist has validity and depth and exhibits enormous potential for expressing the Jewish experience in the Slavic lands. Much as Gordin himself would remake Russian originals for the Jewish stage, Berko's Ukrainian songs, tinged with Slavic rue and Jewish soul, act as a bridge between who the singer was and who he will be.

At eighteen, Berko/Yegor is persuaded to marry one of his adoptive family's daughters, Marusya. The marriage is not a happy one, for it is unnatural: Berko/Yegor *is* Marusya's brother—not by blood but by upbringing and history. Jews and Slavs are kindred, and as always in Gordin's writings, the family is the source of the most painful sufferings, the most lasting damage, and the most dangerous threats. Familiarity has bred contempt in Marusya, but Berko/Yegor ignores the villagers' advice to beat her into submission. When Marusya leaves him, neighbors tease him by calling him "Berko." He leaves the village, thinking that he will find understanding only among his Jewish birth family. Just as unexpectedly as Berko had arrived in the Ukrainian village, he vanishes, leaving his adoptive family grieving.

When Berko returns to the shtetl, like Rip Van Winkle or Urashima Taro of Japanese folktales, only the oldest Jews remember him. He learns that when his parents discovered where their son had gone to live, they mourned and wept and finally left the shtetl and their shame for America. Berko/Yegor is shocked: "To America! He had no idea where this country was, but he knew, or he guessed, that it was terribly far away and that to get there was beyond human strength" (46). America is the other side, *yene velt, tot svet*, a world not to be reached by the living. Berko is not prepared to make that journey, so he is reabsorbed into the shtetl. He is sent to the ritual bath, given Jewish clothing, and is renamed Dov-Ber.

Thus does the third act of his life begin. He is married off to an old maid who will put up with his broken Yiddish and who pities him for his sojourn among the goyim. They have children, and he finds work as a carter—his Ukrainian father's profession, a link that signals his continuing attachment to his old life among the peasants. Berko/Yegor/Dov-Ber—whose identities multiply along with his names—is pious and passionate in his prayers, but every year, around Easter, he disappears. This period of absence continues for years, with no explanation.

> No one guessed that it was not only Berko who lived in these divided circumstances but Yegor, who had spent the best years of his life in another world, in completely different circumstances. His receptive and impressionable nature could not easily part with what he had perceived, could not forget what he had experienced and felt. (48)

Berko is drawn constantly to his old life, and when he discovers a small bronze cross on a shredded string in the road one day, he slips it around his neck, underneath his shirt. While Berko occasionally touches the cross for comfort, more often he will sing Ukrainian songs to himself, recalling the village and the life that there seems now to him to be "so alluring and wonderful" (49).

When Berko is killed in a carting accident, his body is prepared by the burial society for interment in the Jewish cemetery. To their horror, they discover the bronze cross around his neck. Berko's body is committed to a grave in the ravine outside the town, among the suicides. No one says kaddish for him, and Berko, who had dreamed of an eternal rest in the green and wooded cemetery beside his adoptive Ukrainian peasant father, is instead buried in foul clay soil, unmourned and unmissed.

It is probably a coincidence that this story of a Ukrainian Jew who could find happiness in neither the Christian nor the Jewish world appeared in the very month that Gordin left his homeland forever. Though given to overstating both the pastoral charms of peasant life and the grimness of Jewish life, the story recapitulates the conflict facing all of the characters in Gordin's Russian fiction. Caught between cultures, languages, and worlds, always longing for one when in the other, Gordin's heroes and villains find the push-pull of Christian and Jewish cultures intolerable, and often fatal. Berko/Yegor's tragedy is not that he *wants* to be a Slav when he is among Jews and a Jew when he is among Slavs. His tragedy is that by upbringing, language, and elective affinity, he is both Slav and Jew. But it is clear from this story and from Gordin's many others on Jewish life that there is no compromising or negotiating between these identities: one has to make a choice. Berko did not, and could not. But Jacob Gordin did. When Gordin left Russia, he would memorialize the land again and again in Yiddish as a lost father figure, a beloved tyrant, an intimate stranger. The land that was lost could be recovered only in literature, in a form that could be remade for a new audience, and in a new medium.

What did Gordin leave behind in Russia? He left a fractured literary persona, a selective literary assimilation into Russian culture and society through its language and literature. Through fiction and journalism Gordin crossed borders, blurred distinctions, and eluded the limitations imposed by faith, class, and ethnicity. Yet this fluidity—the very thing for which he condemned his protean Jewish protagonists and villains—was in truth his own. It was through fiction again that he would manage one more self-invention. It would be the most successful of all: when Yakov Gordin became Jacob Gordin, Yiddish playwright, journalist, and tireless cultural activist on the Lower East Side.

Figure 1. Jacob Gordin, photographed in 1887 in Elisavetgrad. From the Archives of the YIVO Institute for Jewish Research.

Figure 2. Jacob Gordin with two members of the Spiritual-Biblical Brotherhood, Evgenii Gar and Rozalia Fainzilberg. Elisavetgrad, 1880s. From the Archives of the YIVO Institute for Jewish Research.

Figure 3. Bertha Kalich, who originated the role of Ettie in *Di kreytser sonata* in Yiddish and performed the same role in *The Kreutzer Sonata* in the English translation on Broadway. From the New York magazine *The Theater*, July 1905.

Figure 4. Gordin, photographed in New York in the 1900s. From the Archives of the YIVO Institute for Jewish Research.

CHAPTER FOUR

The Perils of Performance

Di kreytser sonata *(1902)*

Sex, violence, and classical music: Lev Tolstoy's *Kreitserova so-nata* (*The Kreutzer Sonata*, 1889) offered all of these to shocked readers in Europe and America. But Jacob Gordin went further still when he adapted the novel for the Thalia Theatre in 1902. Into Tolstoy's already inflammatory polemic, Gordin added im-migration, a thwarted conversion to Christianity, two illegitimate pregnancies, agrarian utopianism, a double homicide, and trade unions, as well as several musical numbers. Gordin's Tolstoyan drama proved so popular that it was translated into both English and Russian, performed in three different productions on Broad-way, frequently staged and revived in Moscow and St. Petersburg, and made into a film in 1915.[1]

Its melodramatic turns have tended to obscure the Yiddish *Kreyt-ser sonata*'s complex interrogation of its source material, and the play has generally been dismissed as having little to do with Tolstoy's original.[2] Reviewers regarded it as a savvy commercial undertaking only slightly redeemed by its efforts to pique an audience's interest in Beethoven and Tolstoy.

The desire to capitalize on the notoriety of Tolstoy's work by pro-ducing a Yiddish stage adaptation reflects not just a pursuit of box-office profits but an enormous public interest in Tolstoy's art and poli-tics. *Kreitserova sonata* itself had been available in Yiddish translation since 1895.[3] Yiddish speakers could read translations of Tolstoy's complete works and see Gordin's own translation of *Vlast' t'my* (*The Power of Darkness*, 1901): *Di makht fun finsternish*.[4] In 1904 Gordin also adapted *Voskresenie* (*Resurrection*, 1899), for the stage as *Tkhieshamey*, and in 1911 Jacob P. Adler would score a notable success with his Yiddish production of *Zhivoi trup* (*The Living Corpse*, ca. 1900). The *Forverts* offered volumes of Tolstoy as a subscription incentive, and the Yiddish press published interviews with Tolstoy and assiduously reported his pronouncements on war, patriotism, the Russian government, and his excommunication by the Orthodox Church.[5] For New York's Yiddish press, Tolstoy was the model of an artist's commitment to literature, social justice, and personal integrity.[6] In radical circles of the Jewish intelligentsia, Steven Cassedy notes:

> Tolstoy was a hero both because of what they perceived as either anarchist or socialist views in his writings and because of his undying commitment to the welfare of the Russian peasants; to others he was a false prophet; to political moderates and conservatives, he was an object of curiosity as the head of a growing international movement; to all, he was a powerful symbol of resistance.[7]

Hutchins Hapgood's (1869–1944) sensitive profiles of the turn-of-the-century Lower East Side's Russian-Jewish immigrants also found that Russian radicals "look up to Tolstoi and Chekhov, and reject all principles founded upon more romantic and genial models."[8] Gordin's play takes serious issue with that idealization.

Gordin's adaptation of Tolstoy's novel was the culmination of many years of engagement with the Russian writer's art and ideas. But despite the playwright's reputation in America as a passionate follower of Tolstoy, the reality was more complicated.

In 1886, "Yakov Mikhailovich" published a point-by-point rebuttal of an article by the essayist Aleksandr Skabichevsky (1838–1910) that evidences Gordin's detailed knowledge of Tolstoy's philosophical writing. Countering Skabichevsky's argument that the level of violence in a society diminishes as its intellectual development increases, Yakov Mikhailovich notes:

> Count Tolstoy says that surfaces are deceptive, that violence is evil, and that suffering has not diminished with the expansion of scientific knowledge; that barbarism has not vanished, but merely taken on a different appearance, and that relationships between those nearest to us have taken on a much more aesthetic, superficially glossy and adaptable character, but that this has not been matched by an increase in moral knowledge, or love, or justice; that evil has only adopted more refined forms and sophisticated devices, as a result of

which the sum of misfortunes, and the victims of violence, injustice, and oppression, have remained the same.[9]

These ideas return in full force in Gordin's adaptation of *Kreitserova sonata*, as the Yiddish playwright uses the drama to explore the dangerous allure of surface deceptions and glossy exteriors.

In 1890, "Ivan Kolyuchii" also made pointed criticism of *Kreitserova sonata* in a comic story of a young couple whose marriage takes a wrong turn after they read Tolstoy's novel. While the wife, Lipochka, dismisses Tolstoy's advocacy of chastity in marriage as absurd, her husband, Fyodor, becomes convinced that he can only show his true respect for her by acting in a "brotherly" fashion. He mopes about, averting his eyes, but Lipochka still has to look after the house and baby, suggesting that male retreat to the realm of impracticable theory is a form of exploitation itself, because it requires women's shouldering even more of the work of family life. Both husband and wife eventually realize that there is no place for Tolstoy's ideas in the day-to-day affairs of work and family.[10]

In an 1893 address to the Russian Social Democrats Society, Gordin further dismissed Tolstoy's late works as adding nothing new to the writer's worldview, a characterization that is reiterated in 1904's "Realism and Romanticism."[11] The onetime realist "has become a romantic in his old age. He has begun longing for the old Christian past."[12]

The divisive confrontations that the Spiritual-Biblical Brotherhood had weathered in 1889 after the Glodossy fiasco could not have lent any further luster to Tolstoy's prescriptions for the transformed life. That disappointment, as well as the continued thwarting of Gordin's desire to farm in America, is evident in *Di kreytser sonata*'s depiction of a Russian immigrant's disastrous attempt to make himself over into an American farmer.

Gordin substantially reorganizes and reinterprets his source text, and in the process, he offers an original critical perspective that departs significantly from traditional readings of it. Some of the arguments presented in Tolstoy's work, regarding the economic exploitation of women by men (and that of Jews and gentiles), were wholly in accordance with Gordin's own views. But Gordin was as staunch an advocate of "free love" as he was of Beethoven's music, and his play finds neither guilty of inciting the violence with which they are associated in Tolstoy's novel. Gordin's play suggests that the Russian novel is really about the dangerous powers of fiction itself, both as literary art and as social performance. Gordin's play, in turn, examines the manifold destructive effects of performance, pretense, and literary fiction on one Russian-Jewish immigrant family.

KREITSEROVA SONATA

Tolstoy's novel takes the form of a monologue by a repellent antihero, Pozdnyshev, an acquitted wife-murderer who tells an unnamed narrator whom he encounters on a train the tale of his stormy marriage. This framing device brackets a tale that begins with Pozdnyshev's recollection of his dissolute youth spent frequenting brothels. He finds nothing shameful in this account, nor does he find it absurd that he allows himself what he would not tolerate in a prospective wife. Still, Pozdnyshev wishes the innocent girl to whom he becomes engaged to know what his life has been like before marriage. He shows her his diary, and although she is horrified by his promiscuity, she does not break off the engagement.

The marriage that follows is not a happy one, but sexual passion masks the hate that Pozdnyshev and his wife feel for each other. Children are born, but they do little to quell the couple's enmity. After one difficult birth, the wife—who is never named in the novel—is advised to have no more children. Her doctors instruct her on means of contraception, and Pozdnyshev is horrified to see how happily she embraces this option.

No longer hampered by yearly pregnancies, Pozdnyshev's wife finds time to enjoy herself, and she resumes playing the piano. Her interest in music brings a violinist called Trukhachevsky into the family circle. The two begin to practice Beethoven's *Kreutzer* Sonata for a recital. Their musical collaboration leads to Pozdnyshev's suspecting that his wife and the violinist are lovers, although there is never any evidence that this suspicion is actually true. Pozdnyshev leaves for a few days on a business trip, and he receives a letter from his wife that mentions that the violinist dropped off some sheet music. Enraged, Pozdnyshev returns home to find his wife having dinner alone with Trukhachevsky. In a fury, he stabs her to death. Only when she is dying does Pozdnyshev see her as a human being and not as a sexual object.

The lesson that Pozdnyshev draws from these events is that marriage demeans men and women because it legitimizes the destructive sexual instinct. Only when it is conquered can human beings devote themselves to fulfilling God's true plan: altruistic connection with one another, empathy, and the betterment of human lives. It would be better to live an entirely chaste life, argued Tolstoy himself in an afterword, than to give in to the erotic desires that dehumanize men and women alike.

Both Tolstoy and his spokesman Pozdnyshev implicate disparate social and cultural forces in the pernicious legitimization of sexual passion. The church's elevation of marriage to a sacrament, overstimulating music, duplicitous literary fiction, provocative clothing, rich foods, indolence, and contraception all contribute to the dehumanization of women and invite women's retributive exploitation of men through male sexual weaknesses. Each form of sensual aesthetic stimulation (particularly that offered by the arts) is a diversion that makes possible a universal avoidance of the "truth" that sexuality is a force of destruction, not an expression of love. It is Pozdnyshev's self-appointed task to reveal the truth of our dissembling and the toll that it exacts.

Music was long the object of Tolstoy's troubled affections, and it is impugned in *Kreitserova sonata* as the most "dangerous" art, the one most likely to rouse unproductive emotions and license unseemly appetites of the kind that lead Pozdnyshev to murder. Many critical analyses of the novel take their cues from Tolstoy himself and argue that the novel's title reflects its aesthetic preoccupations, as well as Tolstoy's own numerous pronouncements on music in letters and diaries and in *Chto takoe iskusstvo?* (*What Is Art?* 1898).[13]

Gordin's adaptation, however, absolves music of any destructive role in instigating the murders with which *Kreytser sonata* concludes. This point is only one of many in which Gordin parts ways with Tolstoy. Where Tolstoy indicts church-sanctioned sexual oppression in marriage, Gordin rails against the hypocrisy of Jewish patriarchal authority. Where Tolstoy argues for chastity, Gordin advocates sexual emancipation. And where Tolstoy implicates music in his novel's violent end, Gordin uses Tolstoy's own *Kreitserova sonata* as an agent of destruction.

DI KREYTSER SONATA

Gordin's play opens in the Pale of Settlement at the turn of the nineteenth century. At rise, it is revealed that Ettie Friedlander has tried to convert to Christianity in order to marry her Russian officer lover, by whom she is pregnant. The plan is foiled, and in despair Ettie's lover kills himself. To protect the family reputation, Ettie's father, Raphael, plans to marry her to an ambitious musician, Gregor Fiedler, and pack them both off to America. "There no one will ask when you were married, and no one will count the months after the wedding."[14]

When informed of her fate, Ettie, nervously clutching a book, dutifully agrees to the plan:

> *Ettie*: As you think best, Papa. (*She presses the book to her heart.*)
>
> *Raphael*: (*In a friendly tone.*) Well, why are you standing? Sit down. (*She sits.*) What is that book?
>
> *Ettie*: This is volume eleven of Tolstoy's works . . . in this book . . . I will tell you the truth, Papa . . . (*Frightened.*)
>
> *Raphael*: (*Warmly.*) There, there, now, you can talk calmly about a book. What is it?
>
> *Ettie*: This? This is . . . this is *The Kreutzer Sonata*. I've just read the first chapters . . . Oh, it makes life so ugly, so much uglier than I had thought before.
>
> *Raphael*: A book cannot make life ugly. Man makes life ugly. As you have made this life ugly for yourself . . . Give me that book! (11)[15]

Raphael hands the book to Ettie's poisonous younger sister, Celia. The powers of Tolstoy's novel are such that Ettie's merely holding it forces her to tell the "truth"; clearly, cannot be trusted with such stirring material. Ettie symbolically buries her past in the novel by putting her lover's photograph and his last letter to her between its pages. She will do her father's bidding, provide her child with a father, and preserve the family honor by fleeing to New York.

Ettie confesses her sins to Gregor in a manner that recalls Pozdnyshev's (and Tolstoy's own) confession to his fiancée; Gregor is unfazed by Ettie's sexual indiscretion: "Ah, who among us has not had love affairs? And how many love affairs! As I live and breathe, I can't even begin to count how many times I've been in love" (20). Gregor is disturbed, though, when he learns that Ettie is pregnant by her lover, a circumstance that will become the focus of bitter recriminations as the play unfolds. Ettie swears to be faithful to Gregor, but warns that she will never love him. For now, Gregor reckons that Ettie's dowry provides sufficient compensation for a loveless marriage.

Seven years later, Ettie, Gregor, and Ettie's son, Albert, are living in Manhattan, where Gregor is the director of a musical conservatory. The rest of the Friedlander and Fiedler families join them in America. Ephraim, Gregor's exuberant klezmer musician father struggles with the regulations and fees of the musician's union. Raphael buys a farm in Connecticut and tries to live a Tolstoyan dream of agrarian redemption. The farm is losing money and baffles his family, who is mystified by a wealthy businessman's need to spend his twilight years working the land. The family remains in the city, where Celia and Gregor carry on a torrid affair while rehearsing Beethoven's *Kreutzer* Sonata.

Beethoven's work figures in a musical competition among Ephraim, Gregor, and Celia. Following Ephraim's performance of a soulful klezmer variation, Gregor and Celia enter the fray with the first movement of Beethoven's sonata. Ephraim—the authentic folk artist—is spontaneous, sincere, and joyous. But Gregor and Celia—depraved, cynical, trained professionals—do not entirely conform to the image of "bad" artists that Tolstoy outlined in *Chto takoe iskusstvo?* In Gordin's play, "bad" artists may be morally corrupt, but they are entrusted with introducing the audience to the redemptive powers of secular, non-Jewish music. The work of art is impervious to corruption, even though it requires a performer as mediator between artist and audience.

Ettie finds that when her spouse plays Beethoven she forgets all the anguish that he has caused her. On learning the sonata's title, Ettie says to herself, "*The Kreutzer Sonata!* The book . . . I need to find it and finish it . . . " (38). Out of sight of others, Celia tells Gregor, "When we were playing the sonata I suddenly recalled how Tolstoy described the effect their playing had on his heroes . . . My heart suddenly began racing and the sweet sounds began to merge with the fire in your eyes . . . Were you always to play that way, I would always love you . . . " (43).

It is less Beethoven's music, though, than Tolstoy's novel that impresses Ettie and Celia; the latter sees Pozdnyshev's wife and Trukhachevsky as the "heroes" (*heldn*) of the novel and unwisely casts herself and Gregor in their roles. For Ettie, too, music prompts her to recall Tolstoy's novel. Later, when Ettie spies her sister and husband embracing, she extracts a promise from Celia that she will end the affair; it is a promise that Celia does not keep.

Act 3 is set on Raphael's farm at Christmas, where Ettie finds her copy of *Kreitserova sonata*, and after rereading her lover's letter she decides, "I will relive the whole terrible drama again, and then I will destroy it, purge everything, forget . . . " (52). Gazing at her dead love's photograph, Ettie reflects, "I belong now to another, to whom I have sworn to be true" (52). Gregor snatches the letter from her, but Ettie betrays a will of steel and commands him to return it. Somewhat fearfully, Gregor does. The act includes a raucous scene of song and dance involving caroling farmers, the performance of a wistful Russian song by Ettie, and Celia's revelation to Gregor that she is pregnant.

The final act takes place months later, in Ephraim's fledgling music school. Raphael has come into town for supplies and to beg Gregor for money to save the farm. Gregor refuses and swans off to the opera with Celia, who is lately returned to New York after an unexplained absence of several months. When it is inadvertently revealed that Gregor and Celia are actually visiting their illegitimate child, Ettie confronts them. She had tried to ignore their affair, out of a feeling that she had no right to cast stones. But this revelation pushes Ettie over the edge. Why does Celia suffer no consequences, while she, Ettie, has endured such torment and misery? Hysterically, she cries, "That was your last lie! There will be no more lies!" [. . .] Did you think that you'd live out your whole life with opera, songs, and lies? There are no more songs! The terrible end is coming!" (89). Gregor tries to calm Ettie by claiming, "Only you are dear to me, only you are truly mine!" (90). But Ettie answers:

> Yours! I know what it means to be "yours"! Your property! My body belongs to you! My body has belonged to you since I was born and will belong to you until I die! When you need my body, you love me. When you love me it means you need my body! You see that I'm cared for, I am dear to you like any piece of property is to any owner! My body interested you, but you murdered my soul every day ten times over! With every look you trampled my human feelings underfoot! I've lived with you for nearly ten years, and never for a minute have you ever thought of me as a person—only as a woman, as a wife, as a servant! You never would or could understand me. You never would or could know what I've endured in that time. I swore to endure and be silent—I have been silent and borne more than I needed! Enough! (90)[16]

Gordin's gender switch renders Ettie both Pozdnyshev and his nameless wife, a position that Celia mocks by accusing her sister of poaching this speech from Tolstoy's *Kreitserova sonata*. Ettie warns Celia to stop laughing and seizes a bottle of carbolic acid from the bag of supplies that Raphael has left on the piano. Threatening to burn out her sister's eyes, Ettie exclaims, "So that you can't look at other people's husbands!" (91). If Celia is hideous to men, screams Ettie, perhaps then she will remember that she is a mother; like Pozdnyshev, she hopes that the maternal instinct will trump the sexual one. When Gregor and Celia wrest the bottle of acid from her, Ettie reaches for

Raphael's loaded revolver, also lying (conveniently) on the piano. She shoots Gregor and then pumps the remaining five bullets into Celia. The curtain falls as Ettie collapses, delirious, crying to her nanny that she cannot see. The audience is left not knowing Ettie's ultimate fate.

Clearly, Gordin was not interested in a straightforward transfer of Tolstoy's novel to the Yiddish stage. Instead, Gordin emphasizes those aspects of the original text that coincide with his own aesthetic and political biases. This treatment is particularly in evidence with regard to music, which Gordin exonerates entirely of any culpability in the play's tragic end.

Gordin's defense of music is perhaps not surprising, given that music features prominently in nearly every one of his plays. While Yiddish theatrical convention all but required musical elements in drama, the symbolic significance that Gordin attaches to music suggests that his use of it was less a capitulation to public demand than a conscious aesthetic strategy. In an essay titled "Drama," Gordin describes the range and depth of the playwright's art itself in musical terms. He aligns the playwright with the pianist, a solitary voice that blends with the orchestra but nonetheless remains a distinct, guiding presence:

> The piano is a unified entity, a common force of sounds. The talented pianist commands a great sea of sweet, strong, and powerful tones; he harmonizes, creates varied combinations, and plays on all manner of feelings . . . Among the arts, the drama occupies a position that is analogous to that of the piano among musical instruments. The playwright has all of the arts at his command. He has in his hands an immense sea of disparate psychological tones; he has an ocean of colors, a world of feelings and ideas. He has only to combine these to suit his own desires . . . [17]

Gordin's *Kreytser sonata* features both "bad" musicians and "good" ones, but no morally corrupting forces are attributed to the works of Beethoven, or to the opera that makes a late appearance in act 4. Rather, it is literary fiction, in particular Tolstoy's *Kreitserova sonata*, that plays a pivotal role in the play's dénouement.

From her first appearance, clutching a volume of Tolstoy, Ettie Friedlander demonstrates a powerful identification with fiction, such that her father has to confiscate the offending material, lest it prove too stimulating. But Tolstoy has already awakened her to the ugly truth of human relations, and no amount of pretense can now conceal it. Though Ettie acts as a dutiful daughter, devoted mother, and obedient wife, her family regards her as simply playing a role. She is accused of reiterating an "old routine" (an alte shtik), of behaving like a "big hero" (a gantser held) (31, 55). As Ettie begins to unravel she intones, "I am afraid I will depart from my role . . . the end is coming! The end! The end!" (Ikh hob moyre, ikh vel aroys fun mayn role . . . der sof kumt! Di ende! Di ende!) (87). Ettie herself sees that she is playing a role and goes so far as to emphasize the Germanic *ende*, used to describe dramatic and novelistic "ends," in contrast with the more conversational Hebraic *sof*.[18]

Part of the failure of Ettie's performance is owing to the incompatibility of her adopted roles with the one that has been established for her from act 1, that of the fallen woman. Fallen women in nineteenth-century fiction are typically accorded few narrative options—social exclusion, removal of their children, death, or all three, as in the case of Tolstoy's Anna Karenina. But Ettie is a woman of the twentieth century and suffers none of these traditional consequences; she departs from this "role" as well. Ettie's final act of rebellion is to depart even from the role of Pozdnyshev's wife, to take up that of Pozdnyshev himself. This act of literary homage, which would appear to confirm age-old Platonic suspicions of the perilous powers of mimesis, reflects the symbolic and practical functions that Gordin's play assigns to Tolstoy's novel. The novel is an agent of revelation; a repository for Ettie's memories, romantic dreams, and ideals; a catalyst for family antagonism; and a model for conduct. It is a far more potent and volatile work than Beethoven's and is the real focus and namesake of Gordin's play.

Ettie is in many respects an ideal reader in that she exhibits exactly the reaction that Tolstoy intended *Kreitserova sonata* to elicit ("it makes life so ugly, so much uglier than I had thought before"). Awakening readers to the lies around them was the first step to seeing the truth and to making efforts to live by that truth—in Tolstoy's case, his heretical variety of radical Christianity. Yet the means through which this awakening is effected—literary fiction—was fundamentally suspect. Tolstoy's own doubts about literary fiction's suitability as a vehicle for aesthetic and moral reform led him in the 1880s to repudiate his own novels, including *Anna Karenina* (1873–77) and *Voina i mir* (*War and Peace*, 1865–68), as "bad" works of art that served no redeeming social or aesthetic purpose. While the enlightening mission of *Kreitserova sonata* presumably absolved it of charges that it was also a bad work of art, the medium nevertheless remained open to suspicion. Gordin's dramatic emphasis on literary fiction's potential to act as a stimulant to extreme action is one measure of just how dangerous it could be.

That Gordin attaches significance to Tolstoy's work as the pivot on which the drama's violent solution turns raises the question as to whether this treatment has any relevance for interpretation of Tolstoy's novel itself. Does fiction, rather than music, contribute to the downfall of the protagonist in *Kreitserova sonata*? Gordin's play suggests that the novel has an ambiguous relationship to the question of literary prose's suitability as a vehicle for moral reform. Are Tolstoy's postcrisis doubts about the legitimacy of prose concealed under a surface attack on the dangers of musical performance? Do the themes of "role-play" and "pretense" that figure prominently in Gordin's play echo similar preoccupations in Tolstoy's work? Finally, Gordin's play suggests that a potential resolution of the tensions roused by music and fiction lies in a third art, one in which Tolstoy had perhaps even less confidence as a moral medium: theatrical performance.

These arts are linked in Tolstoy's novel by Pozdnyshev, whose distaste for them stems from his loathing of "pretense" (*pritvorstvo*). Under this heading Pozdnyshev lumps all activities invested with any degree of artifice or convention, be it the arts, personal appearance, or social relations. He draws no distinction between the ethical and the aesthetic dimensions of pretense, takes no account of the blurring of the feigned and the creative in the word *pritvorstvo* itself. Novels, plunging necklines, and arranged marriages are all symptoms of the same disease.

Pozdnyshev's morbid preoccupation with pretense merges most vehemently with his loathing of the visual display of performance, rather than with the aural experience of music, a trait that is emphasized through pervasive references in *Kreitserova sonata* to appearances actual and metaphoric. References to glittering eyes, surreptitious glances, imagined pictures, vision, and perception communicate both Pozdnyshev's distrust of and exquisite susceptibility to visual phenomena and his desire to avoid seeing what he regards as "the truth." Indeed, the novel's very first lines point to the fatal role of the visual in determining its murderous conclusion. The biblical epigraph from Matthew 5:28, "But I say unto you, that every one that looketh on a woman to lust after her hath committed adultery with her already in his heart," presents the eye, not the ear, as the agent of the adulterous fall.

If Tolstoy had previously invested the visual with the potential for experience of the sublime, in *Kreitserova sonata* the visual is disconnected from higher possibilities. When appearances and vision are invoked, the danger of their being mere pretense and deception is always suggested by a concomitant reminder of the ease with which appearances are manipulated.

Pozdnyshev is first described by the "executive narrator"[19] as avoiding the other passengers and busying himself with reading, gazing out of the window, smoking, eating, and drinking tea (*PSS*, 27: 7–8). Each of these activities is a means of diverting attention from Pozdnyshev's true purpose in boarding the train, which is to make his anguished confession. Pozdnyshev's most obvious dilatory and illusive device is his smoking, which is both a means of "intoxication" and a way of creating a literal smoke screen.[20] When not actually smoking, Pozdnyshev describes the illusions that people create in terms of "fog" (*zatumanivat'*). Of his fraught married life, he remarks, "To live like that would have been awful had we understood our situation; but we neither understood it nor saw it. In this lies both man's salvation and punishment, for when a man lives wrongly he can befog himself so as not to see the wretchedness of his situation" (*PSS*, 27: 45).

Pozdnyshev's drinking strong tea is another form of intoxication, which Tolstoy underlines by describing it as "really like beer" (*PSS*, 27: 16).[21] Neither is Pozdnyshev's eating above suspicion; if "gastronomic chastity" is an essential component of the moral life, then abstention from pleasurable food is the first step toward controlling more troubling passions.[22] It is no accident that Pozdnyshev's catching his wife dining with Trukhachevsky is tantamount to catching them in flagrante delicto.

Looking out of the window provides Pozdnyshev with a temporary escape, but the reflective glass always returns him to the business at hand. As the executive narrator describes, "He suddenly rose and sat down next to the window. 'Excuse me,' he muttered, and with his eyes fixed on the window he sat silently for about three minutes. Then he sighed heavily and again sat opposite me" (*PSS*, 27: 47). "He again turned his eyes wearily to the window, but that same instant, continued, apparently making an effort to control himself" (*PSS*, 27: 48).

Reading is for Pozdnyshev likewise a means of consumption, intoxication, escapism, and illusion. To Pozdnyshev, books nurture fatal delusions of romance and marital happiness, and the double meaning of *roman* in Russian as both "romance" and "novel" serves as a

punning pretext for the contrast of novelistic romance with the ugly
reality of conjugal relations. In answer to a woman passenger's remarks that love is a preference for one person for one's whole life,
Pozdnyshev snorts, "Oh, but that happens only in novels and never
in real life" (PSS, 27: 13).[23] The association of narrative fiction with
pretense is reiterated in Pozdnyshev's tirade against novels' contribut-
ing to the fiction of male chastity before marriage. Men, complains
Pozdnyshev, are "married" dozens, perhaps hundreds or thousands of
times before they are legally wed:

> And everybody knows this and pretends [*pritvoryayutsya*] not to
> know it. In all the novels they describe in detail the heroes' feelings,
> and the ponds and bushes by which they walk, but when describ-
> ing their great love for some maiden, nothing is written about what
> has happened to him, this interesting hero, before: not a word about
> his frequenting certain houses, or about maids, cooks, other people's
> wives. If there are such improper novels, then they're not put into the
> hands of those who most need to know all of this: unmarried girls.
> In front of these girls they first pretend [*pritvoryayutsya*] that this
> debauchery, which fills half the life of our towns and even villages,
> does not exist at all. Then we are so accustomed to this pretense
> [*pritvorstvu*] that finally, like the English, we ourselves truly begin to
> believe that we are all moral people and live in a moral world. (PSS,
> 27: 21–22)

As the passage continues, Pozdnyshev's diary—ostensibly a work of
nonfiction—is accorded powers of revelatory truth that counter the
illusions of fiction. Like the "true" word of God with which *Kreitserova sonata* opens, nonfiction has the power to awaken one to reality.
In contrast, Gordin's play uses fiction itself—Tolstoy's *Kreitserova sonata*—as a source of terrible truths. Where Tolstoy and Gordin con-
verge is in their confidence that fiction has the power to affect conduct. Pozdnyshev's vile fictions are complicit in the social conspiracy
that hoodwinks innocent girls into depraved marriages. Ettie's favor-
ite novel reveals to her the scope of this conspiracy but offers her no
escape route from it, save by the violent means that Pozdnyshev himself takes.

The passage in which Pozdnyshev heaps scorn on novelistic coy-
ness is noteworthy for its use of what might be called the "accumulative mode," that is, Pozdnyshev's racking up strings of nouns and
adjectives to describe the lies of life. Here he urges the executive narrator to "look at those unfortunate, despised women and at the highest society ladies: the same costumes, the same fashions, the same

perfumes, the same exposed arms, shoulders, breasts, and tight skirts over prominent bustles, the same passion for little stones, for costly, shiny things, the same amusements, dances, music, and singing" (*PSS*, 27: 23).

The accumulative mode is employed to describe the horrors of wedding preparations and rich food: "And moreover there was that ridiculous custom of giving candy, of rude gorging on sweet foods, and all those abominable preparations for the wedding: talk about the apartment, the bedroom, beds, housecoats, dressing gowns, underclothing, toilette" (*PSS*, 27: 27). The progression that the nouns make, from apartment to bedroom, from outer robes to undergarments, suggests an accelerated seduction, which ends with Pozdnyshev's feeling "awkward, ashamed, repelled, pitiful, and above all bored, impossibly bored!" (*PSS*, 27: 28).

The accumulating disgust with which Pozdnyshev describes marital sleeping arrangements is echoed in *Smert' Ivana Ilicha* (*The Death of Ivan Ilich*, 1886), in the accumulation of fatally pretentious decorative items for the protagonist's St. Petersburg apartment: "Looking at the as yet unfinished parlor, he could see the fireplace, the screen, the whatnot, the little chairs here and there, dishes and plates on the walls, and the bronzes, as they would be when everything was in place" (*PSS*, 26: 79). In the same paragraph, Ivan Ilich receives the blow that will kill him. In the paragraph that follows, the decor is linked with affectation and appearances:

> In actuality it was the same thing that is found in the houses of people of moderate means who want to be like the rich, and who therefore only resemble others like themselves: there were damasks, dark woods, flowers, carpets, and bronzes both dark and shiny—all the things that people of a certain class have in order to look like other people of that class. (*PSS*, 26: 79)

It is clear that the accumulative mode parallels the accumulative instinct, but Pozdnyshev's use of it to describe human beings' capitulation to the seductions of food, sex, and material goods suggests that for him words themselves are an object of gluttony. Pozdnyshev may reject the disgusting compulsions that he describes, but his linguistic attachment to them through his relentless monologue suggests that he has far from divested himself of their vicarious pleasures. Pozdnyshev merely substitutes a linguistic "intoxication," consisting of overzealous detail and accelerating enumerations of weaknesses and vices.

Pozdnyshev's use of the accumulative mode is more than a verbal tic, however, and suggests a link with literary fiction in his discussion of what is "natural." Things that are natural and essential are pleasant from the outset; things that are inherently depraved, like sex, smoking, and marriage, are not. Pozdnyshev's preference for natural and unmediated responses, rather than for prolonged periods of acclimation, echoes Tolstoy's own preference for immediate and comprehensible art. The linkage of the two in the accumulative mode suggests that Pozdnyshev's verbal profligacy itself parodies the techniques of mimetic fiction. Amy Mandelker argues that Tolstoy's rejection of the same is encapsulated in his description in *Chto takoe iskusstvo?* of literature that is "imitative."[24] Imitation (*podrazhatel'nost'*) consists in the writer's supplying "in the minutest details the external appearance, faces, clothing, gestures, sounds, and living spaces of the characters, with all the events met with in life" (*PSS*, 30: 114). If Pozdnyshev's antiliterary bias accords with Tolstoy's own painful renunciation of his precrisis fiction, this bias sharpens considerably the irony of Pozdnyshev's fate. For what greater torment could there be for a man who despises fictions than his becoming a storyteller himself?

Yet if literary fiction is the early focus of Pozdnyshev's ire in *Kreitserova sonata,* how does musical seduction become the source of such anxiety in the latter half of the novel? That music should be the focus of Pozdnyshev's fears at all seems unlikely, as we are told that he himself once played an instrument (*PSS*, 27: 53) and that he "loved music very much" (*PSS*, 27: 54).[25] Music becomes objectionable because experience of it does not exist outside of performance, and for Pozdnyshev, performance is indivisible from pretense. The shift begins when Pozdnyshev's wife meets Trukhachevsky; their excitement at playing together is conveyed not through music but through nonverbal, visual exchanges, which Pozdnyshev takes for feigning:

> But catching sight of me, she immediately understood my feeling and changed her expression, and a game of mutual deception began. I smiled pleasantly, pretending that I liked it very much. He, looking at my wife as all lechers look at beautiful women, pretended that he was only interested in the topic of conversation—namely, that which no longer interested him at all. She tried to seem indifferent, though my false smile of jealousy, which was familiar to her, and his lewd gaze, evidently excited her. I saw that from their first meeting her eyes gleamed particularly bright and, probably as a result of my jealousy, it seemed as if an electric current had been established between them, evoking a unanimity of expressions, glances, and smiles. (*PSS*, 27: 53)

Pozdnyshev himself falls into pretense when listening to his wife's performance: "Although I pretended [*pritvoryalsya*] to be interested in the music, I was tormented by jealousy all evening" (*PSS*, 27: 54).

It is pretense, rather than music per se, that stokes Pozdnyshev's simmering rage the following day, when he fumes that his wife wants "to insult me, degrade me, disgrace me, and lay the blame on me" (*PSS*, 27: 58). The shift of the accumulative mode from nouns and adjectives into verbs suggests intensified rancor on Pozdnyshev's part, setting the stage for the violence to come.

On the night of the Beethoven concert, Pozdnyshev notes his wife's appearance of "feigned nonchalance" (*pritvorno-ravnodushnym vidom*) and her attempt to conceal her nervousness with a feigned appearance (*pritvornym vidom*) at the piano (*PSS*, 27: 60). Pozdnyshev's famous tirade against the "irritating" properties of music, which make him feel what he does not truly feel, understand what he does not truly understand, and do what he is normally incapable of doing, is not, however, a spur to his jealous rage but a brief, if illusory, respite from it.

Similarly, in Gordin's play, when Gregor plays, Ettie is able to forget who he is and to forgive him for his ill treatment of her. Although Pozdnyshev characterizes the music's effect on him as "terrible," he also sees "new possibilities" and realizes, in a moment of epiphany: "So that's how it is, not at all as I once thought and lived, but that way, something in my soul seemed to say to me. What this new thing was that I had discovered I could not explain to myself, but consciousness of this new condition was very joyous" (*PSS*, 27: 62). Far from provoking him to kill, the music awakens in Pozdnyshev a feeling of joy: "I felt lighthearted and merry the entire evening" (*PSS*, 27: 62). When Pozdnyshev bids his wife good-bye and leaves two days later on a business trip, he is still "in the very best and calmest of moods" (*PSS*, 27: 63).

What alters his mood so disastrously? "The following day a letter from my wife was brought to me," Pozdnyshev explains (*PSS*, 27: 63). He describes her letter in the accumulative mode, reserved for expressing his loathing of indulgence, consumption, and lies: "She wrote about the children, about uncle, about nanny, about shopping, among other things, and, as if it were the most commonplace of things, that Trukhachevsky had stopped by, had brought some music that he had promised, and had promised to play again, but that she had refused" (*PSS*, 27: 63).

Pozdnyshev remembers the glances and the smiles, and an evil inner voice tells him, "Yes, it's all over" (Da, vse koncheno) (*PSS*, 27: 64). Music, we have been told, "only agitates, but does not lead to a conclusion" (tol'ko razdrazhaet, ne konchaet) (*PSS*, 27: 61). The Beethoven sonata in particular concludes with a "completely weak finale" (sovsem slabyi final) (*PSS*, 27: 62). The task of "finishing," with its unmistakable sexual connotation in Russian, is left to the letter and the sexualized violence that it triggers. Pozdnyshev's characterization of the letter by means of the accumulative mode suggests that he regards it as a work of duplicitous fiction, a disguise for a tryst under cover of talk of children, uncles, nannies, and shopping. Pozdnyshev lights cigarette after cigarette, "so as to befog myself and to not see the contradictions" (*PSS*, 27: 64). The next morning he dashes off to Moscow.

As Richard F. Gustafson and Liza Knapp have noted, toward the end of Pozdnyshev's story events in it begin to coincide with the framing narrative related by the executive narrator.[26] The half darkness of the predawn train carriage parallels the story of Pozdnyshev's rising at dawn to travel to Moscow; when Pozdnyshev describes feeling on the journey like an animal in a cage—jumping up, approaching the windows, and pacing the carriage—he does the same as he narrates his story. His words and actions become a performance, as time past and time present are collapsed into one in a phenomenon that Peter Brook has called "theatrical re-presentation."[27]

"Re-presentation" does not highlight the distortions that have been introduced to Pozdnyshev's narration of events; rather, it emphasizes their inescapable similarity, their eternal repetition. This abolition of the past through performance, its rendering as an event that is part of a living present, is Pozdnyshev's unique punishment. He lives only to tell the tale, and his agonized monologue is an act of penance because it requires him to invest his performance with truth and sincerity in order to "infect" his audience. For Pozdnyshev's violence, inflamed by his fatal inability to distinguish between the ethical and aesthetic dimensions of "pretense" and "performance," he pays a high price: there is no rest, no exit from the role he has fashioned for himself. Pozdnyshev's performance ends only in time for him to board another train in his railway-theatre purgatory, to tell another audience his terrible tale. Far from being a poor spokesman for Tolstoy's views, Pozdnyshev is a cautionary example, proof that the wages of sin is worse than death; it is eternal performance, eternal reenactment of the sin itself.

For Jacob Gordin's work, reenactment of Ettie's sin is a matter of practice, but condemnation of performance and pretense is more difficult in an art that necessarily obfuscates the distinctions between what is and what appears to be. In *Di kreytser sonata*, "pretense" and "role-play" do not lead to a critique of the artistic medium itself, but refer to the veneer of bourgeois propriety that the Friedlanders work furiously to sustain. Pretense is the social code that necessitates Ettie's unhappy marriage, the family's immigration to the United States, the lies surrounding her son's parentage, and the concealing of Celia and Gregor's own child. Shoring up this facade is his characters' attachment to titles, reputations, costly clothing, and jewelry, which lend the appearance of prosperous assimilation into American society. Gregor works the most successful transformation, remaking himself as "Professor Fiedler," establishing his own conservatory, and lavishing expensive gowns on the indifferent Ettie while refusing to loan money to her desperate father.

The accoutrements of Gordin's realist stage at first suggest a parallel with the linguistic accretions and "imitation" of Pozdnyshev's accumulative mode. With its detailed interiors, props, costumes, and colloquial language and the deliberate linkage of its fictional reality with the actual New York and with Russia, Gordin's realism is avowedly "imitative." But there is no suggestion in *Di kreytser sonata* that Gordin chafed against the strictures of the realist stage's "unnecessary truth" as did so many of his contemporaries in Russia and Europe.[28] Gordin retains an orthodox commitment to scenic verisimilitude, making it difficult to equate the verbal clutter of Pozdnyshev's fevered monologues with the material objects on Gordin's stage.

But if words regulate Pozdnyshev's existence, measure out his sins in adjectives, nouns, and verbs, then Ettie's is measured in figures—in dollar amounts, fees paid, and miles traveled. Figures denote Ettie's literal worth in the sum of her dowry, the number of Gregor's lovers, the cost of Raphael's watch, the price of passage to New York, union dues, the streets of midtown, the acreage of Raphael's farm, the taxes owed on it, Albert's true age, and the miles from Russia to America. Ettie is even given to paraphrasing Pozdnyshev himself, when she notes of her married life, "As always, two days in love, two weeks of conflict. [. . .] Of a thousand married couples, as I see it, nine hundred and ninety live as I do" (48). The surfeit of numbers in Gordin's play at times approaches the absurd, as when Ettie and Celia's ne'er-do-well brother, Samuel, asks Raphael: "Papa, why do you need the

farm? With your capital you could have seventy-seven thousand busi-
nesses right here in New York. When there was a panic on the stock
market my broker made eighty-four thousand dollars in exactly sixty-
five minutes—eighty-four thousand to a cent, I swear" (41).

Gordin's representation of the accumulative mode as the accumulation of financial capital pervades the play in seemingly inconsequen-
tial remarks that reflect an obsessive concern with numbers. Natasha,
the Friedlander's peasant nanny, argues with Celia in the play's opening exchanges about the girl's age—is she seventeen or eighteen? Celia
snarls, "You can't even count past eleven" (6). The loving Natasha's
ignorance of numbers and time is also played for laughs, as when she
wonders why Christmas comes twelve days earlier in America than
it does in Russia. Knowing nothing of the peculiarities of the Orthodox Julian calendar, she assumes that Americans are just in a hurry
to celebrate (47).

Ettie, by contrast, is alternately vague and calculating about money. In act 1, she discusses her dowry with Raphael:

Raphael: [. . .] I have promised him only twenty-five hundred for
the dowry, not five thousand, as I figured on giving before. Why are you looking at me like that?

Ettie: Papa, don't be angry, but I think he might treat me
better if you didn't scrimp.

Raphael: (*Angrily.*) Scrimp? I know what kind of a dowry you de-
serve! Five thousand! I must say . . . (11)[29]

In act 4, however, when Ettie begs Gregor for a loan for Raphael's
farm, she asks, "Gregor [. . .] how much money do you have? You
have never once told me, and I have never asked" (77). Yet four pages
later she is pressing her mother, Khava, to give the six hundred dollars
that Ettie "knows" she has in the bank to Raphael for the taxes (80).
The extent to which money defines identity is most pronounced in Raphael's negotiations with Gregor over Ettie's dowry. Raphael propos-
es to give Gregor twenty-five hundred immediately after the wedding:

Gregor: I know . . . and the truth is, twenty-five hundred is not at
all bad.

Raphael: I will not deceive you. She was long ago promised for five
thousand.

Gregor: Oh! You want to take twenty-five hundred away from me because now you are unhappy with her?

Raphael: That is what she thinks. I can say to you that I will take no thing away . . . Three years after the wedding you will receive the remaining twenty-five hundred, with interest. Do you hear me? Friedlander's word is as good as a Kaiser's bond. Yes! With interest . . . Of course, that's if you are living as people should . . . and if she has no reason to complain . . . (18)[30]

The terms of Ettie's sale necessitate the pretense that her marriage is happy. Ettie's rebellion against this role and her treatment as an object of trade comes to the fore in her climactic speech to Gregor. Likening herself to a piece of property, Ettie repudiates Gregor's ownership, declaring that she will no longer be trod upon (90). When Celia mockingly notes that Ettie's long monologue was taken from Tolstoy's novel, she is, in a sense, speaking the truth. Tolstoy's ascetic and anticapitalist ideals were congruent with Gordin's own, and Ettie's response bears out Pozdnyshev's warning that the exploitation of women turns them "not into helpers but enemies" (*PSS*, 27: 36).

Ettie's revenge is not in the form of retaliatory economic exploitation but by Pozdnyshev's own violent means. Just as Pozdnyshev finishes his monologue only to board another train in search of a confessor, Ettie's only certainty is another night's performance, during which she will "relive the whole terrible drama again." For both, eternal reenactment of their sins is sentence itself.

Tolstoy's novel attempts to cast Pozdnyshev's purgatorial existence in a more productive light in an afterword in which the writer outlines a radical Christian alternative to the life of violent sexuality and sensual indulgence that his novel describes. For Gordin's audience, of course, Tolstoy's religious solution is hardly feasible. The crucial failure of Raphael Friedlander's farm in *Di kreytser sonata* also casts doubts on the other key element of Tolstoy's program—agrarian redemption. This solution, to alienated labor, to Jews' concentration in "parasitic" professions, may have seemed promising in peasant Russia but was less practicable in the United States. Only one of the factors that Tolstoy finds complicit in the ills that plague his characters—performance—emerges in Gordin's play as anything like a redeeming feature.

By categorizing pretense and performance in *Di kreytser sonata* as a social and economic condition, rather than an artistic one,
Gordin exempts music, theatre, and literature from Tolstoy's assess-
ment of them as destructive forces. Music, whether it is Beethoven's
compositions, opera, or Jewish folk music, is absolved of culpability
in murder. Literature itself, while stimulating and provocative, is a
source not of lies but of terrible truths that society is not prepared to
address. Performance as a theatrical mode is a key element in Gordin's own recommendations for Jewish renewal and redemption, for
this is the proper domain of art itself—the communal experience of
the theatre, whose enlightening aspirations offer a more productive
example of the performance that is the target of Pozdnyshev's and
Tolstoy's opprobrium. *Di kreytser sonata* bears witness to Gordin's
steadfast commitment to his medium, despite the corrupting potential
that always threatens to render "performance" mere "pretense." The
play is both evidence of his continuing debt to Tolstoy and a sign of
his emancipation—a Jewish son's acknowledgment of, and liberation
from, his Russian father.

CHAPTER FIVE

Don't Look Back

Orphan *in the Underworld (1903)*

The reviews were not so good.

"We have seen all kinds of filth, all kinds of disgusting images in the form of plays and other 'literary goods' but—may God preserve you—no one from the 'realist' daubers has until now had the chutzpah to put such a thing as Gospodin Gordin's *Orphan* before the public."[1] The *Morgen zhurnal* (Morning Journal) added its voice to the *Yidishes tageblat*'s (Jewish Daily News) howl of outrage by condemning *Khasye di yesoyme*'s "so-called 'realism' as one of the alien elements that have been brought here with the impure and unnatural Russian culture," which needed to be "purged from the Yiddish stage for the good of the entire Jewish population."[2] The *Tageblat* couldn't agree more: "The last ten years have seen the production of plays on the Yiddish stage which have gradually and severely undermined Jewish family life, Jewish youth, and Jewish morals."[3] They were sure that some kind of justice, somewhere, somehow, would be meted out, because "the sacredness of the Jewish family has been ruined, the honor of the Jewish home has been shamed, and this is thanks to Jacob Efimovich Gordin."[4]

Khasye di yesoyme, the story of a naive country girl's seduction and ruin by her cruel city relatives, is one of Gordin's least violent and least political plays. It boasts no inflammatory depictions of Orthodox Jews as arsonists (*Egel khazkhav*, [The Golden Calf, 1895]), or pimps (*Dvoyrele meyukheses*, [Dvoyrele the Aristocrat, 1896]), or venal industrialists (*Got, mentsh, un tayvl*). Gordin's usual targets of

opprobrium—the subjugation of women to tyrannical family interests, the grasping middle classes—are presented in a less exaggerated
way than they are in *Di kreytser sonata* or *Di shkhite* (The Slaughter, 1899). Didactic impulses are largely subordinate to artistic ones,
and the play's links with its Russian literary sources are not likely to
be appreciated by the uninitiated. Yet the scandal that *Khasye* generated dwarfed all other protests over Gordin's works. Blaming Gordin
for encouraging everything from prostitution and divorce to a rash of
suicides, *Khasye* led the conservative press to launch sustained salvos
against the writer, his admirers, and his plays.

The furor over *Khasye* was due partly to a generally heightened
sense of Jewish vulnerability and injury after the devastating pogroms
in Kishinev in the spring of 1903, but also to what conservatives saw
as the intolerably expanding powers of leftists in the immigrant community.[5] Long embroiled in fierce polemics with the Orthodox *Tageblat* and *Morgen zhurnal*, Gordin's notoriety had reached something
of an apogee at the time of the play's premiere on October 2, 1903,
at the Thalia Theatre. As one of the most visible adherents of leftist
causes, Gordin was a natural target for conservative ire, especially
as his plays, which seldom enjoyed the broad appeal of Goldfaden or
Lateiner, were having a particularly good run at the box office.

The manufactured nature of the controversy is strikingly apparent
in the contrast between the play's New York reviews and the ones it
received in Poland and Russia, where *Khasye* was widely performed
after 1905. In Warsaw, Mark Arnstein (1878–1942) held up Gordin's play as a "subtle, psychologically deep creation."[6] Another Warsaw reviewer of the performance by the Kaminsky company called
it "one of the best things in the repertoire of the Yiddish theatre"
and remarked on the beauty of *Khasye*'s poetic language and the
psychological verity of its characters.[7] Even Yitskhok Leybush Peretz (1852–1915), who felt that Gordin's works generally "straddle the
line between trash [*shund*] and art," wrote a long and detailed review of the play and found the third act particularly powerful.[8] An
Odessa production in the summer of 1906 by Avrom-Alter Fishzon's
(1843/48–1922) company was the subject of lavish praise in the *Odeser folksblat* (Odessa People's Paper), whose reviewer was particularly taken with Khasye's lyrical descriptions of her native village.[9]
A review in St. Petersburg's *Der fraynd*, of Ester-Rokhl Kaminska's
(1870–1925) 1907 performance as Khasye, described the play as
"suffused with a spare and noble poetry, awaft with the scent of the

Ukrainian steppe and the sounds of the quiet, melancholy melody of the Dnieper's waves."[10]

Eastern European responses to the play as an aesthetic work rather than as a political phenomenon underline the artificiality of the 1903 scandal, but New York's enraged conservatives were correct in several respects. Gordin's play is very much about sex, and death, and Jewish destiny, as befits a work that unfolds in a modern underworld. Veering between tragedy and comedy, disquieting stillness and antic despair, *Khasye di yesoyme* is a contemporary Jewish variation on the classical *katabasis*, or descent to the underworld. It is set in the city of Ekaterinoslav, which is rendered as an infernal otherworld, a shrine to economic exploitation, whose denizens fill their days and nights with card games, adultery, and drunken sprees. The play's engaging heroine makes the mythic journey that is traditionally undertaken as a voyage of self-discovery, a test of maturity, or a search for knowledge of a nation's fate. Khasye is orphaned Israel itself, the unwilling exile who succumbs to the seductions of the underworld and never makes the triumphant return home. Her one-way journey ends in the infernal city, as classical circularity is supplanted by a linear American transit, one that replicates the journey of those who also departed their own homelands and came to stay in another.

Khasye survives exile in the monstrous city in part by resurrecting memories of a beloved home in lyric flights that poeticize and compensate for the loss. But the substitution of poetic text for actuality proves so successful that when Khasye has an opportunity to actually return home, she chooses not to. The guilty pleasures of exile prove more powerful than the remembered happiness of paradise, whose joys appear as such only because they are lost. Significantly, the play reiterates Gordin's old indictment of Jewish immigration but renounces the pastoral ideal that had so animated his years in Russia, when the fruitless pursuit of agrarian redemption consumed and finally dismembered his Spiritual-Biblical Brotherhood. While the end to the pastoral dream is pointedly articulated in the destructive failure of the Friedlander farm in *Di kreytser sonata*, *Khasye*, written in 1901, represents its first abandonment and admission of surrender to the city. It is a bitter acknowledgment that the satisfactions of life in exile are so manifold and seductive that return to the "true" Jewish homeland, be it the Russian countryside or Palestine itself, may be impossible not only practically but psychologically.

Khasye's realization that a lost poetic home is more fruitful as an idea than as a reality is drawn from the Russian literary work that is the play's source text, Ivan Turgenev's novella *Asya* (1858), of which Gordin's *Khasye* is a dark and warped inversion. Where *Asya* is set in a sunny, summery German town on the Rhine, *Khasye* unfolds in the gloomy, prison-house interiors of Ekaterinoslav. Instead of treating the graceful, idle lives of young, expatriate Russian nobles, Gordin details the machinations of the Jewish merchant class. Where Turgenev's heroine makes a successful escape in the final pages of the novella, Gordin's ends a suicide. What links the two works and worlds is their preoccupation with the nature of exile and the ways in which its distances—geographic, social, temporal—facilitate the creative process and its recuperation of the past.

Gordin's point of departure is the narrative structure of Turgenev's novella, which takes the form of a backward glance at long-lost love. Used as well in Turgenev's *Pervaya lyubov'* (*First Love*, 1860), *Faust* (1856), and *Stepnoi korol' Lir*, this framing device typically takes the form of an older man's reminiscences of his youth and lost love. The device is, as Charles Isenberg argues, an attempt "to stabilize the meaning of a turning point in the teller's erotic life," to turn thwarted desire into a narrative of romantic renunciation.[11] It is as much about artistic creation as it is about romantic failure, for the narrative itself becomes a substitute for romantic happiness, a "celebration of the spirit in poetry, if not in the world."[12]

Khasye di yesoyme treats the "backward glance" as fundamentally orphic, in that it requires the sacrifice of the actual object of desire for its artistic representation. Gordin's play examines the process of loss and recuperation from the viewpoint of both the artist-creator and the romantic object, both the one who restores in art what is lost in reality and the one who is herself lost to the underworld. Gordin's Khasye is both Orpheus and Eurydice, just as in *Di kreytser sonata* Ettie is both Pozdnyshev and his nameless wife. The conflation in Khasye of male and female, artist-creator and romantic sacrifice, fundamentally reorders the emphases of Turgenev's work. In *Asya*, the male artist-narrator's transformation of the object of his affections into an aesthetic creation is presented as a means of possessing in art what he could not in reality. But Gordin treats the aesthetic transformation of living life into static art as a kind of death itself and drives the point home in the play's "kingdom of shades" setting, in pervasive references to death and dying, and by his heroine's suicide.

Turgenev's novella is principally a study of the artist's evolution and estrangement, a melancholy *Künstlerroman* that weighs the ambiguous returns of nostalgia. *Asya*'s elegiac meditation on the abyss that separates men and women, youth and age, lived experience and emotional remove finds that these distances may be bridged only in retrospect and only in art, but Gordin's play questions even that. In *Khasye di yesoyme*, the distances that separate classes, sexes, and sensibilities are insuperable, but art, too, is powerless to close the gap or provide a measure of retrospective solace. Art is irrelevant in the world of *Khasye di yesoyme*, where the artist's poetic memories of home fall on indifferent ears, and the lyric impulse that is born of longing and fostered in the grim confines of Gordin's city will ultimately be claimed by it. The eternal tensions in Gordin's work in both Russian and Yiddish—the drive to communicate, made possible by the urban institutions of the press and stage, and the drive to escape to the imagined simplicity and authenticity of the agrarian life—meet in *Khasye di yesoyme*, which finds that the "naïve, anarchic primitivism" of the rural idyll can be satisfied only in death.[13]

ASYA (1858)

In Gordin's day, *Asya* was best known for Chernyshevsky's reading of it as a political allegory.[14] Chernyshevsky characterized the novella's narrator, "N.N.," as a rootless, weak-willed "superfluous man" who preferred words to deeds and observation to participation. For Chernyshevsky, N.N. is the paradigmatic Russian intellectual, incapable of positive political action and ever willing to sacrifice the reality of the present for the dream of a better future. This valid but reductive reading had unfortunate consequences for the highly personal and poetic *Asya*, which has little in common with the radical agenda imposed on Turgenev's art by instrumentally minded critics.

The sacrifice that *Asya* enacts, a renunciation of a transient happiness in life for the more permanent solace of art, finds expression in a number of Turgenev's works, particularly in *Dvoryanskoe gnezdo* (*A Nest of the Gentry*, 1858). *Asya* observes its narrator's failed romance with the eponymous heroine, a mildly eccentric young girl whom he meets on holiday in the German town of S—— (Sinzig). She is traveling with her older brother, Gagin, with whom N.N. strikes up a friendship based on a shared sensibility and an interest in painting. Over the course of a few weeks, the three dine and talk and roam the countryside, and Asya falls deeply in love with N.N. He finds the story of her origins (she is the daughter of a serf and Gagin's father) off-putting, however, and half convinces himself that Asya would not make a suitable wife. Only too late does he realize his mistake, but by then, Asya and Gagin have left, never to be seen by him again. The narrator ends his days a lonely bachelor, reflecting on the elusiveness and unknowability of happiness.

N.N.'s relationship to the past and to his own self is filtered through the consciousness of the older man who narrates the tale from the present, and who offers ironic contrast to the thoughtlessness of his younger self. Their divergences are emphasized in the younger self's blithe incomprehension of events, people, and his surroundings and in their divergent pursuits: the older N.N. of the past, the younger of the future.

The rootless young N.N. is a wanderer, a tourist who declares that he will go "anywhere, so long as it's forward" (*PSS*, 7: 74), as he re-sists what Jane T. Costlow has called the "sirens of stasis."[15] Traveling aimlessly, avoiding any serious engagements and declaring a positive distaste for the "extraordinary mountains, precipices, and waterfalls" around him (*PSS*, 7: 71), N.N. is an ironic variation on the romantic traveler as artist and audience. N.N.'s preference is for perpetual mo-tion and avoidance of reflection and rest, pauses that function for him only as unwanted reminders of death.

> The traveler—man, the secular pilgrim—is halted by an affecting im-age. And something peculiar in the image, or the suspension itself of habitual motion, or an ensuing, meditative consciousness, brings him into the shadow of death. That shadow is lightened or subsumed as the poem proceeds, and the unusual image pointing like an epitaph to the passerby is transformed into a more internal inscription testify-ing of continuance rather than death: "The music in my heart I bore, / Long after it was heard no more."[16]

Unlike Wordsworth's "halted traveler," whose regard is filtered through an exquisite subjectivity that seeks to examine every facet of the poet's emotional responses, Turgenev's narrator avoids the "poi-son of reflection."[17] Only his falling in love with Asya will briefly halt his motion forward, a development that generates an anxiety that is signaled through invocations of Goethe's *Faust*, which offers a cau-tionary example of the perils of pausing to savor the moment.

Watching a lively student chorus in a tavern where he meets Asya and Gagin—in a scene that recalls Auerbach's cellar from *Faust*—the narrator wonders if he shouldn't join the group. A Russian woman's voice behind him paraphrases Faust, as if in answer to the narrator's own thoughts: "Let's stay a little longer" (*PSS*, 7: 74). Gagin, a young Russian nobleman, and seventeen-year-old Asya, a hoydenish child-woman with boyishly cropped hair whom Gagin introduces as his sister, stand behind the narrator. The young men strike up an immediate friendship, but N.N.'s relationship with Asya is more complicated. She "seems not yet completely developed" (*razvita*) (*PSS*, 7: 75), is as changeable as quicksilver, and is in constant, erratic motion. "Not for a single moment did she sit quietly; she stood up, ran into the house and ran right out again, sang something under her breath, laughed frequently not at anything that she heard, but at the various thoughts that came into her head" (*PSS*, 7: 77).

Initially rather annoyed by Asya's eccentricities, N.N.'s interest in her grows as she emerges as the reflective surface par excellence. Her lack of a fixed character means that she can be molded to suit his needs.[18] When N.N. experiences a momentary spasm of homesickness for Russia, the next day Asya "seemed to me a completely Russian girl" (*PSS*, 7: 85). As the trio passes a group of "prim" English tourists, Asya "holds herself primly." The narrator interprets this behavior as her "apparently wanting to play a new role for me, the role of a proper and well-brought-up lady" (*PSS*, 7: 83). When N.N. reads Goethe's *Hermann und Dorothea* aloud to Gagin, the next day Asya appears "thrifty and staid, like Dorothea" (*PSS*, 7: 88). Falling asleep one night, N.N. thinks of Asya and realizes, "She's made like Raphael's little Galatea" (*PSS*, 7: 85). Indeed, she is Galatea, and he her Pygmalion, but N.N. will reverse the mythological order by transforming the living woman into the static work of art.

N.N.'s evolution as an artist is contrasted with that of the would-be painter, Gagin, whose conscious desire to *be* an artist almost certainly means he is *not* one. Looking at Gagin's drawings, N.N. finds, "There was much life and truth in his sketches, something free and expansive; but not one of them was finished, and the drawing seemed careless and uncertain to me" (*PSS*, 7: 80). Gagin ascribes this incomplete quality to the inevitable disappointment represented by the finished work: "While you dream of work you soar like an eagle and it seems as if you could move the earth—but when it comes to carrying it out, you immediately grow weak and weary" (*PSS*, 7: 80). The flux and motion of the creative process is contrasted with the fixity and stillness of the finished work, a fixity that is also a kind of death.

N.N.'s growing attachment to Asya is complicated by his suspicion that her relationship to Gagin is less than fraternal. They appear to be Russian analogues of Byron and his half-sister, Augusta, as N.N. imputes to his new friends an unsavory carnal relationship.[19] But Gagin and Asya's relationship is more along the lines of that of William and Dorothy Wordsworth, a brother and sister whose happiest times are in travel, and who have no need of lesser, conjugal attachments because their home is always with each other. Asya is the daughter of Gagin's late father and a serf named Tatiana, also deceased. A child of two worlds, at ease in neither, Asya grows up "wild, capricious, and silent, like a little animal" (*PSS*, 7: 92).

Asya's class background and illegitimate birth complicate her appeal for the narrator, even as their intimacy grows. N.N.'s alarm at the arresting powers of emotional entanglements stirs on a boat trip back across the river to his lodgings on the other side:

> Looking all around, listening, remembering, I suddenly felt a secret
> restlessness in my heart . . . I raised my eyes to the sky, but even
> in the sky there was no peace. Covered with stars, it was shifting,
> moving, shivering; I bent down to the river . . . but there too, even in
> these dark, cold depths, the stars were also swaying and trembling; it
> seemed to me there was an uneasy vitality all around me—and alarm
> rose within me as well. (*PSS*, 7: 101–2)

The transitory lure of "happiness" must be resisted, and so the narrator sets out to derail the romantic plot about to engulf him. When Asya arranges to meet to learn his feelings, he bursts out that they must part and that she "did not allow feelings to develop" before rushing his hand (*PSS*, 7: 114). Humiliated, Asya flees. The brother and sister are gone the next morning, and N.N. never sees Asya again. He is left with only a withered sprig of geranium that she once gave him. The narrator reflects, "Happiness has no tomorrow, it has no yesterday, it remembers no past, thinks of no future. It has the present, and not even a day, but a moment" (*PSS*, 7: 117). Only twenty years hence does he give narrative form to experience, as the story itself takes the place of happiness forfeit.

KHASYE DI YESOYME

Gordin's play's treatment of the process of artistic embalming that Turgenev observes is mitigated by its theatrical form, which always literally brings to life what the novelistic text cannot. Where N.N.'s Asya is resurrected as text whose very existence is testament to its subject's absence, Gordin offers a parallel substitution in Khasye's textualization of her own lost love—her Ukrainian home.

Act 1 opens on a richly furnished merchant's home in Ekaterinoslav, as patriarch Joel Trakhtenberg saunters in and lasciviously watches the maid set the table for a card game. She is one of a perpetually changing cast of Russian housemaids who are fired by Freyde, Trakhtenberg's hysterical wife, as soon as her husband and son, Vladimir, have had their fun with them. The Trakhtenberg men's taste for non-Jewish females vexes Freyde enough to take in her niece, fifteen-year-old Khasye, as a maid. Although a "wild" country girl, at least Khasye is "one of our own" and can be trusted to be discrete, where "strangers" cannot.[20]

The Trakhtenbergs have many charms. Daughter Carolina steals from her mother, as does handsome wastrel son Vladimir, who sulks when chided for the number of hours and rubles spent drinking and romancing chorines at the local *café-chantant*. Their party guests—local demoiselles and Carolina's lawyer fiancé, Mark—titter at lewd humor and offer no evidence of the civilized life of the city that the Trakhtenbergs boast of to Khasye.

She is brought to Ekaterinoslav by her father, Mordecai (Motye), because she does not get along with her stepmother, Toltse. With five young children in the house, there is no room for Khasye. When she appears, she is marked not as "one of our own" (*eygene*) but as a "stranger" (*fremde*), by the Ukrainian peasant dress and boy's jacket that she wears, by the wildflowers that she clutches, and for her habit of naively speaking the truth. Khasye is referred to initially as a *khokhlyushka* (a belittling term for a Ukrainian), an insult that is varied throughout the play: she is also called a "wild animal," a "horse," an "ass," and a "devil" (40, 45, 53, 56, 68). When it emerges that she was called Asya in her home village, Vladimir wonders, "It seems to me that . . . Dobrolyubov had a novel by the name of *Asya*?" (37). Carolina sniffs that the author was Turgenev. And there the matter ends. There is no question of their perceiving parallels between their own lives and the literature that shapes them, as in *Der yidisher kenig lir*. There is no possibility of literature's having a terrible, revelatory force as in *Di kreytser sonata*. Such things simply do not matter in Gordin's Ekaterinoslav, where people may play the piano or recall that there was someone called Dobrolyubov, but they do not care. Art is only a diversion.

Less a vertically ordered Hell in the Christian mold than it is a

Sheol or Hades for sinners and saints alike, Ekaterinoslav is reminiscent of other modern Jewish underworlds. Like Yakov Mikhailovich's dusty Golta, or Sholem Aleichem's Kasrilevke, movement into it is lateral, and escape is possible, but the Trakhtenbergs have no desire to leave it for they are masters of the realm.

Khasye is a native of another land, whose beauties she describes in what is literally a foreign tongue in the Trakhtenberg salon. Explaining her wildflower bouquet using Russian and Ukrainian words for many of the blooms, Khasye remembers:

> [. . .] When we were on the road and I would catch sight of wild-flowers in the field I would jump out of the cart and run to pick them . . . and so the goyim wouldn't let Papa hit me. To him, everything is a sin! If a Jewish girl picks wildflowers she's already a shikse to him . . . And I love wildflowers . . . You see, this is lovage, this is baby's bonnet, periwinkle, daisies, wild thyme, cornflowers, clover, yellow rocket, and this is Ivan-da-Marya . . . I know all the wildflowers and all the grasses in the field. (40)[21]

The flowers are an obvious symbol for Khasye herself, who is also torn from her native field, certain to wither and die. But they also establish her literary sisterhood with the doomed peasant girl Akulina, from Turgenev's "Svidanie" ("The Tryst"), in *Zapiski okhotnika* (*Notes of a Hunter*, 1847–52).

Akulina is trusting, naive, and pregnant by her faithless lover, a lackey with aristocratic pretensions. Meeting with him in the forest, she too clutches a bouquet of wildflowers—marigolds and cornflowers, tansy and forget-me-nots—whose names and medicinal properties she lists. Akulina's bored seducer drops the proffered cornflowers as carelessly as he abandons her. She weeps with grief as the sun sets and an autumn wind picks up, while a raven, the folkloric envoy to the land of the dead, flies overhead. Turgenev's narrator, witness to the forest tryst, picks up the abandoned cornflowers. "I returned home; but it was a long time before the image of poor Akulina left my mind, and her cornflowers, long withered, are with me still" (*PSS*, 4: 269). The young girl whose remembered image and withered flowers remain long after she is gone is reiterated in the conclusion to *Asya*, and Gordin links both in Khasye, whose story will follow the same trajectory as Akulina's, from innocence to seduction, abandonment, and death.

The image most poignantly evoked by Khasye's running into the field to gather flowers, though, is that of Persephone. Demeter's daughter too is picking flowers in a meadow when seized from the land of the living and brought to her uncle's dark palace. Like Hades, Khasye's uncle Joel Trakhtenberg is associated with wealth and incestuous appetites, and he will likewise show erotic interest in Khasye in act 2. But where Persephone has Demeter to plead for her annual reprieve from the underworld, Khasye's mother is dead; as a child of nature, she is cut off from her remaining source of nurture in Ekaterinoslav. Khasye's own sense of foreboding about the city is explicit in a speech to Motye in act 2:

> I had signs on the road: tall white poplars. A well with a cross . . . a hill . . . windmills . . . the sun shone, I walked and sang . . . (*She is lost in thought.*) Then the night came. The darkness came to meet me, like a black priest with a broad, black cloak, and wrapped everything in it, wrapped everything in it . . . And it became so quiet. That's when I began to be frightened: I thought that the mermaids with the green hands were creeping toward me from the water . . . from the woods the old forest spirit was whispering . . . fiery eyes were gleaming in the grass . . . I walked so quietly that I heard the stalks of rye say something to the field, heard the sky tell a secret to the earth and the stars wink and whisper: yes, yes! My shadow was so large that I was afraid to look around . . . I was very afraid to cry aloud . . . my tears flowed in the quiet . . . No one should hear an orphan cry . . . the night was silent and the darkness covered my tears. (49)[22]

The landmarks of Khasye's bright world are Slavic, from the wells with crosses and the priests' robes to the mythical creatures that populate its streams and woods: the *rusalka*, a malevolent water spirit intent on drowning the unwary, and the whispering woods that are the haunt of the demon *leshii*. Her fear before them is a presentiment of death itself, which sweeps over her as shadows and silence. Her monologue abruptly switches tack, though, as she laughs and adds, "No, I will not make such a journey a second time. I'm already truly a native here" (49).

Khasye's acceptance of her fate extends to her stalwart submission to the torture that she suffers at the hands of the Trakhtenbergs. Vladimir, looking for extra cash to supplement his drinking and whoring allowance, steals a diamond brooch from his sister and hides it in the ashes of the stove, to be retrieved later and pawned. Khasye, who lives in the kitchen like a latter-day Cinderella, sees him hide the brooch but says nothing. When Freyde and Carolina beat her, demanding that she return the brooch that they are certain she has stolen, Khasye is silent. Vladimir, whether from guilt or admiration of her fortitude, returns the brooch to a spot where it will be discovered. Absolved, Khasye laughs at her torture, and the others join in with barely controlled hysteria.

In act 3, Vladimir invents a pretext to return home from a family outing to the theatre and finds Khasye in the parlor adorned in Ukrainian dress. Vladimir declares his love, but he also confesses that he is "a little afraid" of her (70). Khasye feels the same, but for her, love and fear are one, a truth that Turgenev's N.N. could not fathom.

> Even when I was in the village I would think of you. And as I was coming here, I don't know why, but I would start trembling when they mentioned your name. But I soon understood what kind of a trouble you are and I resolved to protect myself from you as from the angel of death . . . I kept waiting for you to woo me like the other swine, but you didn't . . . I began to wait. Then it grieved me. Then I cried quietly a few times. Yes, I cried that I was such an unfortunate one, and that when I wanted misfortune to come to me, it did not . . . well (*embarrassed*). Finally, misfortune has come to me and I am a fortunate one. (71–72)[23]

Vladimir is Khasye's angel of death; she knows this, has always known this, but as Peretz noted, "she throws herself into the abyss with her eyes open."[24] As they sit in the parlor, pretending to be in Khasye's village, the two hear the distant music of a choir singing on a ship somewhere on the Dnieper. The "distant music" motif is borrowed directly from Turgenev's *Asya*, in a scene in which Gagin and the narrator, dining outside the town, hear the sounds of music from the tavern they have just left. Both agree, "Close by, someone else's waltz will never do—it's just vulgar, coarse noise—but at a distance, it's marvelous!" (*PSS*, 7: 77). Distance provides an imaginative space that turns noise into music and irritation into charm. The creative possibilities of estrangement are evident in Khasye's own reading of the ship's "distant music," and it evokes for her a mythic image of the soul's passage to the world beyond. "When I want, I close my eyes and I see a great body of water and on the water, a ship. When I see the ship sail far, far away, my heart starts to ache and I think, where is it going, and who is guiding it?" (73).

Their brief idyll is interrupted first by Motye and then by the Trakhtenberg family. As Vladimir gleefully announces his engagement to Khasye, the Trakhtenbergs' shock is less than their outrage at Khasye, Vladimir, and Motye's eating leftovers in the parlor. This blurring of

class-defined spaces is truly shocking: "They've made a pogrom! This
is a scandal!" (81). Although Khasye repeats again and again that
Vladimir does not really mean to marry her, that he has just been
drinking, and that she rejects his proposal, by act 4 the two are wed.[25]

Khasye, not quite eighteen, lives in poverty with Vladimir and
their infant daughter. The Trakhtenbergs have disowned Vladimir,
and he spends Khasye's meager earnings in his usual fashion: on
drink, cards, and prostitutes. Khasye tells the visiting Motye that she
is weary, lonely, and homesick, but she loves her daughter and husband and tries to remain cheerful. Asking after her girlhood friends
and town, Khasye sighs, "There, everything is blooming and growing
right now . . . and here everything is dry and wilts. Oh, when I remember, I long so for my younger years . . . " (91). But all is not as she
remembers; a tree she loved has long since been devoured by starving
goats; Toltse is pregnant again; and Motye's continually bemoaning
his "poverty, poverty" underlines the distance between Khasye's rosy
memory of home and its grim reality. The conditions that impelled
her leaving have not improved, but Khasye's sentimental attachment
to home does not change. She has too much invested in the memory
to permit its revision.

Vladimir, meanwhile, has come up with a scheme involving a
feigned suicide attempt to shock his family into taking him back into
the fold. The plan entails sending Khasye and the baby back to the
village "just for a while" (96). But the place for which she longs is not
one to which she actually wants to return: "It should be good for me
there, like in the Garden of Eden . . . but Vladimir, I cannot live there
without you" (97). The compensations of exile—adult knowledge—
make return to Eden impossible. Resigned and calm, Khasye agrees
to go because she has already decided to take her own life.

The Trakhtenbergs arrive, alarmed by Vladimir's threat to kill
himself but delighted by the news of Khasye's impending departure.
As they scatter to buy things for her trip, Khasye remains, agonizing
over leaving her child behind. But she cannot bring herself to harm the
infant. Carefully dissolving phosphorous matches in water, Khasye
drinks the poisonous brew. As she lies dying, the family returns and
is witness to her agonies. She gives her daughter to her father, asking
him to raise the child in their village home.

> Oh, I remember that when I was a child I would sit alone by the river
> and throw a stone into the water, and I would wait . . . The stone
> would sink, as I am sinking now into the abyss of death . . . And

a breeze would rush from the old trees to the dry reeds and it
seemed to me that someone there was whispering: Asya is already
gone . . . (*more softly*) Asya is already gone . . . (*very softly*) Asya is
already . . . gone . . . (*She dies.*) (110)[26]

Khasye's imagining her own watery oblivion echoes the scene of
Asya's narrator's gazing into the waters of the Rhine, but where he
remains on the surface, Khasye plunges in and sinks to the depths.
Turgenev's N.N. is ever the observer, but Gordin's Khasye is both actor and author, narrating her own end, writing herself out of her own
story.

Turgenev's abundant use of reflective surfaces—in the river cross-
ings that N.N. makes daily to meet with Gagin and Asya, in Asya's
own character that reflects her surroundings and the moods of those
whom she encounters, in the text's mirroring of scenes and characters
from *Faust*—is replicated by *Khasye di yesoyme*'s acting as another
reflective surface. Gordin's play refracts and inverts Turgenev's original: the sunny Rhine takes on darker hues as the Dnieper, the girl
who is serf and noble finds form in one who is Jewish and Ukrainian,
and she who eluded capture in the Russian novella is trapped in the
Yiddish drama. But if *Asya* is Turgenev's mirror, and N.N.'s journey
a "confrontation of self with earlier self,"[27] is *Khasye* Gordin's own
reflection, his own *Künstlerroman*?

Khasye's character might be read as a cipher for Gordin himself:
the agrarian reformer wrenched from his pastoral Ukraine, interned
in the infernal city, where he too is misunderstood and abused, leaving behind an orphaned child (that time-honored personification of
the Yiddish theatre itself).[28] But, of course, Gordin spent his entire
life in cities and was never a farmer, and while his longing for home
was as real as it was creatively fruitful, *Khasye* suggests that exile has
its own rewards.

And in this lies part of the explanation for New York's conservative critics' rage over *Khasye*, whose heroine might plausibly be read
as a personification of orphaned Israel: motherless, in exile, the child
of a loving but distant father who has more children than he can care
for and who is never around to protect his eldest, best-loved child.
The orphan finds comfort in exile with memories of home, rendered
in a hypnotic prose that weaves fantasy and folklore with an ardent,
if blinkered, view of the place of origins. In the city the orphan is se-
duced by an assimilated Jew who has taken a gentile name and adopted the worst of stereotypically gentile habits. Drawn to the "an-

gel of death," the orphan Khasye's only joy is in her obviously fertile union with her destroyer. She dies in exile, without ever glimpsing home again.

It is not only urban, gentile blandishments but also sexual knowl-edge—the fruit of rebellion and the concomitant of death itself—that makes Khasye's underworld exile preferable to return to the home land. But her grim end can hardly be said to constitute a rousing en-dorsement of life in the diaspora. Neither can Khasye's death be said to offer a bracing example of the life fully lived, rather than observed from a distance that facilitates its transformation into safely static art. Turgenev's N.N., who spends his twilight years in lonely bachelor brooding, appears to have gotten the better end of the deal by remain-ing safely removed from direct engagement with life and love.

The only possible consolation that *Khasye di yesoyme* offers is it-self, for in it Gordin achieves a work of genuine originality, one that moves well beyond his source material and into uncharted waters. For in Gordin's heightened psychological realism, in his commitment to bear witness, to rectify through the mimetic power of the theatri-cal image, his *Khasye* begins to look like something very different, something very much like symbolism.

GORDIN THE SYMBOLIST?

At first glance, such a development seems unlikely given Gordin's em-phatically stated links with the civic and political biases of realism and his own dramas' careful attention to their characters' individu-alized psychology. Symbolist writers argued that the cluttered sur-faces and detailed psychological portraits of realism were meaning-less, nothing more than a mask for what was really important: the interior life, the mystery of the terrible absolute that lay behind the deceptive facade of reality. Where realism saw man as a product of his environment, symbolism's interest lay in metaphysical man and in the ineffable and intangible aspects of existence to which art might be a conduit.[29] Symbolism's focus on the enigmatic eternal promised to reconnect alienated, realist man with his own spirit and to restore the theatre's ecstatic, communal potential, which realism had traded away for physical man and the myriad problems of his world.

How exactly symbolist theatre would restore metaphysical man to the stage, though, was a problem of no small order. In an effort to discourage their audiences from seeing the symbolist stage as an extension of reality itself, symbolist writers attempted to short-circuit rational, intellectual responses to their art by creating worlds that had little reference to empirical reality. Dramas like Maurice Maeterlinck's (1862–1949) *La Morte de Tintagiles* (1894) incorporated dance and rhythmic motion and repetitive, singsong dialogue, and set their action in antique-interplanetary-postapocalyptic-underwater realms. The results were not a complete success.

Anton Chekhov's (1860–1904) *Chaika* (*The Seagull*, 1895) offered a parodic précis of the symbolist dramatic experiment in Konstantin's abortive play-within-a-play, which features the immortal lines, "All is cold, cold, cold. All is empty, empty, empty. All is terror, terror, terror."[30] As Chekhov makes clear, audiences for symbolist plays typically responded with confusion or derision. ("Something smells like sulfur. Is that part of the effect?")[31] Actors' efforts to embody fantastical creatures—mermaids and world-spirits and medieval saints—sat ill with their training in creating characters based on observation of life. In trying to divorce itself from everyday reality, symbolist theatre found itself tethered ever more tightly to it by the stubbornly real actor. Some theorists proposed doing away with performers altogether and replacing them (with their annoying unions, demands for remuneration, and resistance to symbolist drama) with puppets.[32] Even Vsevolod Meyerhold's (1871–1940) attempt "to soothe the audience with a vision of harmony and to induce participation in a corporate mystical experience akin to the medieval miracle play," bore little fruit, as audiences complained of boredom with the static, pictorial quality of the finished product.[33]

Gordin's own execrable experiments in this variety of symbolist drama illustrate how impracticable it really was as theatre. *Der unbekanter* (1904) and *Oyf di berg* (1906) each offer characters representing personified abstractions ("Hopes, Dreams, Spirits"), portentous verse prologues, and deadly soliloquies on the woeful fate of man.[34] *Oyf di berg* features an inadvertently hilarious setting in the Catskill Mountains, among vacationing ghetto Jews carousing at a summer resort. The spectacle of the enraged "Spirit of the Catskills" wreaking vengeance on proto-Grossinger's patrons was mildly chided by the *American Hebrew* as "a confusing, unreal, and ofttimes tedious drama," but Dovid Pinski is surely right in calling *Oyf di berg* "stillborn."[35] While Zalmen Zylbercweig attributed the failure of the play to Gordin's inability to produce a drama set in America, the symbolist fixation on the ethereal and otherworldly is at least as much to blame for the many turgid dramas produced according to its precepts.

The only genuinely symbolist drama emerges from plays that bear a surface likeness to realism. Only plays that create a world that looks like our own, but is not, that has some anchor in reality, but is not itself real, can make us pause to consider which is the true world and which the reflection. Only absolute fidelity to character produces from an act of impersonation a creative entity in its own right, one that has dimension and breath and speech but is not itself real, and makes us wonder at our own potential to harbor other selves and other natures. It is the realist quest to see truly, to be alive to the process of revision that is life itself, that can offer us a glimpse of the weird, quivering, restless world that exists just beyond our field of vision.

Khasye di yesoyme's transparent realism, its very fidelity to the visible world and to human character, is what permits us to glimpse what lies beyond it. As Andrei Bely noted, "An instant of life taken by itself as it is deeply probed becomes a doorway to infinity. Like a loop of life's lace, it is nothing by itself; it outlines an opening into that which is behind it."[36] Gordin's play does not need to launch undulating choruses of chiton-clad sylphs across the stage or chant dithyrambs to dead gods, because his Khasye is real and palpable, and thus her fear of the night and the fantastical creatures it shelters is itself real and palpable. The actor is not an impediment to the symbolist drama but the essential link between the invisible and the real. In *Khasye di yesoyme*, Gordin's fidelity to the psychologically real character transforms the play's surface verisimilitude into something new and strange on the Yiddish stage.

Many of the techniques that *Khasye* employs that enable it to shift from the realist to the symbolist are typical of Gordin's work as a whole. One of his distinguishing means of establishing character is to assign to villains and comic characters alike repetitive verbal tics. The repetitions are shorthand for a character's worldview and dramatic action; thus Joel Trakhtenberg will remind the audience again and again, "I am a businessman" (Ikh bin a kommertsheski mentsh) and a "liberal man" (a liberaler mentsh), and warn that it is best "not to have anything to do with your relatives" (nisht hobn tsu ton mit eygene). Freyde will insist again and again that she will make a human being out of Khasye ("Ikh makh zi far a mentsh"), and Vladimir will always complain, "Are you going to lecture me?" (Vilst mir zogn musar?), after which he will always sing a few lines from a popular Russian song. The repetition of the word "mentsh" underlines how far Freyde and Joel Trakhtenberg are from being human themselves, a gulf that widens further by their mechanical repetition of the same phrases again and again. Are they in thrall to some larger, malevolent force, which renders them unable to respond with the flexibility of the fully human? If the fundamental law of life is "the complete negation of repetition,"[37] how is it that Freyde and Joel and Vladimir look to be alive, and human, but are not? Only Khasye is without such verbal tics, and only she appears by comparison with those around her to be fully realized, fully human. She exists at the nexus of the real and the simulated, the living and the dead, in a world that mirrors our own with unsettling precision.

The play's contemporary period and setting is similarly grounded in the real, and Gordin enumerates its topographic particularities in Khasye's memories of meadows and rivers and willow trees. By contrast, Gordin's Ekaterinoslav is also real, but its darkened, underworld aspect is far from the world his heroine knows. Yet it too appears at first glance to have much in common with our world and with the real city that bears the same name:

> *Khasye*: Why are they so quiet, like strangers? (*She looks around.*) It's light here and happy . . . People are singing and playing cards and back in our village, so late at night, it's quiet and dark . . . or people have long been asleep, or they're arguing, or the children are crying . . . (*Cheerful.*) They're ours? And like a fool, I was afraid of them . . . I thought that educated people would be sitting with big books, like the Gemara, and studying . . . And they're just playing cards . . . Ha ha ha! They're playing cards in the middle of the week! What, does Ekaterinoslav have Hanukah in the summer? (*Laughter.*) (33)[38]

The lamps are a necessity, for in Ekaterinoslav it is always darkest night, always deepest winter. And because none of the play's action is set outside Ekaterinoslav or the claustrophobic interiors of its houses, the existence of the world outside becomes increasingly tenuous, a matter only of Khasye's memories, Motye's weary reports, and the distant sounds of riverboats. So forceful is Ekaterinoslav's baleful influence that Freyde predicts that Khasye, like any other shade, will forget the life she led before: "In my house she'll soon forget all of those village things" (43). But she does not. Khasye looks ever backward over her shoulder to the world that she left behind.

> Well, papa's gone and I'm still here among the strangers . . . (*Sighs. Starts to iron.*) In Korotshikrak right now there are clear, cold mornings. Over the river you can see a town in another *guberniya* . . . a water tower . . . smoke goes from the chimney columns to the

skies . . . (*Irons and sings softly, "Oh mama, mama, don't marry me off."*) (52)[39]

Pauses and ellipses are characteristic of Khasye's speech in general, but they are especially pronounced in her remembrances of her beloved village. Khasye's act 2 speech to her father, in which she recalls their trip to Ekaterinoslav, is particularly marked in this respect: "I had signs on the road: tall white poplars. A well with a cross . . . a hill . . . windmills . . . the sun shone, I walked and sang . . . (*She is lost in thought.*) Then the night came. The darkness came to meet me, like a black priest with a broad, black cloak, and wrapped everything in it, wrapped everything in it . . . And it became so quiet" (49). The cadences of her speech are not quite conversational, the ellipses leaving gaps between words that suggest a corresponding gap in the familiar reality that she describes, one which by its resemblance to our own does not eliminate the possibility that we may find such fissures as well, perhaps where we least expect them.

Gordin's observation of the physical world, which Khasye describes in lucid prose, effects what Bely described as the shift that realist drama makes, almost imperceptibly, to symbolism:

> The realist artist, still true to himself, involuntarily sketches, along with the surface of life's texture, also that which is revealed in the depths of the instants' labyrinths, parallel to one another. Everything remains the same in his depiction, but is permeated by *something different*. He himself does not suspect whereof he speaks. Tell such an artist that he has penetrated *the world beyond*, and he will not believe you. After all, he worked from without. He studied reality. He does not believe that the reality he depicts is no longer, in a certain sense, reality.[40]

Through Gordin, Khasye's haunted memory and the language that reconstitutes it link one world to the other. In their connection of the realist and the symbolist, the rural and the urban, the Russian and the Yiddish, the old world and the new, similarities are mirrored and differences questioned. In *Khasye di yesoyme* Gordin makes us believe that hell is here, and looks very much like a place we know, and that the people in it may in fact be us. But he also lets us see that paradise is here as well, in this world, although we may never return to it again.

CHAPTER SIX

Homecoming

The future of Yiddish theatre is in Russia![1]

—JACOB GORDIN (1906)

Eva Lioznova's letter to her brother, Yasha, begins in good Russian-Jewish style, with a scolding for his not writing more often to her and to their younger sister, Masha. With equal vigor Gordin's elder sister enthuses over performances of *Der yidisher kenig lir* and *Di shkhite* that they had seen in Melitopol, in southeastern Ukraine. "My dear brother, you can't imagine the pleasure Masha and I got from them. It was as if we could see you ourselves, and hear your clever words. When they performed *King Lear* all the men were crying. How painful it is to have such a famous brother and to not be able to see him!"[2]

That Gordin's plays were being performed at all in his homeland—albeit with some difficulty, as the letter also notes that the troupe was shortly shut down by the police—was not a development that many would have predicted a little more than a decade before, when Nicholas II assumed the throne. Nicholas hewed closely to the path taken by his father, Alexander III, who maintained strict controls on the press and political opposition, while promoting the growth of domestic industry.[3] Financing this expansion through high taxes on the peasantry and massive foreign investment proved effective but unpopular. Mounting evidence of popular discontent—strikes in the mid-1890s in Moscow, in St. Petersburg's textile mills in 1896–97, at the Putilov munitions works in 1904—failed to convince Nicholas of the necessity, if not the inevitability, of political as well as economic change.

But it was not until Russia became embroiled in a war with Japan that things came to the point of real crisis.

Russia had been expanding into the Far East since the 1850s and in 1891 had begun construction of the Trans-Siberian Railway, linking Moscow and Vladivostok. Japanese anxieties about Russian encroachment in this region, and suspicion that Russia would not hold to a proposal to carve up Manchuria and Korea between them, led to a preemptive Japanese strike against Russian forces on February 8, 1904. The war that followed was short, devastating, and humiliating for Russia. An armistice was hastily declared and a peace swiftly concluded in August of 1905, in part because Russia was careering into chaos at home.

1905

The year had begun with the events that became known as "Bloody Sunday," when the tsar's guard fired on a crowd of peaceful demonstrators in St. Petersburg. The massacre sparked unrest throughout an empire that was already fuming over the Russo-Japanese war, and by the summer of 1905, basic industries had shut down, segments of the army and navy were in revolt (most famously, the sailors of the battleship *Potyomkin* in Odessa), and nationalities that had long chafed under Russian rule seized the opportunity to broadcast their discontent.[4]

While Soviet histories portrayed the uprisings of 1905 as a protosocialist revolution, most of the rebellions that convulsed the Russian empire had little in the way of socialist protest about them. Horrific pogroms in Odessa, Voronezh, and Gomel were echoed in miniature in smaller towns and did not cease with year's end. Nicholas's concession to the riots and general strikes of 1905 was the October Manifesto, a promise to grant a constitution to limit the monarch's powers. Nicholas agreed to convene a Russian parliamentary body, the Duma; censorship regulations were relaxed, rights of assembly were established, trade unions were legalized, and the remaining peasant debt to the state for the Emancipation of 1861 was nullified.

But unrest, pogroms, and political assassinations continued, and much of the Russian countryside was under martial law in the winter of 1906–7. In Melitopol, where Jews formed self-defense leagues and troops were barely able to suppress the mobs, Gordin's sister noted that their "little constitution" had a high price, as she described the violence visited with particular severity against the Jews.[5]

The immigrant community in New York watched these events unfold with a mixture of dread and hope. Gordin declared that a Japanese victory in 1905 would "kill the prestige of the Czar," and he welcomed Russia's opening to Japan's "light and culture."[6] Gordin raised funds for the *Potyomkin* sailors, and he took the new constitution as an assurance of "the freedom of the Jew in Russia" and thus an argument against renewed calls for Jewish cultural and territorial autonomy.[7] Gordin remained convinced that Jews were too much enmeshed in the world around them, too polyglot, and too cosmopolitan to be swayed by "narrow" nationalist programs.[8] The only nations, he thundered in a public debate in 1905 with the Bundist advocate Chaim Zhitlowsky (1865–1943), were those of the oppressed and the oppressors, those who labored, and those who consumed. Their struggle would bring forth only one nation: mankind.[9]

Gordin's optimism regarding Russia's Jews stood in stark contrast to his bleak prognostications for their future in America and in particular for their theatre. Now into his second decade as a Yiddish playwright, there were signs that the Golden Age of New York's Yiddish theatre was coming to a close, a casualty of assimilation, anglicization, and the shifting fortunes of show business.

JACOB GORDIN, THE DIRECTOR

Flush with the success of *Safo* and *Di kreytser sonata*, and poised to make his plays part of the profitable mainstream, Gordin had assumed directorship of the Thalia Theatre for the 1903–4 season. Gordin and the Thalia's business director, Leopold Spachner, declared that the theatre would only stage plays "produced by the pen of Jacob Gordin, or those approved by him."[10] It was a risky undertaking, given the variability of Gordin's popular success and the inroads that the cinema and music halls were making on the theatre's traditional audience base.[11] The Thalia, moreover, would not be able to stage plays such as *Der yidisher kenig lir*, because Jacob P. Adler had the exclusive right to perform them in his People's Theatre. In the Thalia's first season, with Bertha Kalich (1874–1939) and Keni Liptzin (ca.1863–1916), the repertoire included their exclusive hits *Safo*, *Di kreytser sonata*, *Di shkhite*, and *Mirele efros*, with the remainder of the repertoire made up of new Gordin plays.

The only hit of the 1903–4 season was *Khasye di yesoyme*, and its success owed more to scandal than to art. That *Khasye* was actually written two years earlier, in 1901, suggests that Gordin was having difficulty, even with his colossal energies, in running a theatre, writing its repertoire, berating its audiences almost nightly from the stage, supporting a large family, and editing his own short-lived monthly theatre journal, *Di dramatishe velt* (The Dramatic World).[12] Nor did the situation improve in the following year, when his actors Kessler and Kalich decamped to Adler's theatre, taking *Safo, Kreytser sonata,* and *Got, mentsh, un tayvl* with them. The opening, too, of a fourth Yiddish playhouse, the enormous Grand Theatre, put further pressure on the Thalia's ability to attract the increasingly elusive Yiddish theatre patron.

Even before the Thalia Theatre's lackluster 1904–5 season, Gordin spared no haste in declaring, "The Jewish theatre in America has no future."[13] At a symposium on modern drama in July of 1904, Gordin located the source of the Yiddish theatre's malaise in the popularity of "infinitely more vicious and purely narcotic amusements" (i.e., the music hall) and younger Jews' preference for English-language theatre. As ever, Gordin had no kind words for the Great White Way, whose actors he dismissed as "wooden manikins that move on the stage like phantoms, talk like marionettes, dress like dolls, and sigh sentimentally of love, drying their tears of disappointment with a perfumed handkerchief."[14]

Two years later, after yet another scandal surrounding the production of Gordin's new drama, *Tares hamishpokhe* (The Purity of the Family, 1904), which had serious repercussions for his relationship with the *Forverts*, Gordin's prognosis was bleaker still.[15] In a deeply pessimistic article titled "The Future of the Yiddish Theatre" (Di tsukunft fun idishen teater), published in *Di tsukunft* in 1906, he offers a bitter indictment of Jewish America and an obituary for its immigrant theatre. Gordin compares the American Yiddish theatre to a large, unblemished, but completely tasteless cucumber, nurtured in the hothouse conditions of immigrant New York. As life improved for the Jews of Russia, immigration to the United States would drop off, halting the influx of new audiences.[16] Assimilation and anglicization inevitably hastened the Yiddish stage's demise, but the other cause of its decline was the pursuit of profit, an American obsession that perverted all cultural production. In contrast, Gordin holds up the shining example of Russia, where material success for writers and artists is only a "means to an end." That end is "love of one's people and the collective spiritual interests of the Jewish masses," values that are "entirely alien to the Jewish American intellectual." Here in the

United States, Gordin notes, "anyone who retains the smallest bit of idealistic striving in his writing is reckoned a Russian fool."[17]

Gordin's diatribe smacks of his most recent fallings-out with Abraham Cahan, now restored as editor of the influential *Forverts*. Their long, reciprocal accumulation of professional slights had plumbed new depths in 1904, after Cahan, with considerable justice, found Gordin's dramatic efforts in *Tares hamishpokhe* less than praiseworthy.[18] Their ensuing feud resulted in the *Forverts*'s retracting its crucial support of Gordin's newest plays and marked the beginning of Cahan's determined assaults on Gordin's character and dramatic legacy.

"Di tsukunft fun idishen teater" also suggests that Gordin had reached a point of exhaustion in his own writing. Gordin had never had success with plays that were set entirely in the United States, and as this article implies, his American milieu no more inspired him now than it had in 1891. "The 'settled' American Jew," Gordin declares, "is very uninteresting. He is a shallow and flat subject, who trades in real estate, plays poker, gambles on the stock market and bets money on political candidates and racehorses. The old forms of Jewish life are quietly vanishing here, without obvious struggle and without dramatic confrontations."[19] As for the "unsettled" American Jew— the recent immigrant—"it is very difficult to observe and describe a life that has not as yet taken definite form." Gordin's dramas had always explored the tensions inherent in the experience of immigration, between the past and the present, being and becoming, but now he turned, like an old and tired man, to castigating the young and looking nostalgically to the past.

The younger generation of immigrant Jews was rapidly becoming American, and Gordin predicted that their children would prefer American sports and "vulgar American amusements."[20] Jewish audiences would not be the only ones to desert the Yiddish theatre. "A Jewish American intellectual, even if he knows only a little English and can find a customer for his scribblings, will no longer write in Yiddish because the goyim pay better."[21] The only hope for the future of the Jewish theatre, Gordin declares, lies in Russia:

> in Russia, where life gives the drama rich, inexhaustible material, where the struggle between the old and the new generations continues, between old traditions and new ideals, where there are the first beginnings of a great movement for liberation and the important work of enlightenment. In Russia, where the Jew lives now not for material interests, where the intellectual works not simply for pay,

where the masses are not ignored, where love of the people is not just
a phrase, where there are noble traditions in literature and high aims
in art, where there is a learned school of criticism, and great cultural
works, where wanton youth is not respected, nor respectable people
humiliated.[22]

Gordin's vision of the lost land, idealized here almost beyond recognition, is certainly a product of the guarded optimism for Russia in the
immediate post-1905 period. In some respects, he was right about the
vibrant Russian-Jewish culture that flowered in the years before the
First World War, when Russia would indeed present fertile ground for
the growth of the Yiddish theatre. Gordin himself would never make
it back to his homeland, but his plays would, as the Yiddish theatre
was reborn in the Russian empire.

IN DER ALTER HEYM

In October of 1913, a columnist for Russia's leading theatre journal,
Teatr i iskusstvo (Theatre and Art) breezily declared, "The most
fashionable themes are Jewish themes. The most profitable plays
are those with Jewish content."[23] Russian theatregoers did indeed
evince a strange and fevered interest in the lives of the empire's most
maligned minority. Between 1903 and 1917, there were more than a
hundred Russian-language productions of plays with Jewish themes
and subjects performed in St. Petersburg alone.[24] These included
translations of Yiddish dramas like Sholem Asch's (1880-1957) *Got
fun nekome* (*God of Vengeance*, 1907); original plays by Jewish
dramatists writing in Russian, such as Semyon Yushkevich (1868–
1927) and Osip Dymov (1878–1959); and also works by ethnic Russians like Evgenii Chirikov (1864–1932). From light comedies to
mordant satires, domestic dramas, and woolly minded symbolist experiments, the repertoire's formal variety stood in stark contrast to
its thematic unity.

Russian interest in "Jewish" plays seems to have been sparked by
the pogroms in Kishinev in April 1903, events that had the dubious
distinction of launching a new genre—the pogrom play.[25] The most
famous of these was Chirikov's *Evrei* (*The Jews*, 1903), which framed
the murderous attacks as an eruption of ethnic, religious, gendered,
and class conflict. Drawing parallels between Jewish suffering and
that of the Russian nation as a whole, Chirikov's Marxist-leaning
drama was applauded by one reviewer who argued that "attending a

performance of *The Jews* could in no small way aid in the development of a viewer's political consciousness."[26]

The extraordinarily popular Jewish repertoire offered its audiences a heady mix of politics, violence, melodrama, and ethnography, a combination that left critics mystified. The eminent critic and editor Aleksandr Kugel (1864–1928) noted that the popularity of Jewish plays among urban Russian theatregoers stood in suspicious contrast to popular distaste for Jews themselves. He suspected that these plays provided Russian audiences with opportunities for public preening over their own open-mindedness and accounted for at least some of the repertoire's longevity and popularity.[27]

Given that Jews never exceeded more than 2 percent of the population of St. Petersburg, even at its height during the First World War, Kugel's assumption that ethnic Russians made up the majority of audiences for the Jewish repertoire is a fair one. But the city's hunger for theatrical Judaica was certainly abetted by its Jewish community, which was lively, educated, and extremely interested in Jewish culture. The loosening of censorship restrictions after 1905 meant that it was only a matter of time before Yiddish-language theatre itself would return to the city.[28]

Yankev Spivakovski's (1852–1919) "German-Jewish" operetta theatre was the first to reach the capital in March of 1905, and thereafter, Yiddish theatre became a fixture of St. Petersburg's theatrical life.[29] Initially, East European companies relied on the traditional repertoire of Goldfaden and Lateiner plays, but as demand grew, publishers turned to the latest American repertoire. Gordin's plays were some of the most widely available printed texts.[30] Between 1902 and 1908, two dozen different Gordin plays were cleared by the St. Petersburg censor.[31] Gordin's correspondence of the period confirms his awareness of his plays' production in Russia.[32] His trip to Germany and Austria-Hungary in 1907 was made in part to assert some control over the proliferation of unauthorized texts and to appoint individuals to oversee the collection of royalties.[33]

Gordin's plays, in both Yiddish and Russian, soon found their way to the imperial capital, where audience appetite for topical, ethnographic, and violent plays made his popular success almost certain. Critical esteem was less forthcoming, but in no way can Abraham Cahan's assertion that Gordin's plays were "laughed at" by Russian critics be supported.[34]

ST. PETERSBURG

Avrom (1867–1918) and Ester-Rokhl Kaminsky's Warsaw-based company was widely credited with introducing Gordin's plays to the Russian capital.[35] The Kaminsky company's 1908 and 1909 tours went down in theatre history as triumphs, but its dramatic repertoire was the subject of debate.[36]

The arrested development of the Yiddish stage in Russia after the 1883 "ban" meant that though its theatrical practice had managed to survive the difficult years, its dramatic tradition had not. The repertoire of Goldfaden and Lateiner plays, or what Pinski termed the "first act" of Yiddish drama, was soon augmented with its "second act" Gordin plays, as well as with those of Gordin's successors.[37] The effect was a strange, ahistorical lineup. St. Petersburg's critics saw Sholem Asch's *Got fun nekome* (1907) before they saw *Der yidisher kenig lir* (1892). Pinski's *Yankl der shmid* (Yankel the Blacksmith, 1907) had its premiere in the same week as *Mirele efros* (1898). What had in the United States been a clear and marked evolution, with Gordin forming the crucial link between generations, looked in Russia to be a chaotic jumble of dramatic styles. Side by side with the symbolism of Peretz Hirshbein (1881–1948), Gordin's work would indeed have looked curiously old-fashioned, but Russian reviewers proved sensitive to the disordered genealogy of the Yiddish theatre. Reception of Gordin's plays, the awkward middle children in the Yiddish dramatic family, took full account of his works' contributions, as well as their deficiencies.

One of Gordin's earliest Russian translators, S. M. Ginnerman (Gen), whose text of *Mirele efros* was an enormous success for Moscow's Korsh theatre in 1910, railed in the pages of *Teatr i iskusstvo* against the repertoire of Goldfaden epigones, "whose literary and theatrical merits bear comparison with fairground clowning of the lowest level" and whose proliferation had reached as far as "Kiev, Odessa, and even St. Petersburg."[38] The august Aleksandr Kugel was less harsh in his judgment of the "operettas blended with farce" that had been the mainstay of Russia's Yiddish repertoire before 1905. But like Gen, Kugel welcomed the new American repertoire and the evidence that it offered of the "particularly intense national life" of American Jews.[39] Kugel did not rate Gordin's native talents particularly highly, yet he found that Gordin's "theatrical effects are tried and true, and aspects of everyday reality are faithfully observed, but with broad strokes that give actors as much freedom as they need."[40]

"Victor" from *Teatr i iskusstvo* also offered praise for the Kaminsky company and the writer whose plays were its mainstay:

> For the first time genuine drama and genuine actors have appeared on the Jewish stage. In performance are the plays of the popular young American writer-actor [*sic*] Jacob Gordin. Gordin is the Jewish Ostrovsky, albeit in miniature. His creations are deeply realistic, depict everyday life, and are very theatrically effective. That the "Yiddish Literary Theatre" has rejected the old repertoire of farces, fantastical *féerie* shows and operettas and shifted to Gordin's dramas is a great service.[41]

For "Victor," as for many other critics, the chief contribution of Gordin's dramas was that they gave rise to "real actors." He marveled at the thirty-eight-year-old Ester-Rokhl Kaminska's range, as she played the teenaged Esterke Rappoport in *Di shkhite* one night and the elderly Mirele Efros the next. Kugel remarked of *Mirele efros*: "I must say that it is his best play, and not without considerable literary merits. In the title role Madam Kaminska portrayed the Jewish 'Queen Lear.' The author treated the history of a Jewish family very adeptly, and its depiction of everyday life and psychology was convincing. This is a play that should be translated into Russian."[42] Indeed, Kugel's own publishing house translated Gordin's plays in 1910.[43]

When the Kaminsky company returned to the capital in 1909, now with works by Sholem Asch, Mark Arnstein, Peretz Hirshbein and Sholem Aleichem, Gordin's plays nevertheless remained in the repertoire.[44] Reviewers again noted that "even with all his faults, Gordin's plays have two valuable traits: the dramatic quality of their subject matter, and the faithfulness of their representation of the everyday reality of patriarchal Jewish life."[45] Though chided for his prodigious, sometimes workmanlike output that "balances on the line between drama and melodrama," there was consistent praise for Gordin's "living" characters, "photographic" realism, and the rich roles that he provided Yiddish actors.[46] Gordin's plays were widely credited with transforming Ester-Rokhl Kaminska from a good actress into a great one, and Arnstein remarked on how, as Khasye, she had grown overnight into an "immense, great artist."[47]

What, then, is the basis for Abraham Cahan's account of the alleged mockery of Gordin and his plays in Russia? The allegation was made in a series of articles that Cahan published in the *Forverts* between February and April of 1908, in which he subjected Gordin's writing to rigorous, if prejudiced, examination.[48] Accusing Gordin of a lack of originality at best and plagiarism at worst, Cahan titled one of his articles "Vos denkt men in rusland vegn gordinen" (What They Think of Gordin in Russia, March 15, 1908). In his memoirs, Cahan describes this article as his revelations of the truth about the Kaminsky company's Gordin repertoire, of which Cahan says that Russian critics "held very unflattering opinions."[49] In fact, "Vos denkt men" is just a reprint of an article by Jacob Zerubavel (1886–1967) from Warsaw's *Roman-tsaytung* (The Novel Newspaper). In an unflattering critique, Zerubavel compares Gordin's plays to the primitive, tendentious works of early maskilic writers. The article has nothing at all to do with the reception of Gordin's plays in St. Petersburg, however, because the Kaminsky company had not yet performed there, and would not for another five weeks. In his memoirs, Cahan claims that "Vos denkt men" is a translation of a review of *Mirele efros* from the Petersburg newspaper *Rech'* (Speech). It is this review, rather than Cahan's duplicitous representation of it, that bears closer examination.

The Kaminsky troupe opened in St. Petersburg on April 15 [28], 1908, with a performance of *Di shkhite*, Gordin's hugely success-ful 1899 vehicle for Keni Liptzin. Set in Russia, the tragedy revolves around young Esterke, who is married off to Betsalel Rappoport, a dissolute, wealthy widower, who abuses and insults his young wife and cavorts in their home with his mistress. Featuring scenes of grind-ing poverty and frantic gaiety, the play ends with Rappoport's mur-der at the hands of Esterke. In its initial run in New York, the *Com-mercial Advertiser* had described the play as having "a psychological idea, clothed in bloody symbolism, underlying a series of scenes rich in detailed representation of the sordid, humorous, pathetic, coarse, everyday passions of the proletarian Jewish world of Russia."[50]

The reviewer for *Rech'*, "Kean," was less than impressed, and his review derides the weepiness of Jewish theatre in general and of *Di shkhite* in particular. Kean took special exception to the play's repre-sentation of Russian Jewry:

The Slaughter is a play that was written in New York by a long-ago émigré from Russia, Jacob Gordin. Perhaps it is because of this—that this distant Russian emigrant preserved in his memory only the recollections of his childhood—that the life of Russian Jews appeared before him at a double distance.[51]

Kean found the infant immigrant's characters unbelievable and his actors unnatural, "although, perhaps, not without talent." He also argued that *Di shkhite* reiterated clichés of Yiddish dramaturgy as a whole:

> *The Slaughter* has a "plot." It'll be the plot of tomorrow's *Mirele Efros*, and the day after tomorrow, of [Zalmen Libin's (1872–1955)] *Broken Hearts*, and after that it'll be the familiar plot of *The Stranger*, and so on. One of two characters will be the hero, the other will be the incarnation of evil. If the first one is a woman, then the second will be a man, and vice versa. They'll be duly married, during which everyone will sing and joke and be cheerful. But insulted love will demand revenge, and the one who is not the hero will be stabbed— of course with a very large knife covered with a lot of red blood. And then everyone will cry very loudly, so that in the upper galleries they'll also start to cry and a lot of them will even have hysterics . . .
> Thus is the playwright's objective attained, and friends of the Jews who understand the "corrupt German dialect" will come to the theatre to study everyday Jewish life.[52]

In fact, none of the plots of *Mirele efros*, Libin's *Gebrokhene hertser* (Broken Hearts, 1903), or Gordin's adaptation of Tennyson's *Enoch Arden, Der fremder*, resembles that of *Di shkhite*, and only *Der meturef* (The Madman, 1905)—a disturbing work that resembles Gothic horror crossed with Eugene O'Neill's *Desire under the Elms*—bears any resemblence to Kean's supposedly typical Yiddish dramatic plot. But accuracy rarely gets in Kean's way, as is evident in his critique of *Mirele efros*.

By the next night, Kean has warmed up to the actors. But his distaste for Gordin, whom he refers to throughout as "the American denizen," seems to have grown exponentially.

> "The American denizen" took a small group of very talented people, outfitted them in patterned rags and a coarsely and falsely assembled atmosphere, put them out on the stage and said, "Give the audience a drama from life in which the human elements drown in the Jewish ones."[53]

What Kean appears to object to in Gordin is the wealth of ethnographic detail that "since the time of the late founder of the Yiddish theatre, Goldfaden, has been regarded as essential in every Yiddish play."[54]

Kean has no more love lost on *Mirele efros* than on *Di shkhite* and finds (with some justice) that the Jewish Queen Lear is such a despot in the first act that she quite exhausts sympathy in the last. Regretting that "the American denizen" could not merely have ended the play with Mirele's expulsion from her home, Kean opines that the American love of happy endings trumped good dramatic sense: "In accordance with established laws, it was essential for the author to ensure the triumph of the heroes and a happy ending to the play."[55]

Much of the reviewer's pique fixates on the fact that Gordin's plays are American and have the sheer chutzpah to depict Russian-Jewish life. What does an American know from Russia? Kean's fantasy runs amok, as he imagines Gordin "in his sealed glass container, deprived of the true breath of life, with a weightless worldview, without any fixed centers, establishing the laws of Russian-Jewish existence."[56] American critics, of course, were wont to locate the source of Gordin's dramatic sense elsewhere: "Mr. Gordin is a Russian whose standards of fitness and art are different from the Anglo-Saxon standards. This difference makes it possible for Mr. Gordin to present things on the Yiddish stage in a manner shocking to the aesthetic feelings of an American."[57]

Kean continues, with mounting bathos and a physics unhinged from earthly laws: "And with their bright, sparkling, indisputable theatrical talents, his performers have to press forward the entire reserve of their artistic feeling in order not to burn in that airless space, and so that none nearby are burned, or warmed around them. In this is the entire tragedy of modern Jewish drama."[58]

There is much in Kean's shrill, abstruse, and bizarre reviews that is simply incoherent. He criticizes Gordin's plays for their violence but also for their happy endings. He derides them as unconvincing portraits of Russian-Jewish life, yet worries that non-Jews will take them for the real thing. Certainly, Abraham Cahan is within rights in singling out Kean's vituperative columns as being unfavorably disposed to Gordin's dramas, but the balance of critical opinion tends in the opposite direction; Kean's views constitute a distinct minority. Russian critics did acknowledge the role that Gordin's dramas had played in fostering performers like Kaminska. Or as Noyakh Prylucki (1881–1941), a perennial reviewer of the company in Warsaw, proclaimed in a 1909 debate, "It was not Kaminska who created Gordin, but the other way around—it was Gordin who created Rokhl Kaminska!"[59]

One of the most sensitive responses to the Kaminsky troupe and its Gordin repertoire was Stepan Gavrilovich Petrov's (1869–1941) 1909 review of *Mirele efros*. A non-Jew, Petrov wrote under the pseudonym "Skitalets" (Wanderer), reflecting both his subject matter and his own early career as a performer in Mark Kropivnitsky's traveling Ukrainian theatre troupe. Petrov initially approached the prospect of literary Yiddish theatre with some trepidation:

> I had managed to see Jewish troupes several times before, and the experience had been most depressing. Third-rate vagabond players performing brainless fairground puppet-show plays in some sort of syrupy half-German language that no one in the entire world speaks. It was strange and absurd to think that this was the theatre of the Jews—the theatre of a people whose members had given so much to world drama and to the theatre arts all over the world . . .
>
> *Mirele Efros* was on at the Kommissarzhevsky theatre in a jubilee benefit performance for Madam Kaminska, to honor her fifteen years as a stage artist. The theatre was filled to overflowing, almost entirely with the Jewish public. I listened attentively to the entire play and was enriched by the discovery that the Jewish theatre is not a myth or a fairground attraction, but an artistic entity that is as capable as any other theatre of reflecting the soul, the life, and the idealistic aspirations of its people . . . Madam Kaminska is a superb actress. She's not, of course, [the celebrated Italian actress Eleonora] Duse, but I think that for Jewish reality Duse would be a bit of an extravagance. Duse is art that carries you to the skies, and the daily life of the Jews drags out on earth. Madam Kaminska is a marvelous, real talent. In the role of Mirele Efros she commands that slender hint of irony that is three-quarters of the Jewish soul. Madam Kaminska presents a truly artistic image—human and national at the same time.[60]

Actors, Gordin's first and best readers, found depth and range in texts whose peculiar intensity owes both to Gordin's own ardent pursuit of earthly "truth" and to his plays' powerful engagement with their "higher" source works. In Eastern Europe, divested of their immediate and local, hot-button political relevance, unprejudiced by hectoring authorial curtain-speeches or newspaper wars of words, the plays might be appreciated or rejected for what they were—works of art.

In Russia Gordin never enjoyed the status of an avant-garde writer as he had in New York, and the next generation of Eastern European Yiddish playwrights and entrepreneurs, having benefited from Gordin's innovations, were quick to distance themselves from him. When Peretz Hirshbein opened his Yiddish art theatre in Odessa in January of 1909, his company "had from its very first steps painted itself as an anti-Gordin theatre, and had taken a sharply oppositional position to Gordin and his successors, and would not acknowledge that their plays had any connection to literature."[61] Arguably, one of the greatest services that Gordin could render the twenty-seven-year-old Hirshbein and other Yiddish playwrights of the younger generation was the belief that Gordin's work dominated the Yiddish dramatic tradition. Without tradition, there can be no rebellion; Gordin's plays made rebellion possible, offering a launching point for the "third act" of Yiddish drama.

Hirshbein's theatre collapsed after two years, perhaps because he took little note that Gordin's plays pleased audiences who found the sometimes etiolated aestheticism of Russian art theatre and its Yiddish cousin somewhat wanting. Gordin's dramas continued to find popular audiences in Russia and the Soviet Union for many years and were revived thoughout the next decade and into the period of the New Economic Policy (1921–28).[62] In Poland, Gordin remained in the repertoire of the legendary Kaminsky company. His plays found new audiences, too, in film adapations of *Der yidisher kenig lir*; *Di shkhite*; *Got, mentsh, un tayvl*; *Khasye di yesoyme*; *On a heym* (Without a Home, 1907); and *Mirele efros*.[63]

There was no truth to the myth promulgated by Abraham Cahan that Gordin was the object of Russian critics' mockery. But Cahan's assertion that no one in Russia recognized Gordin as a Russian writer was perhaps closer to the mark.[64] Gordin was not a Russian writer anymore, and it took his plays' return to Russia to reveal that their author had, in fact, been home—in America—for many years. Only Yiddish allowed Gordin to cross metaphoric borders, to reclaim his Russian writing, to rewrite his Russian past, and to transcend actual ones, making him, albeit briefly, into a genuinely international playwright.

THE OTHER SIDE

The subject of borders is addressed directly and with great poignance in an essay of 1907, one of a series written for the journal *Di varhayt* (The Truth) after Gordin's trip that year to Germany and Austria-Hungary, where he had sought treatment for the cancer that would claim his life two years later.[65] "A yidishe shtetl baym rusishen grenets" (A Jewish Town by the Russian Border) elides its own literary and linguistic borders by rewriting an earlier scene from one of the last stories that Gordin published in Russia. It reframes the subjects that Gordin addressed as a Russian writer and suggests their partial resolution in Yiddish.

The Yiddish essay reconfigures a scene from a story called "Strannyi portnoi" (The Strange Tailor), published in 1890 in *Knizhki nedeli*. That story's hero is Gerts Shneiderzon, a minimally observant, impoverished tailor whose indifference to money earns him a reputation for strangeness. The story offers an array of small-minded Jewish bankers, landlords, and businessmen, but the true villain of the piece is the pogrom that ruins the hero's modest happiness.

Initially, Gerts has no fear of the mob, telling his wife, "They'll see that a poor man lives here, a craftsman, and they'll leave—you'll see. Let Leyb Pupik the banker worry . . . Why should we?"[66] He believes that pogroms are a show of peasant rage at their supposed exploitation by Jewish bankers and merchants. But the fury of the pogrom forces Gerts and his family to hide for two days in the attic of an abandoned, broken-down mill. Screams and the sounds of breaking glass reach them from the street. When they emerge from hiding, the effects of the pogrom are writ large on Gerts's dramatically aged face and newly white hair. The family leaves for America and prospers there, but after a few years, Gerts returns.

> He missed Russia, longed for it. Gerts could not forget his native land, where he was raised and had spent his youth and the best years of his life, where the bones of his ancestors lay, where every patch of earth was full of memories, where everything was so familiar, and close, and easy to understand . . . He felt lonely and alien in that faraway land, and he wanted to be with his *own* again.[67]

Like a latter-day Jacob, unable to bear the idea of being buried in Egypt, the profane land of exile, Gerts is unable to bear the idea of dying in America, of having his body laid to rest in foreign soil. Gerts returns to his Russian homeland, where the graves of his parents lie. Russia is a graveyard, but it is still home. The old tailor talks often of his children, shows all and sundry their photographs. But after every conversation, he will "leave the photographs in the hands of the one to whom he is speaking, and turn away, to hide his tears."[68]

Gordin returned to this image in the autobiographical "Yidishe shtetl baym rusishen grenets," in which he describes how he and a companion set out one day from the city of Lemberg (present-day L'viv) for the poor shtetl of Varish, on the Polish-Russian border. The town is separated from Russia by a stream and a border checkpoint. By the water's edge are a Jewish cemetery and a ruined watermill. The mill is silent, its wheel unturning, but the stream of water flows and babbles around it. Gordin stands looking at the cemetery, and the mill, and the green Russian fields beyond.

It is a symbolically loaded scene: the river separating the past from the present, the person you were from the one you have become, life from death, stillness from motion. The Russian and Polish-Jewish landscapes are almost identical—the same blue skies and green fields are on either side of the border—but they are ever separate, barred by artificial but uncrossable borders. The broken mill—an image, as in "Strannyi portnoi," of desolation and impotence, of utility squandered—is still and silent. The water that flows around it is time itself, unheeding of man's schemes, indifferent and alive, while the works of men rot, collapse, and die. Gordin looks to Russia, and his heart pounds:

> From this side of the border, as I look over, I look as a stranger, one
> who was expelled, shut out. But when I was on the other side, for
> almost thirty-nine years I felt that I was at home. For decades I said
> and wrote: our Russia, our people, our zemstvo, our public schools,
> our press, our literature . . . and now I stand on the other side by a
> Jewish cemetery, and I look back at the land of which I have so many
> sweet and painful memories, where I was born and raised, where the
> graves of my father and mother are, where my two poor sisters still
> live, where my best and dearest friends still live, and I know not what
> to call this land: my fatherland? My homeland? The graveyard of my
> past? The tomb of my future? Oh, Russia! I turn away from my com-
> panion, so he will not see my tears . . . [69]

The passage's conscious reconstruction of its Russian precursor and echo of Gordin's long-ago conversation with Vladimir Korolenko about "our Russian people, our zemstvo, our Ministry for Public Education" reiterates the persistent preoccupations of Gordin's literary and public life. But their expression in Yiddish, in a deeply personal essay that incorporates details of Gordin's actual as well as fictional past, also suggests a kind of reconciliation and return. Gazing at Russia, he stands on the Jewish side of the border. Thinking of the past, he wonders about the future.

Standing on the grounds of a Jewish cemetery, Gordin offers a clear-eyed appraisal not only of his own demise but of the art that had been his life for nearly two decades. Perhaps only when he saw the Yiddish theatre and the Yiddish language vanishing over the horizon, as did his Russian homeland, could this language and this art of expedience become objects of nostalgic longing themselves. And perhaps like his tailor hero, Gordin also "wanted to be with his *own* again," if only at the very end.

THE FINAL ACT

After many months of declining health, Jacob Gordin died of esophageal cancer a little after midnight on June 11, 1909. His death, at the age of fifty-six, was greeted in New York's immigrant Jewish community with an outpouring of public grief, the operatic heights of which, some suspected, owed more than a little to feelings of guilt.[70]

By 1909, Gordin no longer commanded the public notice that he had even a few years earlier. Audiences were changing, and so was their theatre. Since 1905, inexpensive and informal music halls, vaudeville houses, and nickelodeons had been making inroads on the Yiddish theatre's audience, and an economic depression in 1907–8 further cut into box-office takings. The runaway success of unabashedly commercial plays like Boris Thomashefsky's production of *Dos pintele yid* (The Essential Spark of Jewishness) in the 1909–10 season seemed, to the radical intelligentsia, to sound the death knell for the literary repertoire that Gordin had championed.[71] His passing marked the end of the Golden Age of the American Yiddish theatre, the end of its supremacy as a creative, intellectual, and commercial hub on the Lower East Side.

Yet even before Gordin's death, his work was coming in for sharp critical reappraisal. The harsh judgment on Gordin's work that Abraham Cahan had passed in the pages of the *Forverts* in 1908 may have been chiefly motivated by a desire to settle old scores, but his opinion of Gordin's legacy echoed misgivings voiced by the more impartial Dovid Pinski. In *Dos idishe drama* (The Yiddish Drama), a series of articles originally published in 1908 in the newspaper *Der arbayter* (The Worker), Pinski noted the pivotal role that Gordin's work had played in encouraging the literary ambitions of the Yiddish theatre in America, and he praised Gordin's vivid characters and genuinely theatrical sensibility. But for Pinski, Gordin's practice of adapting non-Jewish writers could not but result in a deracinated Yiddish drama, one that imbibed gentile writers' inevitable indifference to uniquely Jewish issues and problems.[72]

While conceding that it was normal for Yiddish writers to be strongly affected by the "foreign" literatures (*fremde literaturn*) of their host nations, Pinski observed that despite the vigor and influence of Russian literature on Russian-Jewish writers, Yiddish drama in the Russian empire was actually *less* imitative of Russian models than was Yiddish drama in America.[73] Yiddish dramatists in the Russian empire felt no need to Judaize the content of non-Jewish works or themes for their own plays. Whatever the deficiencies of the dramas of Peretz, Asch, or Hirshbein (and Pinski was happy to point these out), they were "Jewish to the core. They address Jewish subjects and Jewish problems, questions from the Jewish past, present and future. Onto the stage step authentic Jewish types; there is no makeup or Jewish costuming, from beneath which goyim peer out."[74] Reflecting a deep-seated belief that Eastern European Jewish culture represented the most authentic version of Jewishness itself, the Russian-born Pinski makes little reference to the historically unique culture of Jewish America or to its potential for providing authentic Jewish content for new plays. Exactly as Gordin did in 1906, Pinski locates the Yiddish theatre's future in Russia.

Pinski advocates creative autonomy (*zelbstshtendigkayt*) for Jewish playwrights, a call that echoes an important shift in the post-1905 period in Russia itself, when the old appeals for Jewish assimilation and integration gave way to advocacy of a more independent Jewish aesthetic and political life.[75] The brilliant, secular Jewish culture that emerged in the last decades of tsarist rule, particularly evident in the flowering of Yiddish and Hebrew arts and letters, looked to be proof of a vital Jewish culture that could flourish independently of its non-Jewish neighbors. That Jewish literature, theatre, music, and visual arts continued to thrive, even when hope for real reform of the Russian government ebbed away after 1907, appeared to detach the question of Jewish cultural emancipation from the more problematic one of Jewish political emancipation.

What, then, was left for the arts of the politically emancipated but culturally "inauthentic" Jews of America? Surely, the American Yiddish drama's own *zelbstshtendigkayt* lay not in its growing closer to its Eastern European cousin but in separation from it and from the perception that American Jewish culture was innately inferior to that of Eastern Europe. Yet the very success of a play like *Dos pintele yid*, which offered a comic treatment of the cultural and linguistic divide between immigrants and American-born Jews, led committed intellectuals like Pinski to gnash their teeth over the Jewish stage's apparent capitulation to crass commercialism, a characteristic that was felt to be a poisonous American accretion.[76]

The Yiddish drama in America might now no longer have to look to gentile models or to feel its own inadequacy so acutely, but Pinski nonetheless asserts its inferiority to Eastern Europe's Jewish stage. His recommendations for the American Yiddish stage envision for it a character defined less by generic and stylistic categories like realism or symbolism than by its *inhalt*, its content. The content of the next generation of Yiddish plays, he argued, would reflect the historically unique culture of the Jews and their life in a contemporary world still largely defined by that history—one that did not, apparently, include that of Jewish America. While by no means aggressively nationalistic, Pinski's vision is far from the old liberal ideal that Gordin had promoted in his public and creative work. Gordin's unwavering belief in the necessity of Jews' participating in the cultural and civic life of their homelands, his call for broad recognition that Jews were inextricably a part of the places they called home and that Jews and non-Jews could only benefit from recognition of their mutual interests and culture, looked timid when compared with the evidence of what Jews could accomplish on their own. What Gordin believed in, ironically, had more relevance to Jewish America than to Jewish Russia. It seemed as if the modern Yiddish drama that Gordin's innovations had fostered now had little use for the very ideals that were instrumental in its own creation.

Gordin's success in expanding the linguistic, thematic, and formal range of the Yiddish drama meant that younger playwrights, more confident of their technical skills and their right to address a broad variety of subjects on the stage, might explore avenues that those who went before could only help indicate. This freedom is nowhere more evident than in what despairing intellectuals on the Lower East Side saw as the demise of a literary repertoire.

But surely the competition offered by the commercial theatre was evidence not of decline but of a theatrical and dramatic tradition whose shifts and starts, range and variety, were proof positive of its very vitality. Avrom Goldfaden's genius had been to harness existing Yiddish performance traditions to a poetic dramatic sense and a gorgeous musicality, beginning a theatrical revolution that only catastrophe could halt. Joseph Lateiner and Moyshe Hurwitz crafted from these origins a Yiddish drama that turned Jewish pride, unabashed sentimentality, and predictably reliable catharsis into a commercial juggernaut that won the Yiddish theatre a central place in the cultural landscape of American immigrant life. Jacob Gordin was no less a part of this theatrical and dramatic continuity. He merged the melodramatic and the literary, the Jewish and gentile, old country and new, in dramas that expanded ideas about what Yiddish plays could do, and should do. His dramas were essential in encouraging playwrights, critics, actors, and audiences to look upon the Yiddish stage as an art in its own right, one that was as true to the ancient, divided Jewish soul as any other art form. Gordin's vision and his methods were not a betrayal of Jewish autonomy, or a capitulation to fears of Jewish inadequacy before the giants of gentile art, but an assertion of Jewish entitlement to that art, of Jewish and gentile community through art.

It is easy to dismiss Gordin's contribution to the creation of a modern Yiddish drama, as Pinski does, as being an adroit bit of midwifery, rather than a genuinely original effort. But what Gordin did bring into the world was a sense that the Yiddish drama could be more than a jester, could do more than offer salve for injured pride or temporary flight from a world that pressed with more than its ordinary share of pains on the Jewish people. Gordin's avowedly literary plays made it possible for Yiddish drama to lay claim to an intellectual tradition and ambition that might otherwise seem to have little place in popular American culture.

It is Gordin's framing the modern Jewish experience in aesthetic as well as sociopolitical terms that made his work important in his own day and relevant for ours. For if Jewish history is increasingly seen and approached within a broad, multiethnic, and interdisciplinary scholarly framework, which itself approximates the complex connections, ambivalences, and collaborations of Jews and their host nations, then the study of Jewish art and culture too must necessarily be a part of this process and must reflect its multiplicity. The twentieth century's betrayal of Gordin's internationalist and integrationist ethic, of his unwavering belief in the necessity of Jews' participation in the larger culture of their native lands, does not negate the value of what his plays accomplished in their time and place or what they might hold for future scholarship on the history and culture of Russian Jews and their own Russian-Jewish diaspora.

If, as Walter Benjamin notes, "an orientation toward practical interests is characteristic of many born storytellers," then Jacob Gordin may certainly be counted among those writers who include agricultural advice, or warnings about gaslight, or "bits of scientific instruction" in their texts.[77] "The[ir] usefulness may, in one case, consist in a moral; in another, in some practical advice; in a third, in a proverb or maxim. In every case the storyteller is a man who has counsel for his readers."[78] Perhaps a fourth type of storyteller might be added to Benjamin's list: the one who is interested in the practical business of how stories themselves are made. This is the storyteller who leaves clues with which his audience might trace the intricate designs of fiction itself, designs to which his own works lay claim, even as they divulge the guild's closely guarded secrets. Jacob Gordin is just such a storyteller. Beneath the helpful discussions of Beethoven, the utility of a medical education, or the folly of mistaking the city's glitter for gold, he is always deeply engaged with his source texts, mulling over their meanings, testing their inconsistencies, remaking them for new audiences. It is this aspect of Gordin's writing that holds the greatest interest today, long after the practical advice has been dispensed, and probably ignored. His plays are a Jewish contribution to a dramatic tradition that is both Russian and American, and they belong to both nations, as well as to their own. If Russian and Jewish cultures hesitate still to regard the other as *eygene*, as one's own, despite their long, fraught, remarkable history, perhaps what might be learned from the tenaciously internationalist and pugnaciously inclusive Gordin is that what you think is most alien, most strange, and most distant from yourself is actually you, and always was, all along.

INTRODUCTION

1. See Steven Cassedy, *To the Other Shore: The Russian Jewish Intellectuals Who Came to America* (Princeton, N.J.: Princeton University Press, 1997); Melech Epstein, *Profiles of Eleven* (Detroit: Wayne State University Press, 1965); Jacob Gordin, *The Jewish King Lear: A Comedy in America*, trans. Ruth Gay, with notes by Ruth Gay and Sophie Glazer (New Haven, Conn., and London: Yale University Press, 2007); B. Gorin [Yitskhok Goydo], *Di geshikhte fun idishen teater. Tsvey toyzend yohr teater bay iden* (New York: Spetsiele oyflage fun "Forverts," 1929); Hutchins Hapgood, *The Spirit of the Ghetto*, ed. Moses Rischin (1902; repr., Cambridge, Mass.: Belknap Press of Harvard University Press, 1967); Irving Howe, *World of Our Fathers: The Journey of the East European Jews to America and the Life They Found and Made* (1976; repr., New York: New York University Press, 2005); Beth Kaplan, *Finding the Jewish Shakespeare: The Life and Legacy of Jacob Gordin* (Syracuse, N.Y.: Syracuse University Press, 2007); Kalmen Marmor, *Yankev gordin* (New York: YKUF, 1953); Nahma Sandrow, *Vagabond Stars: A World History of Yiddish Theater* (New York: Harper and Row, 1977; repr., Syracuse, N.Y.: Syracuse University Press, 1996); Bettina Warnke, "Reforming the New York Yiddish Theater: The Cultural Politics of Immigrant Intellectuals and the Yiddish Press, 1887–1910" (Ph.D. diss., Columbia University, 2001); Morris Winchevsky, *A tog mit yankev gordin* (New York: M. Mayzel, 1909); and Zalmen Zylbercweig, *Di velt fun yankev gordin* (Tel-Aviv: Hadfus "Orli," 1964).

2. Notable exceptions to this tendency are Dovid Pinski's early discussion of Gordin's best-known dramas in *Dos idishe drama: Eyn iberblik iber ihr entviklung* (New York: S. Drukerman, 1909), 15–34; Joel Berkowitz's illuminating analyses of Gordin's Shakespeare adaptations, in *Shakespeare on the American Yiddish Stage* (Iowa: University of Iowa Press, 2002); and Leonard Prager's "Of Parents and Children: Jacob

Gordin's *The Jewish King Lear,*" *American Quarterly* 18, no. 3 (1966): 506–16. See also Iska Alter, "King Lear and *1000 Acres,*" in *Transforming Shakespeare: Contemporary Women's Re-visions in Literature and Performance,* ed. Marianne Novy (New York: St. Martin's Press, 1999), 145–58; and Kenneth Wishnia, "Yiddish in Amerike: Translating Multilingual Texts; Jacob Gordin's 'Moses, Jesus Christ, and Karl Marx Visit New York,'" *MELUS* 28 (Summer 2003): 203–15.

3. The term *intertextuality* is Julia Kristeva's. See Kristeva, *La révolution du langage poétique* (Paris: Seuil, 1974); *The Kristeva Reader,* ed. Toril Moi (New York: Columbia University Press, 1986); and Kristeva, *Desire in Language: A Semiotic Approach to Literature and Art,* ed. Leon S. Roudiez, trans. Thomas Gora, Alice Jardine, and Leon S. Roudiez (Oxford: Basil Blackwell, 1980).

4. See Yuri Tynyanov, "Dostoevskii i Gogol' (K teorii parodii)," in *Arkhaisty i novatory* (Prague: Priboi, 1929; Ann Arbor, Mich.: Ardis Publishers, 1985), 412–55; page reference is to the Ardis edition. See also Tynyanov, "O parodii," in *Poetika, istoriya literatury, kino* (Moscow: Izdatel'stvo "Nauka," 1977), 284–310.

5. See Jacob Gordin, *Der yudisher kenig lir. Drama in 4 akten fun J. Gordin* (Warsaw: Tipografiya I. Starovol'sky, 1907); and Gordin, *Evreiskii Lir. Drama v chetyrekh deistviyakh,* trans. D. Rozenblit (Odessa: Izdatel'stvo "Odesskie Novosti," 1912).

6. See Sophie Glazer, "Reading *The Jewish King Lear,*" in Gordin, *The Jewish King Lear,* xiii–xv, 142–43, 156.

7. See Chone Shmeruk, "Hebrew-Yiddish-Polish: A Tri-lingual Jewish Culture," in *The Jews of Poland between Two World Wars,* ed. Yisrael Gutman, Ezra Mendelsohn, Jehuda Reinharz, and Chone Shmeruk (Hanover, N.H., and London: Brandeis University Press, by the University Press of New England, 1989), 285–311.

CHAPTER 1: AMERIKA

1. On the origins and character of the *purimshpil,* see B. Gorin, *Di geshikhte fun idishen teater,* 1: 19–63; and Nahma Sandrow, *Vagabond Stars,* 1–20. Ahuva Belkin treats the *purimshpil*'s often erotic and grotesque subject matter in "The 'Low' Culture of the *Purimshpil,*" in *Yiddish Theatre: New Approaches,* ed. Joel Berkowitz (Oxford and Portland, Ore.: Littman Library of Jewish Civilization, 2003), 29–43.

2. On Haskalah drama, see Jeremy Asher Dauber, *Antonio's Devils: Writers of the Jewish Enlightenment and the Birth of Modern Hebrew and Yiddish Literature* (Stanford, Calif.: Stanford University Press, 2004); and Joel Berkowitz and Jeremy Asher Dauber, introduction to *Landmark Yiddish Plays: A Critical Anthology,* ed. and trans. Joel Berkowitz

and Jeremy Asher Dauber (Albany: State University of New York Press, 2006), 1–72.

3. On the Broder singers, see "Broderzingers un folkzingers," in Zalmen Zylbercweig, ed., *Leksikon fun yidishn teater* (New York: Farlag "Elisheva," 1931), 1: 216–36; and B. Gorin, *Di geshikhte fun idishen teater*, 1: 132–49.

4. On Goldfaden and the beginnings of Yiddish theatre, see Alyssa Quint, "The Botched Kiss: Abraham Goldfaden and the Literary Origins of the Yiddish Theatre" (Ph.D. diss., Harvard University, 2002); Jacob Shatzky, ed., *Hundert yor goldfadn* (New York: YIVO Institute for Jewish Research, 1940); and Zylbercweig, *Leksikon fun yidishn teater*, 1: 275–367.

5. On Goldfaden's progress in Russia, see Hillel Zolotarov, "Der onfang fun der yidisher drame in rusland," in *Suvenir tsu yankev gordins tsenyeriken yubileyum* (New York: n.p., 1901), 23–30. See also Evgenii Binevich, "Nachalo evreiskogo teatra v rossii," Preprint 3 of the Jewish Heritage Society, 1994, http://www. jewish-heritage.org.

6. For the specifics of the government's restrictions on Yiddish theatre performances, see John Klier, "'Exit, Pursued by a Bear': Russian Administrators and the Ban on Yiddish Theatre in Imperial Russia," in Berkowitz, *Yiddish Theatre: New Approaches*, 159–74.

7. On the early history of the Yiddish theatre in New York, see B. Gorin, *Di geshikhte fun idishen teater*, 2: 5–106; and Marvin Leon Seiger, "A History of the Yiddish Theatre in New York City to 1892" (Ph.D. diss., Indiana University, 1960). See also the actor Boris Thomashefsky's entertaining (and probably embellished) account of his own efforts to organize Yiddish theatre in the city, in Thomashefsky, *Mayn lebns-geshikhte* (New York: Trio Press, 1937), 75–88.

8. Howe, *World of Our Fathers*, 460.

9. For details of these business practices, see Warnke, "Reforming the New York Yiddish Theater," 28.

10. Nahma Sandrow, "Romanticism and the Yiddish Theatre," in Berkowitz, *Yiddish Theatre: New Approaches*, 48.

11. John H. James, "The Theatres of the Ghetto," *New York Dramatic Mirror*, July 28, 1900, Jacob Gordin Papers, box 11, folder 193, YIVO Institute for Jewish Research, New York.

12. Warnke, "Reforming the New York Yiddish Theater," 2, 9.

13. For traditional accounts of Gordin's Russian past, see Kaplan, *Finding the Jewish Shakespeare*, 8–33; Marmor, *Yankev gordin*, 12–13, 19–46; Zylbercweig, *Di velt fun yankev gordin*, 76–117; and Zylbercweig, *Leksikon fun yidishn teater*, 1: 392–461. See also Epstein, *Profiles of Eleven*, 135–58; B. Gorin, *Di geshikhte fun idishen teater*, 2: 107–26; and Isaac Turkow-Grudberg, *Goldfaden un gordin. Eseyen un biografies* (Tel Aviv:

"Urli," 1969). See also Gordin's own "Erinerungen fun yankev gordin: Vi azoy ikh bin gevorn a dramaturg," in *Di idishe bine*, ed. Chanan Minikes (New York: J. Katzenelenbogen, 1897), vol. 1 (unpaginated); and *Suvenir tsu yankev gordins tsen-yorikn yubileyum*, 3.

14. Gordin's command of Hebrew remains an object of dispute. Zylbercweig reports that Gordin's contemporary, Mikhl Goldberg, remembered the playwright's Hebrew as being so weak that he kept a notebook of phrases in Hebrew for use in his dramas (Zylbercweig, *Di velt fun yankev gordin*, 77). But both Zylbercweig and Marmor impute to Gordin a proficiency in Hebrew sufficient for him to write articles for *Hamelits* (Zylbercweig, *Di velt fun yankev gordin*, 114; Marmor, *Yankev gordin*, 19). Morris Winchevsky declared that Gordin wrote Hebrew "not at all badly." ("Gordin un lilienblum," *Di tsukunft* 14, no.8 [1909]: 451.)

15. That they communicated primarily in Yiddish coheres with the report of the first imperial Russian census of 1897, which noted that almost 97 percent of Jews reported Yiddish as their mother tongue. For more on Jewish languages and literacy in Russia, see Sarah Abrevaya Stein, *Making Jews Modern: The Yiddish and Ladino Press in the Russian and Ottoman Empires* (Bloomington: Indiana University Press, 2004).

16. On the pro- and anti-Jewish character of the Russian press, see John Klier, *Imperial Russia's Jewish Question, 1855–1881* (Cambridge: Cambridge University Press, 1995).

17. See the list, in Gordin's own hand, of his children's dates of birth, in Jacob Gordin Papers, box 10, folder 181. The U.S. Census for 1900 lists Anna Gordin as having borne eleven children, all surviving.

18. The only evidence for Gordin's working as an actor is suggested by a feuilleton of 1887 for *Odesskie novosti* [Odessa News], which suggests a rueful knowledge of backstage life: "Who is not familiar with the life and circumstances of our provincial actors, those who have not yet managed to become 'names'?—the miserly pay, rudeness of directors, exploitation and swindling of producers, tardy payment of wages, lack of security, cold, hunger, eternal wanderings from town to town; the unbearable conditions, draughty stages, damp dressing rooms, lax morality and total absence of any concept of personal property." (Ivan Kolyuchii [Jacob Gordin], "Fel'eton. Sutoloka odesskoi zhizni," *Odesskie novosti*, May 31, 1887.) There is more concrete acknowledgment of theatre experience in an article in which Gordin recalled his reading Aleksandr Ostrovsky's plays for local peasants, which, he noted, "drew upon theatrical experience." (N.N. [Jacob Gordin], "Teatr v derevne," *Elisavetgradskii vestnik*, August 3, 1889.) No evidence at all can be gathered to substantiate Gordin's claim that he worked as an agricultural laborer.

19. See Yakov Gordin [Jacob Gordin], "Dva slova pravdy v pol'zu 'brat'ev-bibleitsev,'" *Russkii evrei*, 36 (September 3, 1881): 1424–26; and "Ob

obshchestve Elizavetgradskom Dukhovno-bibleiskom bratstve," Gosudarstvennyi Arkhiv Rossiiskoi Federatsii (GARF), Moscow, fond 102,
3-e deloproizvodstvo, opis' 87, ed. khr. 606 (1, 2), 4. All subsequent references to GARF are to this document.

20. On the Progressive Era, see Richard Hofstadter's classic *The Age of
Reform: From Bryan to F.D.R.* (New York: Alfred A. Knopf, 1966);
Arthur S. Link and Richard L. McCormick, *Progressivism* (Arling-
ton Heights, Ill.: Harlan Davidson, Inc., 1983); Michael E. McGeer, *A
Fierce Discontent: The Rise and Fall of the Progressive Movement in
America* (New York: Free Press, 2003); and Peter Berkowitz, ed., *Vari-
eties of Progressivism in America* (Stanford, Calif.: Hoover Institution
Press, Stanford University, 2004).

21. *Memoirs of David Blaustein*, ed. Miriam Blaustein (New York, 1913),
267, quoted in Abraham J. Karp, *Haven and Home: A History of the
Jews in America* (New York: Schocken Books, 1985), 188. The Lith-
uanian-born David Blaustein, who immigrated to the United States in
1886, was superintendent of the Educational Alliance and made these
remarks in 1903.

22. On Jewish socialist New York, see Steven Cassedy, ed. and trans., *Building the Future: Jewish Immigrant Intellectuals and the Making of "Tsukunft"* (New York: Holmes and Meier, 1999); Cassedy, *To the Other Shore*; Howe, *World of Our Fathers*; Tony Michels, *A Fire in Their
Hearts: Yiddish Socialists in New York* (Cambridge, Mass.: Harvard
University Press, 2005); and Warnke, "Reforming the New York Yiddish Theater."

23. Yankev ben Mikhl [Jacob Gordin], "Der pogrom in elizavetgrad (Oys a
privat-brif)," *Di arbayter tsaytung*, August 21, 1891.

24. Advertisement, *Di arbayter tsaytung*, August 28, 1891.

25. Abraham Cahan, *Bleter fun mayn leben* (New York: Forverts Association, 1926), 3: 187.

26. Jacob Gordin, "Di oblave. Oys dem yidishn lebn in rusland," in *Ale
shriftn fun yankev gordin* (New York: Hebrew Publishing Company,
1910), 2: 271. Originally published in *Di arbayter tsaytung*, September
4, 1891.

27. B. Gorin, *Di geshikhte fun idishen teater*, 2: 107–8.

28. Gordin was well acquainted with the Yiddish theatre in Russia and
was given to making dismissive remarks about its repertoire, which he
satirized as consisting of plays called *Rivke and the Gefilte Fish*. See
Gordin's remarks on the Yiddish theatre as "Yakov Mikhailovich,"
"Fel'eton. Po nashim yuzhnym palestinam," *Odesskie novosti*, March
11, 1887; and as "Ivan Kolyuchii," "Progulka po Elisavetgradu," *Elisavetgradskii vestnik*, January 29, 1889.

29. Gordin, "Erinerungen fun yankev gordin."

30. It is not clear whether Gordin's meeting with the actors came before or after he wrote *Pantole polge far dem beys din shloyme hameylekh* [*Pantole Polge before the Court of King Solomon*], a newspaper sketch that was quickly dramatized as a monologue for Mogulesco and then performed again by the actor-playwright Rudolf Marks. This debut was passed over in Gordin's more colorful account of the composition of his first full-length dramatic work, *Sibirya*.

31. Gordin, "Erinerungen fun yankev gordin."

32. Ibid.

33. Warnke, "Reforming the New York Yiddish Theater," 75.

34. For discussion of Belasco's methods and their influence on the realist stage in America, see Lise-Lone Marker, *David Belasco: Naturalism in the American Theatre* (Princeton, N.J.: Princeton University Press, 1975).

35. In the late 1890s, Gordin savaged the "immodesty and cynicism" that the Yiddish theatre learned from its American surroundings. (Jacob Gordin, "Evreiskii teatr v N'yu-Iyorke. Chitano v klube 'Obshchestva Russkikh Studentov,'" June 6, 1897, Jacob Gordin Papers, box 7, folder 108.) Highly critical of the elaborate sets and costumes of the Yiddish stage in America, he found these distracted from the artistic mission of the theatre itself. (Jacob Gordin, "Dos yidishe teater in 19ten yorhundert," *Daily Jewish Herald*, undated clipping [1890s], Jacob Gordin Papers, box 11, folder 194.) Gordin regarded the English-language American stage as frivolous, its only purpose being "to amuse," a trait he attributed to the American audience's being "still undeveloped in matters of art." (Morris R. Finkelstein, "The American Stage: What It Is—What It Should Be—an Interview with Mr. Jacob Gordin, the Famous Playwright," *Echo* 1, no. 2 [April–May 1902]: 1.)

36. Jacob Gordin, "Di tsukunft fun idishen teater," *Di tsukunft* 11, no. 2 (February 1906): 84. This article is reprinted in an edited version in Zylbercweig, *Di velt fun yankev gordin*, 434–41.

37. *Der groyser sotsyalist* premiered January 8, 1892, at the Union Theatre and had only four performances, and *Der pogrom in rusland* (March 18, 1892, Romanian Opera House) had only two performances in the regular season.

38. See Abraham Cahan, "Di yidishe bine: *Sibirya* in yunyon teater," *Di arbayter tsaytung*, November 20, 1891.

39. See, e.g., reprinted in *Ale shriftn fun yankev gordin*: "Drama," 4: 53–62; "Nokh vos darf men teater?" 4: 107–13; and "Drama un roman," 4: 120–22.

40. Jacob Gordin, "Vegn di drame 'pogrom,'" cited by Warnke, "Reforming the New York Yiddish Theater," 89–91.

41. Ivan Kolyuchii [Jacob Gordin], "*Evgenii Onegin* na elisavetgradskoi st-sene," *Elisavetgradskii vestnik*, June 4, 1889.

42. For discussion of Gordin's *Lear* play, see Alter, "King Lear and *1000 Acres*"; Berkowitz, *Shakespeare on the American Yiddish Stage*, 31–51; Rhoda S. Kachuk, "Entering *King Lear* with Shakespeare and His Yiddish Adapter," in *Entering the Maze: Shakespeare's Art of Beginning*, ed. Robert F. Willson, Jr. (New York: Peter Lang, 1995), 145–53; Kachuk, "The First Two Yiddish Lears," in *The Globalization of Shakespeare in the Nineteenth Century*, ed. Krystyna Kujawińska Courtney and John Mercer (Lewiston, N.Y.: Edwin Mellen Press, 2003), 55–67; Prager, "Of Parents and Children"; Albert Waldinger, "Jewish Groundlings, Folk Vehemence, and *King Lear* in Yiddish," *Yiddish* 10 (1996): 121–39; and Paul Yachnin, "The Jewish King Lear: Populuxe, Performance, and the Dimension of Literature," *Shakespeare Bulletin* 21 (Winter 2003): 5–18.

43. In a 1907 meeting in Lemberg with the writer and journalist Gershom Bader, Gordin called *Der yidisher kenig lir* "my first play" and referred to *Sibirya* and *Der pogrom in rusland* as "nothing." Zylbercweig, *Di velt fun yankev gordin*, 327.

44. William Shakespeare, *King Lear*, in the *Arden Shakespeare*, ed. R. A. Foakes (1997; repr., London: Thomson Learning, 2001), 162. All subsequent citations are to the 2001 edition. References are to act, scene, and line.

45. Prager, "Of Parents and Children," 510.

46. Joel Berkowitz was the first to note and comment on this Russian source; see *Shakespeare on the American Yiddish Stage*, 39.

47. Elizabeth Cheresh Allen, *Beyond Realism: Turgenev's Poetics of Secular Salvation* (Stanford, Calif.: Stanford University Press, 1992), 104.

48. Jane T. Costlow, *Worlds within Worlds: The Novels of Ivan Turgenev* (Princeton, N.J.: Princeton University Press, 1990), 35. See also Allen, *Beyond Realism*, especially 100–135; and L. M. Lotman, "Turgenev i Fet," in *Turgenev i ego sovremenniki*, ed. M. P. Alekseev (Leningrad: Izdatel'stvo "Nauka," 1977), 25–47.

49. Costlow, *Worlds within Worlds*, 36.

50. On *Stepnoi korol' Lir*, see Frank Friedeberg Seeley, *Turgenev: A Reading of His Fiction* (Cambridge: Cambridge University Press, 1991), especially 287–93. L. M. Lotman's notes to the *Polnoe sobranie sochinenii* are detailed, although they focus primarily on the sociopolitical implications of the text. See Lotman, "Istochniki teksta," in Ivan Turgenev, *Polnoe sobranie sochinenii i pisem v dvadtsati vos'mi tomakh*, ed. Mikhail P. Alekseev (Moscow and Leningrad: Izdatel'stvo "Nauka," 1965), 10: 482–500. See also Lotman's "Turgenev i Fet," 45–47.

51. Turgenev, *Polnoe sobranie sochinenii*, 10: 186 (hereafter cited as *PSS*). All subsequent citations are to this edition.

52. For Turgenev's letter to Kishinsky, see Turgenev, *PSS*, 7 (1964): 324–25.

53. Like the Shakespearean original, Gordin's *Kenig lir* exists in its own versions of Folios and Quartos, each of which offers events and lines that exist nowhere in the other. This chapter draws on both the manuscript version of Gordin's text and the version thought to have been adapted and performed by Jacob P. Adler's company and published in Warsaw in 1907. While it contains interpolations that are not indicated in the original manuscript, this "Adler" text was considered authoritative enough to serve as the basis of an authorized Russian translation in 1912. This Russian translation, published with the consent of the Gordin estate and by Gordin's old employer, the newspaper *Odesskie novosti*, is a faithful translation of the Warsaw "Adler" text.

54. Berkowitz, *Shakespeare on the American Yiddish Stage*, 41; Prager, 510-11.

55. "Yaffe: Guten Abend! Oh! Ihr frayt aykh nokh alts mit homens mapole—a mitsve oyf ihm. Er hot gezehn nokh far a yohren purim, vos far a shvartsen sof er hot gehat un er iz nokh nit geven forzikhtig und iz nokh amol gekrokhen oyf dem yudele—nu a udai hobn ihm di yudn nokh amol oyf gehangen, es lebt di alte geshikhte mit ihre hamantashen un gragers!" Gordin, *Der yudisher kenig lir*, 4. All subsequent citations are to this edition.

56. Berkowitz, *Shakespeare on the American Yiddish Stage*, 48.

57. The significance of the action's taking place at Purim is explicit in Gordin's manuscript copy of *Der yidisher kenig lir*. Following Yaffe's outburst, Gordin's original text calls for the entrance of a group of Purim players dressed in contemporary costumes. They present a burlesque version of the Purim story, complete with songs and dances. While the show is greeted with delight by the family, Yaffe, predictably, is appalled, and he rants against the "bleating" and "jumping around" of this Jewish theatre, a remark that recalls Gordin's own musings in his *erinerungen* (reminiscences) about Yiddish actors' potential for jumping around on tabletops. See Gordin, *The Jewish King Lear*, 14–15.

58. "Ikh veys, foter, dos du verst veren vider shtark beyz, dokh muz ikh dir zogn di varhayt, az der plan gefelt mir gor nit. Vos hot mir tsugefelen? Dos zol mikh frayen? Dos vos du ferlost uns?! Oder vos du gist mikh iber in di hend fun dem falshen Avrom Harif? Tateniu! Tsushter nit aleyn dayn eygen glik folg mikh, mekhuts es nit! Ikh bet dikh!"

59. "Dovid Moysheles: Ikh vel dir zogn ver do iz der balebos . . . Ikh hob gezen vos do geyt far bay mir in shtub un ikh hob geshvign, ikh hob mikh nisht gemisht, ikh hob gezeyn vi du host mikh un mayne kinder beroybt un bagazlt, un ikh hob geshvign; ikh hob gezeyn vi du host oyf

den dritn monat nokh mayn avek forn keyn eretz-isroel mir oyfgehert
tsu shikn geld un ikh hob geshvign; meynstu az ikh bin a tsubrokhener
sharbn velkhen men ken treten mit di fis? Ganev! Tsvuak! Vilst visn ver
do iz balebos? Ikh! Dovid Moyshele! Shteyt oyf fun ayer erte ven ikh red
mit aykh! Aher gib di shlisl fun di kromen, fun skladen, fun di kasa, di
shlisele gib aher!"

60. "Shrekt aykh nit, ikh vel keynem nit lozn fun aykh keyn shlekhts ton
un dos vos ikh hob aykh amol avekgegebn kert tsu aykh tsurik. Ikh bin
shoyn alt, krank un shvakh. Ikh ken nit fil redn, nor dos vel ikh aykh
zogn, begnigt aykh mit dem vos ir hot, begehrt nit arayntsuhafn in ayere
hend di gantse velt; zayt nor frum, zayt nor gut, nemt zikh arop a musar
fun mir, Dovid Moysheles, oder vi Yaffe ruft mikh, der yidisher kenig
Lir."

61. Zylbercweig, *Di velt fun yankev gordin*, 54.

62. See Ezekiel Lifschutz, "Jacob Gordin's Proposal to Establish an Agricultural Colony," in *The Jewish Experience in America; Selected Studies from the Publications of the American Jewish Historical Society*, ed. Abraham J. Karp (Waltham, Mass.: American Jewish Historical Society, 1969), 252–64. On Gordin's appeal for money to establish a commune, see his 1891 letter to the Baron de Hirsch Fund, Jacob Gordin Papers, box 9, folder 126. See also Gordin's characterization of this episode in "Erinerungen fun yankev gordin."

63. Gordin, "Evreiskii teatr v N'yu-Iyorke." Nina Warnke cites Joel Entin's slightly different account of the same lecture. See Warnke, "Reforming the New York Yiddish Theatre," 74; and Joel Entin, "Leon Kobrin der dramaturg," in Leon Kobrin, *Dramatishe shriftn* (New York: Leon Kobrin bukh-komitet, 1952), xii.

CHAPTER 2: IN THE OLD COUNTRY

1. Gordin arrived in New York on July 27, 1891, on the steamship *Devonia*. *New York Passenger Lists, 1820–1957*; Year: *1891*; Arrival: *New York, United States*; Microfilm serial: M237; Microfilm roll: M237_572; Line: 41; List number: 1112 (Provo, Utah: Generations Network, Inc., 2006), http://www.ancestry.com.

2. Jacob Gordin, "Di shvimende trune (a fantazye)," *Di tsukunft* 1 (January 1892): 44–47. Reprinted, with altered title, in *Yankev gordins ertseylungen*, 3rd ed. (New York: International Library Publishing Co., 1909), 2: 197–204.

3. Modernizing forces like the Reform and Conservative Judaism movements had failed to take hold in Russia. See Benjamin Nathans, *Beyond the Pale: The Jewish Encounter with Late Imperial Russia* (Berkeley: University of California Press, 2002), 146, 149; and Michael A. Meyer,

"The German Model of Religious Reform and Russian Jewry," in *Danzig between East and West: Aspects of Modern Jewish History*, ed. I. Twersky, Harvard Judaic Texts and Studies 4 (Cambridge, Mass.: Harvard University Press, 1985), 67–86. Vassili Schedrin draws direct parallels between a 1909 attempt to establish a Reform-style congregation in St. Petersburg and previous attempts at modernizing Jewish worship in Gordin's Brotherhood and Yakov Priluker's New Israel. Schedrin, "No More Cries! History of the Reform Jewish Congregation in St. Petersburg in the 1900s," December 1997, News Update of the Jewish Heritage Society, http://www.jewish-heritage.org/vspres.htm.

4. Zvi Gitelman, *A Century of Ambivalence: The Jews of Russia and the Soviet Union, 1881 to the Present*, 2nd ed. (Bloomington: Indiana University Press, 2001), xii.

5. Isaac Levitats, *The Jewish Community in Russia, 1844–1917* (Jerusalem: Posner and Sons, 1981), 1.

6. In 1802–4 Alexander I convened a special committee to investigate the possibility of settling Jews on the land in the southern territories of Novorossiya. From 1807 until 1866, the government offered monetary incentives and military exemptions to Jews who settled in Podolsk, Bessarabia, Kherson, and Ekaterinoslav *gubernii* (provinces). By the time Gordin's Jewish sect was formed in 1881, Kherson *guberniya* was home to twenty Jewish agricultural colonies. "Khronika," *Elisavetgradskii vestnik*, March 7, 1886.

7. Idealization of agricultural labor as the cure for the ills of Jewish life had been a feature of Haskalah discourse since the eighteenth century. See Christian Wilhelm von Dohm's (1751–1820) "Concerning the Amelioration of the Civil Status of the Jews" (1781), reprinted in *The Jew in the Modern World: A Documentary History*, ed. Paul Mendes-Flohr and Jehuda Reinharz, 2nd ed. (Oxford: Oxford University Press, 1995), 32–33.

8. Venyamin Portugalov, *Znamenatel'nye dvizheniya v evreistve* (St. Petersburg: Izdatel'stvo avtora, Tipografiya Dr. M. A. Khana, 1884), 43.

9. The Brotherhood's oft-cited founding date of January 2, 1880, is not reliable. Admirers like historian Aleksandr S. Prugavin claimed an 1880 founding date, which detractors were keen to dispute. (Prugavin, "Dukhovno-bibleiskoe bratstvo [Ocherk evreiskogo religioznogo dvizheniya]," *Istoricheskii vestnik* 18, no. 11 [1884]: 398–410; no. 12 [1884]: 632–49].) Painting members of the Brotherhood as publicity hounds cravenly exploiting Jewish suffering for the purposes of self-promotion, Moyshe Leib Lilienblum gave a founding date of 1881. Hillel Zolotarov disputed this date, arguing for the Brotherhood's founding in 1880, although there is little evidence for this earlier date. See Zolotarov [Solotaroff], "Yankev gordin un di 'bibleiskoe bratstvo' (an entfer dem

h'lilienblum)," *Der fraynd*, July 23, 1909; July 24, 1909. Zolotarov's piece is a response to Lilienblum's comments ("Iberige shvokhim" [Excessive praise]) on Gordin's *Der fraynd* obituary (no. 120). For detailed discussion of Lilienblum's *Fraynd* article, see Winchevsky, "Gordin un lilienblum."

10. Nikolai A. Bukhbinder cites a report by a tsarist spy in New York in December 1893. "Iz istorii sektantskogo dvizheniya sredi russkikh evreev. Dukhovno-bibleiskoe bratstvo," *Evreiskaya starina* 11 (1918): 246–47.

11. Ibid., 246. Bukhbinder cites as his source "Gonenie na dukhovno-bibleiskoe bratstvo," *Odesskii vestnik*, no. 137 (1884). One source of their ire was apparently the Brotherhood's success in preaching in Yiddish.

12. Lev Burshtein, "K istorii 'Dukhovno-bibleiskogo bratstva,'" *Perezhitoe* 1 (1908): 38–41. Burshtein was a former member of the Brotherhood. (See his 1924 letter on his sources, Jacob Gordin Papers, box 9, folder 120.) Burshtein cites 1884 correspondence between Elisavetgrad Chief of Police Tsikulenko and district officer Kuznetsov.

13. *Maslianskis zikhroynes: Firtsig yor lebn un kemfen* (New York: Farlag Zerubavel, 1924), cited in Zylbercweig, *Di velt fun yankev gordin*, 89. Nina Warnke notes that in 1901, "the conservative *Tageblatt* (Daily Paper) accused [Gordin] of having founded a sect in Russia in order to 'convert Jews to Christianity,' a reference to his Biblical Brotherhood which rejected all Rabbinic texts and advocated Jewish farming. In fact, the paper claimed, he had to flee to America because incensed Jews drove him out of Russia and now he continued his destructive work among the immigrants." Warnke, "Reforming the New York Yiddish Theater," 168.

14. Emmanuel Ben-Sion [Yakov Priluker], *Evrei-reformatory: "Novyi Izrail'" i "Dukhovno-Bibleiskoe Bratsvto." Opyt sotsial'no-religioznoi reformy evreistva i novoi postanovki evreiskogo voprosa v Rossii* (St. Petersburg: Tipografiya A. Transhelya, 1882), 71. The St. Petersburg censor passed Priluker's book on September 17, 1882, putting the publication date of the *Odesskii vestnik* article somewhere between early 1881 and early September 1882.

15. Rumors of the Brotherhood's foundation reached Priluker, but he knew nothing concrete about its beliefs. "Finally, in one of the southern newspapers, in the *Odessa Courier*, an article by one of the sectarians appeared, in which he outlined the initial premises of the 'spiritual-biblical brotherhood,' its tendencies, and its goals. We will cite this article from the *Odessa Courier* in its entirety, in order to give the reader the opportunity to decide as to the justice of the various attacks and accusations that have been made against the sectarians by the Russian-Jewish press, which regards itself as a competent judge of such matters." Priluker, *Evrei-reformatory*, 68.

16. Ibid., 71.

17. Ibid., 75.

18. A twentieth-century parallel to Gordin's godless, ethical Judaism is suggested by Rabbi Sherwin T. Wine's (1928–2007) Society for Humanistic Judaism, established in 1969. Wine's movement emphasized the ethical dimension of Jewish teaching, eliminated the word *God* from its services, did not recite the Shema, and preached humanism because "it enables man to relate himself to his universe." Dennis Hevesi, "Sherwin Wine, 79, Founder of Splinter Judaism Group," *New York Times*, sec. A, July 25, 2007.

19. Priluker, *Evrei-reformatory*, 77.

20. Ibid., 75.

21. Karaites rejected the Talmud and separated from rabbinical Jewry in the eighth century CE. They were widely viewed as heretics by rabbinical Jews. In tsarist Russia, Karaites were registered separately from Talmudic Jews and were not subject to the residence restrictions that affected the latter.

22. Lilienblum, "Iberige shvokhim," quoted in Zolotarov, "Yankev gordin un di 'bibleiskoe bratstvo.'"

23. Zolotarov, "Yankev gordin un di 'bibleiskoe bratstvo.'"

24. Zylbercweig, *Di velt fun yankev gordin*, 89, 94, 114–15.

25. N. Rovensky [N. Shtif], "Yakov Gordin," *Razsvet*, June 7, 1909.

26. Editorial, *Razsvet*, April 9, 1881.

27. Priluker, *Evrei-reformatory*, 77.

28. A. Firer, "Vozniknovenie novogo tolka," *Razsvet* 15 (1881): 574–76, quoting remarks by a "Brother" published in *Elisavetgradskii vestnik*, no. 35 ([late March] 1881).

29. The only Jewish conspirator arrested for the tsar's murder was Gesya Gelfman. A detailed study of the actual participation of Jews in Russia's revolutionary and terrorist movements is Erich E. Haberer's *Jews and Revolution in Nineteenth-Century Russia* (Cambridge: Cambridge University Press, 1995). For an account of the buildup to the pogroms in Elisavetgrad, see I. Michael Aronson, *Troubled Waters: The Origins of the 1881 Anti-Jewish Pogroms in Russia* (Pittsburgh: University of Pittsburgh Press, 1990), 44–47.

30. "Vnutrennaya khronika: Evreiskii pogrom," *Nedelya*, no. 17 (April 26, 1881): 573.

31. "Korrespondentsii 'Nov. Tel.': Elisavetgrad," *Novorossiiskii telegraf*, April 24, 1881.

32. *Novorossiiskii telegraf*, April 21, 1881.

33. Jonathan Frankel, *Prophecy and Politics: Socialism, Nationalism, and the Russian Jews, 1862–1917* (Cambridge: Cambridge University Press, 1981), 51–52.

34. *Russkii evrei* 27 (July 2, 1881): 1042–47; *Razsvet,* June 19, 1881. See also follow-up commentary on the letter in *Russkii evrei* 28 (July 8, 1881): 1082–86.

35. John Klier, "From Elisavetgrad to Broadway: The Strange Odyssey of Iakov Gordin," in *Extending the Borders of Russian History: Essays in Honor of Alfred J. Rieber,* ed. Marsha Siefert (Budapest and New York: Central European University Press, 2003), 117.

36. A.L. [A.E. Laundau], "Vnutrenee obozrenie," *Voskhod,* no. 7 (1881): 33–38.

37. Marmor, *Yankev gordin,* 39–40.

38. Cahan, *Bleter fun mayn leben,* 3: 8, quoted in Frankel, *Prophecy and Politics,* 52.

39. Simon Dubnow, "Kakaya samoemansipatsiya nuzhna evreev," *Voskhod,* nos. 5–6 (May–June, 1883): 219.

40. *Russkii evrei* 27 (July 2, 1881): 1043; "Elisavetgrad (Korrespondentsiya 'Russkogo Evreya'): Materialy dlya istorii novoobrazovsheisya sekty," *Russkii evrei* 29 (July 14, 1881): 1137–38.

41. Marmor also refers to the rumor that Gordin participated in a committee to aid the families of those arrested for taking part in the pogroms. The source of this rumor is apparently Lilienblum, and Marmor argues (but does not cite his own sources) that Gordin *did* serve on such a committee, although only because the families aided by the committee were also those of men who had been arrested but not charged or convicted of offenses against Elisavetgrad's Jews. Marmor, *Yankev gordin,* 38–39.

42. "Pis'mo v redaktsiyu (Ot Yakova Gordina)," *Elisavetgradskii vestnik,* July 22, 1881.

43. Gordin, "Dva slova pravdy v pol'zu 'brat'ev-bibleitsev.'"

44. "Nam pishut: Iz Elisavetgrada (Khersonskoi gubernii)," *Nedelya,* no. 39 (September 27, 1881): 1298–99.

45. Zylbercweig, *Di velt fun yankev gordin,* 94–99; Marmor, *Yankev gordin,* 30, 43; Bukhbinder, "Iz istorii sektantskogo dvizheniya sredi russkikh evreev." 245. Bukhbinder dates Gordin's alleged sojourn in the countryside to 1881–84.

46. GARF, 1.

47. Marmor, *Yankev gordin,* 31, 43; Zylbercweig, *Di velt fun yankev gordin,* 94, 105; *Suvenir tsu yankev gordins tsen-yerikn yubileyum,* 1; "Gordin, Yakov Mikhailovich," *Evreiskaya entsiklopediya. Svod znanii o evreistve i ego kul'ture v proshlom i nastoyashchem,* ed. Lev I. Katsenel'son and Baron David G. Gintsburg (St. Petersburg: Brockhaus-Efron, 1908–13), 6: 688.

48. Zylbercweig, *Di velt fun yankev gordin,* 105–6; Marmor, *Yankev gordin,* 30; Bukhbinder, "Iz istorii sektantskogo dvizheniya sredi russkikh evreev," 245.

49. Zylbercweig, *Di velt fun yankev gordin.*
50. Jaakoff Prelooker [Yakov Priluker], *Under the Czar and Queen Victoria: The Experiences of a Russian Reformer* (London: James Nisbet, 1895), 42.
51. Yakov Priluker, *Odesskii listok* [Odessa Sheet], January, 31, 1882, cited by Klier, "From Elisavetgrad to Broadway," 116. Priluker includes this list in *Evrei-reformatory,* 79–82.
52. "The Brotherhood's teachings have nothing in common with the initial program of 'New Israel,' which speaks of some sort of stripes and distinguishing marks." Jacob Gordin, "V zashchitu dukhovno-bibleiskogo bratstva—Pis'mo v redaktsiyu," *Nedelya,* no. 45 (November 4, 1884): 1535–36.
53. Rabinovich, a former *maskil* from Kishinev, converted to Protestant Christianity in Germany and was later ordained a Congregationalist minister. See Sergei I. Zhuk, *Russia's Lost Reformation: Peasants, Millennialism, and Radical Sects in Southern Russia and Ukraine, 1830–1917* (Washington, D.C.: Woodrow Wilson Center Press; Baltimore: Johns Hopkins University Press, 2004), 359–62; and Steven J. Zipperstein, "Heresy, Apostasy, and the Transformation of Joseph Rabinovich," in *Jewish Apostasy in the Modern World,* ed. Todd M. Endelman (New York: Holmes and Meier, 1987), 206–31.
54. "Nam pishut: Iz Elisavetgrada," *Nedelya,* no. 3 (January 15, 1884): 102. In a typical example of Gordin's revising his Russian writings for his work in Yiddish, Moses and Jesus were paired up with Karl Marx in the satire "Yezus Kristus un Karl Marks tsu gast in Nyu York" See *Ale shriftn fun yankev gordin,* 2: 193–205. In this sketch, Moses, Jesus, and Marx are hapless greenhorns who compete fruitlessly to find exemplars of the beliefs for which they stand.
55. Venyamin Portugalov, "Nezhdannaya pomekha," *Nedelya,* no. 39 (September 23, 1884): 1293.
56. "Dukhovno-bibleiskoe bratstvo," *Odesskii vestnik,* November 13, 1882.
57. Jews charged with "conversionary activities" could be expelled from any district in which they appeared. See John Klier, *Russia Gathers Her Jews: The Origins of the Jewish Question in Russia, 1722–1825* (De Kalb: Northern Illinois University Press, 1986), 166.
58. Letter from the office of the governor of Kherson province to the chief of police, December 11, 1881, GARF, 4.
59. Ibid., GARF, reel 2, 60, 65.
60. Bukhbinder, "Iz istorii sektantskogo dvizheniya sredi russkikh evreev," 246.
61. Prugavin, "Dukhovno-bibleiskoe bratstvo," 647. In practice, the two organizations seem to have been allied, rather than a single entity; there is no mention of New Israel by name in any of the Brotherhood's gov-

ernment petitions, and Priluker's memoirs continue to refer to his organization as New Israel, up until his emigration from Russia in June of
1891. See also Emmanuel Ben-Sion [Yakov Priluker], "Novye idei sredi
evreev," *Nedelya*, no. 12 (March 20, 1883): 379–80.

62. Prugavin added a footnote: "The 'biblists' who had resettled in America
are terribly impoverished and dream only of returning to their 'brothers'
in Russia." "Dukhovno-bibleiskoe bratstvo," 646.

CHAPTER 3: A RUSSIAN WRITER

1. Leon Kobrin, *Erinerungen fun a yidishn dramaturg: A fertl yorhundert
yidish teater in amerika* (New York: Komitet far kobrins shriftn, 1925),
1: 123. Kobrin notes that his account is based on the reminiscences of
Leon Blank, who played a doctor in *Sibirya*. Adler appears to have emphasized Gordin's Russianness by referring to him as the "famous Russian *pisatel'*, Yakov Mikhailovich Gordin." Howe has an ironic account
of this appeal in *World of Our Fathers*, 468.

2. Advertisement, *Di arbayter tsaytung*, August 28, 1891.

3. On this aspect of the intellectual culture of the Lower East Side, and its
origins, see especially Cassedy, *To the Other Shore*, 3–35; and Hapgood,
Spirit of the Ghetto, 79–85, 109–10, 199–201, 215–18, 223, 232, 234.

4. Both Marmor and Zylbercweig offer identically muddled conflations
of two separate stories by Ivan Kolyuchii [Jacob Gordin], "Berkova
koza (Fantaziya)," *Elisavetgradskii vestnik*, July 3, 1888, and "Rody
razlichnykh rodov (Eskiz)," *Elisavetgradskii vestnik*, November 6,
1888). See Marmor, *Yankev gordin*, 20–21; and Zylbercweig, *Di velt
fun yankev gordin*, 79.

5. N. [Jacob Gordin], "Evreiskie siluety 2. Avramele Shloper," *Knizhki
nedeli*, no. 8 (August 1885): 11. All subsequent citations are from this
edition.

6. N., "Doktor-vykrest," *Knizhki nedeli*, no. 10 (October 1885): 52.

7. N., "Syupriz," *Knizhki nedeli*, no. 10 (October 1885): 57. All subsequent citations are from this edition.

8. N., "Evreiskie siluety: Aptekar' na vse ruki," *Knizhki nedeli*, no. 2
(1886): 120.

9. N., "Evreiskie siluety: Evrei-shtundist," *Knizhki nedeli*, no. 2 (1886):
138. All subsequent citations are from this edition.

10. Yakov Mikhailovich [Jacob Gordin], "Putyovaya zametka," *Elisavetgradskii vestnik*, November 8, 1885.

11. Gordin, "Drama," in *Ale shriftn fun yankev gordin*, 4: 53–62.

12. GARF, 21.

13. See Leah Garrett, *Journeys beyond the Pale: Yiddish Travel Writing in
the Modern World* (Madison: University of Wisconsin Press, 2003); and

Dan Miron, *A Traveler Disguised: The Rise of Modern Yiddish Fiction in the Nineteenth Century*, 2nd ed. (Syracuse, N.Y.: Syracuse University Press, 1996).

14. N.N.—"Nomen nescio," or "I do not know the name."
15. Ivan Kolyuchii, "Fel'eton. Sutoloka odesskoi zhizni," *Odesskie novosti*, May 24, 1887.
16. Jacob Gordin, "The Jewish Drama and Its Effects in America," as reported in "Interesting Symposium on Modern Drama—Methods of Philanthropic Work," *Jewish Assembly Summer Supplement* 29, no. 15 (July 29, 1904): 1, Jacob Gordin Papers, box 11, folder 193.
17. Jacob Gordin, "Realizmus un romantizmus," in *Ale shriftn fun yankev gordin*, 4: 176–84; originally published in *Di tsukunft* (1904). Translated by Steven Cassedy as "Realism and Romanticism," in *Building the Future*, 80–86.
18. Ivan Kolyuchii, "*Evgenii Onegin* na elisavetgradskoi stsene."
19. Gordin, "Realism and Romanticism," 84.
20. Ivan Kolyuchii, "*Evgenii Onegin* na elisavetgradskoi stsene."
21. Alfei [Jacob Gordin], "Malen'kii fel'eton: Real'nyi roman v sovremennom dukhe," *Elisavetgradskii vestnik*, January 8, 1889.
22. See Yan [Jacob Gordin], "Teatr i muzyka," *Odesskie novosti*, June 27, 1887.
23. See David Mazower, "Stories in Song: The Melo-deklamatsyes of Joseph Markovitsh," in Berkowitz, *Yiddish Theatre: New Approaches*, 119–37.
24. Ivan Kolyuchii, "Neskol'ko slov po povodu melodeklamatsionnogo vechera," *Elisavetgradskii vestnik*, March 27, 1888.
25. Yan, "Teatr," *Elisavetgradskii vestnik*, December 4, 1888.
26. Ivan Kolyuchii, "Fel'eton. Sutoloka odesskoi zhizni," *Odesskie novosti*, April 26, 1887.
27. Yan, "Teatr i muzyka: Russkii teatr," *Odesskie novosti*, November 20, 1886.
28. Yan, "Teatr i muzyka: Russkii teatr," *Odesskie novosti*, November 18, 1886.
29. Ivan Kolyuchii, "*Evgenii Onegin* na elisavetgradskoi stsene."
30. Ibid.
31. See excerpts from *Der unbekanter* in *Di tsukunft* 4, no. 3 (1905): 147–50; and from *Oyf di berg*, adapted from Gerhart Hauptmann's "Die versunkene Glocke," in *Di tsukunft* 11, no. 10 (1906): 598–601.
32. Ivan Kolyuchii, "M. G. Savina na Elisavetgradkoi stsene (Pis'mo v redaktsiyu)," *Elisavetgradskii vestnik*, July 3, 1888.
33. Ivan Kolyuchii, "Fel'eton. Sutoloka odesskoi zhizni," *Odesskie novosti*, April 26, 1887.
34. Yan, "Teatr," *Elisavetgradskii vestnik*, December 1, 1888.
35. Ibid.

36. Gordin, "Realism and Romanticism," 82.
37. "N'yu-Iork (Iz nashego korrespondenta)," *Voskhod*, no. 4 (January 24, 1902): 30. Gordin's contemporaries rarely remarked on his "photographic realism" without also noting his actors' "remarkable" faculties. See "A New Yiddish Drama," [undated], Jacob Gordin Papers, box 11, folder 193.
38. Playbill for *Reyzele* and *Der shvartser yid* [The Black Jew], from Boston's Bijou Theatre, 1895, Jacob Gordin Papers, box 10, folder 186.
39. See Marmor, *Yankev gordin*, 43–44; Zylbercweig, *Di velt fun yankev gordin*, 107; Kaplan, *Finding the Jewish Shakespeare*, 31–32; and *Suvenir tsu yankev gordins tsen-yerikn yubileyum*.
40. GARF, ed. khr. 606 (2), listki 90–96. Reports dating from January 26, 1892, allege that Gordin would attempt to return to Russia using an American passport registered to "James Gordin." In February, the Ministry of Internal Affairs circulated notices to all border checkpoints and ports to be on the alert for Gordin and to arrest him should he materialize. He never did.
41. Editorial, *Elisavetgradskii vestnik*, March 5, 1886.
42. "Fel'eton. Prazdnovanie godovshchiny 'Dukhovno-bibleiskogo bratstva' v Elisavetgrade," *Odesskie novosti*, January 10, 1887.
43. Ibid.
44. See Uri D. Herscher, *Jewish Agricultural Utopias in America, 1880–1910* (Detroit: Wayne State University Press, 1981); Joseph Brandes, in association with Martin Douglas, *Immigrants to Freedom: Jewish Communities in Rural New Jersey since 1882* (Philadelphia: University of Pennsylvania Press, 1971); and Ellen Eisenberg, *Jewish Agricultural Colonies in New Jersey, 1882–1920* (Syracuse, N.Y.: Syracuse University Press, 1995).
45. Lifschutz, "Jacob Gordin's Proposal to Establish an Agricultural Colony," 262–63. Lifschutz's source for information on Gordin's visit to Woodbine is a memoir by Anna Dobrowolski-Sherman, a former member of the Brotherhood who immigrated to the United States in November of 1891. She dates Gordin's visit to the New Jersey colony to eighteen months after she had arrived in New York. Unfortunately, Dobrowolski-Sherman's memoirs, preserved at the YIVO Institute, cannot be located.
46. "Nedel'nye zametki," *Nedelya*, no. 7 (February 14, 1887): 236 (italics in original).
47. None of these humiliations register in the feuilletons that Gordin wrote about his trip to the capital. Ivan Kolyuchii merely played the part of the gee-whiz provincial taking in the magnificent sights of Moscow. See Ivan Kolyuchii, "Fel'eton. Peterburg-Odessa (Nechto v rode putyovoi zametki)," *Odesskie novosti*, February 21, 1887.

48. Quoted by Anatolii Stepanovich Butkevich, *Vospominaniya L. N.* (Moscow: Izdatel'stvo Gosudarstvennogo literaturnogo muzeya, 1938), 1: 342, http://feb-web.ru/feb/tolstoy/critics/lg2/lg23337-.htm (accessed December 6, 2007).

49. GARF, 20.

50. Zylbercweig, *Di velt fun yankev gordin*, 86.

51. Fainerman was also the author of a monograph on Tolstoy, *Lev Tolstoy o evreyakh* (St. Petersburg: Knizhnoe Izdatel'stvo "Vremya," 1908). For more on Fainerman's Tolstoy connection, see Galina A. Eliasberg, "I. Teneromo—provintsial'nyi korrespondent L. N. Tolstogo," *Filologicheskie nauki* 5 (2009): 45–55.

52. On the subject of Fainerman, see Tolstoy's letters to his wife, Sofiya, in 1887, in Lev Tolstoy, *Polnoe sobranie sochinenii v 90-i tomakh. Akademicheskoe yubileinoe izdanie*, ed. Vladimir G. Chertkov (Moscow: Gosudarstvennoe Izdatel'stvo Khudozhestvennoi Literatury, 1949), 84: 24–27 (hereafter cited as *PSS*).

53. N. Gusev, *Letopis' zhizni i tvorchestva L. N. Tolstogo, 1828–1919* (Moscow and Leningrad: Akademiya, 1936), 336. Tolstoy's daughter Tatiana was Fainerman's godmother.

54. Butkevich, *Vospominaniya L. N.*, 1: 350; Lev Tolstoy, diary entry for June 26, 1889, *PSS*, 50: 101.

55. Gordin's police file reports that Khilkov allowed the Brotherhood to proselytize on his estate, Pavlovki (a hotbed of evangelical dissident activity), in 1889 (GARF, 23). The police credited Khilkov with heading a division of the Brotherhood in Poltava province, but this role is unlikely (GARF, 21). Although Khilkov insisted on nonviolent solutions to Russia's problems, both police and Orthodox clergy worried about the widespread appeal of his views. See Graham P. Camfield, "From Tolstoyan to Terrorist: The Revolutionary Career of Prince D. A. Khilkov, 1900–1905," *Revolutionary Russia* 12, no. 1 (June 1999): 1–43. For discussion of archival documents relating to official communiqués about Khilkov, see Zhuk, *Russia's Lost Reformation*, 367–70.

56. Butkevich, *Vospominaniya L. N.*, 1: 352–53.

57. Lev Tolstoy, letter to N. N. Ge, March 1890, *PSS*, 65: 48–49.

58. GARF, 21.

59. GARF, 22.

60. Butkevich, *Vospominaniya L. N.*, 1: 351.

61. GARF, 23.

62. Klier, "From Elisavetgrad to Broadway," 120.

63. GARF, 11.

64. The police list those who settled in Glodossy as Fainerman and his wife, Anna (Khana) Lyubarskaya; Butkevich; Mark Gol'dfeld and his wife

(Katya Gol'dfeld); Kel'man Galitskii and his wife, Roza Kogan; Isaak Ostry; and Isaak (Shaya) Burshtein and his wife. GARF, 28, 57.

65. Gordin's Yiddish biographers erroneously report not only that he helped Fainerman establish the colony (Marmor, *Yankev gordin*, 44) but also that he was one of its settlers (Zylbercweig, *Di velt fun yankev gordin*, 107). These errors create a false link between Gordin's nonexistent involvement in the Glodossy exodus and his nonexistent threat of arrest.

66. Tolstoy, *PSS*, 65: 86–88.

67. Dobrowolski-Sherman's memoirs, 61–62, quoted in Lifschutz, "Jacob Gordin's Proposal to Establish an Agricultural Colony," 258–59. See also Gusev, *Letopis' zhizni i tvorchestva L. N. Tolstogo*, 413; and GARF, 67.

68. GARF, 65.

69. "Khronika," *Elisavetgradskii vestnik*, October 1, 1889; "Khronika," *Elisavetgradskii vestnik*, December 1, 1889.

70. GARF, 61; "Khronika," *Elisavetgradskii vestnik*, May 31, 1889.

71. GARF, 68.

72. Ibid., 66.

73. Ibid., 73, dated October 7, 1891.

74. Gordin's close friends Rozalia Fainzilberg, who was Jewish, and Evgenii Gar, who was Russian Orthodox, had married according to the Brotherhood's rites, which did not require them to forswear the religion of their birth. This was in blatant violation of Russian law, which recognized no civil marriage and forbade marriages between Orthodox Christians and members of other faiths. Fainzilberg and Gar moved to St. Petersburg after the closing of the Brotherhood, and they were kept under watch of the local police but were never arrested. They eventually returned to Ukraine and remained in contact with Gordin and former members of the Brotherhood for many years.

75. See Jacob Gordin Papers, box 9, folders 178, 179. One former member of the Brotherhood, Boris Lintser, was arrested—in 1905.

76. Ivan Kolyuchii, "Dovol'no! Dovol'no!" *Elisavetgradskii vestnik*, June 11, 1889.

77. Ivan Kolyuchii, "Razgovory," *Elisavetgradskii vestnik*, July 9, 1889.

78. Ibid.

79. Ivan Kolyuchii, "Pis'mo k chitatelyam," *Elisavetgradskii vestnik*, December 17, 1889.

80. Erdeli had a lengthy tenure in office and retired in 1890 for health reasons. "Vysochaishie Prikazy: Po Ministerstvu Vnutrennykh Del, 7-go sego iyunya," *Pravitel'stvennyi vestnik*, June 9, 1890.

81. Max Paul Friedman, "Beyond 'Voting with Their Feet': Toward a Conceptual History of 'America' in European Migrant Sending Communi-

ties, 1860s to 1914," *Journal of Social History* 40, no. 3 (Spring 2007): 557.

82. Yakov Mikhailovich, "Vykrest," *Knizhki nedeli*, no. 6 (1891): 33. All subsequent citations are from this edition.

CHAPTER 4: THE PERILS OF PERFORMANCE

1. There are two English translations of Gordin's *Kreutzer Sonata*, the first by Samuel Schiffman and the second by Langdon Mitchell. Mitchell's translation was adapted by Herbert Brenon in 1915 for the film version, starring Nance O'Neil as Ettie ("Miriam") and Theda Bara as Celia. There are several Russian translations, the most recent and faithful of which is in *Polveka evreiskogo teatra, 1876–1926. Antologiya evreiskoi dramaturgii*, ed. Boris Entin (Moscow: Dom evreiskoi knigi, 2003), 151–219.

2. See numerous clippings of reviews of Yiddish and English-language productions, in Jacob Gordin Papers, box 11, folder 193. See also Ruth Gay, "Jacob Gordin's Life," in Gordin, *The Jewish King Lear*, 124.

3. The first Yiddish translation appeared in 1895 in *Di tsukunft* in Cahan's own translation (under the pseudonym David Bernstein) and was republished in 1910 in the *Forverts* as part of a posthumous tribute to Tolstoy. The YIVO Institute's catalogs list translations in 1906, 1911, 1914, and 1929, in addition to collected Yiddish editions of Tolstoy's work.

4. Bessie Thomashefsky's memoirs (cited by Zylbercweig, *Leksikon fun yidishn teater* [Warsaw: Farlag "Elisheva," 1934], 2: 424) list Gordin's translation as *Di makht fun finsternish* and date it to 1902. But B. Gorin lists the play as *Di finsternish in rusland* and dates its opening to 1905 (*Di geshikhte fun idishen teater*, 2: 259).

5. Among the many articles on Tolstoy, see in the *Forverts*: "Tolstoy in kampf," March 18, 1901; "Tolstoy oysgevizn fun rusland," April 2, 1901; "Tolstoy tsum tsar," April 21, 1901; "Tolstoy vegn amerike—an intervyu," October 2, 1901; and "Sholem aleykhem un tolstoy," July 19, 1903. In *Di arbayter tsaytung*, see Kh. Aleksandrov, "Tkhies hameysim: Tolstoys letster roman," March 11, 1900; "Graf tolstoy in kheyrem," March 10, 1901; and "Tolstoys protest-briv," August 16 1901. For these I am greatly indebted to Steven Cassedy for his invaluable index of turn-of-the-century New York Yiddish newspapers.

6. See Abraham Cahan, "Realistishe literatur. Zol der shrayber zikh araynmishn in bild?" *Forverts*, December 17, 1903; "In vos beshteyt tolstoys groskayt?" *Forverts*, November 23, 1910; "Tolstoys groskayt als a shrayber," *Forverts*, November 24, 1910; and M. Rozenfeld, "Ruslands neyr-tomed. Gedanken iber graf tolstoy," *Forverts*, November 29, 1910.

7. Cassedy, *To the Other Shore*, 92.
8. Hapgood, *Spirit of the Ghetto*, 199.
9. Yakov Mikhailovich, "Po povodu odnoi retsenzii," *Elisavetgradksii vestnik*, March 19, 1886.
10. Ivan Kolyuchii, "Bezbrachniki (Etyud)," *Elisavetgradskii vestnik*, June 10, 1890.
11. "Beseda o Tolstom," December 24, 1893, Jacob Gordin Papers, box 7, folder 108.
12. Gordin, "Realizmus un romantizmus," 180.
13. See Caryl Emerson, "*What Is Art?* and the Anxiety of Music," *Russian Literature* 40 (1996): 433–50; Emerson, "Tolstoy's Aesthetics: A Harmony and Translation of the Five Senses," *Tolstoy Studies Journal* 12 (2000): 9–17; David Herman, "Stricken by Infection: Art and Adultery in *Anna Karenina* and *Kreutzer Sonata*," *Slavic Review* 56, no. 1 (1997): 15–36; Liza Knapp, "Tolstoy on Musical Mimesis: Platonic Aesthetics and Erotics in *The Kreutzer Sonata*," *Tolstoy Studies Journal* 4 (1991): 25–42; Ruth Rischin, "*Allegro Tumultuosissimamente*: Beethoven in Tolstoy's Fiction," in *In the Shade of the Giant: Essays on Tolstoy*, ed. Hugh McLean (Berkeley: University of California Press, 1989), 12–60; Rimvydas Silbajoris, *Tolstoy's Aesthetics and His Art* (Columbus, Ohio: Slavica, 1991); and Janneke Van de Stadt, "Narrative, Music, and Performance: Tolstoy's *Kreutzer Sonata* and the Example of Beethoven," *Tolstoy Studies Journal* 12 (2000): 57–69.
14. Jacob Gordin, *Kreytser sonate: A drame in fir akten* (New York: M. Mayzel, 1907), 10. All subsequent citations refer to this edition.
15.   *Eti*: Vi du farshteyst, papa. (*Zi drikt dem bukh tsu ir hartsn*.)
    Rafail: (*Frayndlekh*.) Nu, vos shteystu? Zets dikh. (*Zi zetst zikh*.) Vos iz dos far a bukh bay dir?
      Eti: Dos iz der elfter band fun tolstoys verk . . . Do in bukh, iz do . . . Ikh vel dir zogn di varhayt, papa . . . (*Dershrokn*.)
    Rafail: (*Frayndlekh*.) Ze nor, vegn a bukh megstu dokh redn ruiker . . . Vos iz do?
      Eti: Do? Do iz zayn . . . Do iz "Kreytsers sonata" . . . Ikh hob ersht etlekhe kapitlekh gelezen . . . Oy, dos makht azoy mies dos lebn, nokh mieser, vi ikh hob frier gefilt.
    Rafail: A bukh ken dos lebn nit mies makhn. Der mentsh makht mies dos lebn. Ot host du genumen un host zikh dos gantse lebn mies gemakht . . . Aher gib dem bukh!
16. "Dayne! Ikh veys, vos heyst dayne! Dayn eygentum! Mayn kerper gehert dir! Mayn kerper hot dir gehert zind ikh bin geboyrn gevorn un vet dir geheren biz ikh vel shtarbn! Ven du darfst mayn kerper, host du mikh lib! Ven du host mikh lib, heyst es, du darfst mayn kerper! Du zest mikh

obhitn, ikh bin dir tayer, vi yedes eygentum bay yeden eygenthimer! Mayn kerper hot dikh interesirt, mayn zeele ober host du yedn tog tsen mol ermordet! Mayne mentshlekhe gefile host du yedn oygnblik getrotn mit di fis! Kimat tsen yor gelebt mit dir, un du host mikh oyf eyn minut nit betrakht als mentsh, nor als froy, als vayb, als dinst! Host nit gevolt un nit gekent mikh farshteyen. Host nit gevolt un nit gekent visn vos ikh hob far der tsayt ibergefilt. Ikh hob farshprokhen tsu duldn un shvaygn—hob ikh geshvign un ertrogn mer vi ikh hob gedarft! Genug!"

17. Gordin, "Drama," in *Ale shriftn fun yankev gordin*, 4: 53.

18. I am indebted to one of the *Tolstoy Studies Journal*'s anonymous readers for this observation.

19. Van de Stadt, "Narrative, Music, and Performance," 58.

20. After a bitter quarrel, Pozdnyshev's wife accuses him: "Everything is pretense [*pritvorstvo*] to you, you would kill a person and say he was pretending [*pritvoryaetsya*]" (*PSS*, 27: 50). Pozdnyshev's reaction is to lock himself in his room and dream of escape: "A thousand different plans come into my head of how to get revenge on her and get rid of her, and how to make everything right and make it as if nothing had happened. I think about all this and smoke" (*PSS*, 27: 51). Dreaming of death and divorce, Pozdnyshev thinks about how to get rid of his wife: "I see that I am confused and not thinking of what is necessary, but in order not to see that I am not thinking of what is necessary, I smoke" (*PSS*, 27: 51).

21. Richard F. Gustafson also notes the intoxicating properties of the tea. See *Leo Tolstoy, Resident and Stranger: A Study in Fiction and Theology* (Princeton, N.J.: Princeton University Press, 1986), 354.

22. Ronald D. LeBlanc, "Tolstoy's Way of No Flesh: Abstinence, Vegetarianism, and Christian Physiology," in *Food in Russian History and Culture*, ed. Musya Glants and Joyce Toomre (Bloomington: Indiana University Press, 1997), 90.

23. The earlier lithograph version of *Kreitserova sonata* suggested that there was truth in ancient literature but not in contemporary works: "Even if one allows that Menelaus might prefer Helen for his whole life, Helen would prefer Paris, and that is how it always was and is in the world. It cannot be any other way, any more than there can be two marked peas lying side by side in a cartload of peas. Besides, it is not just the unlikelihood of this, but the inevitable satiety of Helen with Menelaus or vice versa. The only difference is that with one it comes earlier and with the other, later. It is only in stupid novels that they write that they loved each other their whole lives. And only children can believe that" (*PSS*, 27: 295–96).

24. Amy Mandelker, *Framing Anna Karenina: Tolstoy, the Woman Question, and the Victorian Novel* (Columbus: Ohio State University Press, 1993), 32, 67-69.

25. Pozdnyshev also lays the blame for the murder on sexual relations ("So you may see how and when that which led me to my 'episode' began" [*PSS*, 27: 17]); on his wife's use of contraceptives ("that which caused all that happened later" [*PSS*, 27: 46]); and on music ("She again enthusiastically took up the piano, which before she had completely abandoned. It all began from that" [*PSS*, 27: 48]).

26. Gustafson, *Leo Tolstoy, Resident and Stranger*, 354-55; Knapp, "Tolstoy on Musical Mimesis, 39.

27. Peter Brook, *There Are No Secrets: Thoughts on Acting and the Theatre* (London: Methuen, 1993), 41–42.

28. See Valerii Bryusov, "Nenuzhnaya pravda," *Mir iskusstva* 8, no. 4 (1902): 67–74.

29. *Rafail*: [. . .] Nadn farshprekh ikh im nor tsvey-un-a-halb toyzend, nit finf toyzend, vi ikh hob frier gerekhent tsu gebn. Vos kukstu mikh on?

    Eti: Papa, zay nit beyz, ikh meyn, er vet efsher zayn beser tsu mir, az du vest nit obshporn . . .

    Rafail: (*Beyz.*) Obshporn! Ikh veys, vifl nadn du fardinst, finf toyzend! Ikh zog dir!

30. *Greguar*: Ikh veys . . . Di varhayt, finf un tsvantsik hunderter iz gor nit shlekht, az var ikh leb. . .

    Rafail: Ikh vil nit leykenen, ir iz geven farshprokhen shoyn lang finf toyzend.

    Greguar: Eh! Vilt ir bay mir obraysn tsvey un a halb toyzend, vayl itst zayt ir mit ir umtsufridn?

    Rafail: Azoy meynt zi. Aykh meg ikh zogn: ikh vil gor nit obraysn . . . Dray yor nokh der khasene krigt ir di ibrige finf un tsvantsik hunderter mit protsent. Ir hert? Friedlenders a vort iz azoy gut vi a kayzerlekher kreditner bilet . . . Yo! Mit protsent . . . gevis, oyb ir vet nor lebn vi mentshn . . . un zi vet nit hobn keyne urzakhn tsu beklogn zikh . . .

CHAPTER 5: DON'T LOOK BACK

1. "4 naye pyesen. 'Di yesoyme oder khasye fun korotshekrank.' Drama in 4 akten fun ya. gordin," *Yidishes tageblat*, [October 1903], Jacob Gordin Papers, box 10, folder 193.

2. "Der kampf gegen 'realizm,'" *Morgen zhurnal*, [October 1903], Jacob Gordin Papers, box 12, folder 195.

3. "Ver grobt di kvorim. Di zelbstmord epidemie unter yidn," *Jewish Daily News / Yidishes tageblat*, October 20, 1903, Jacob Gordin Papers, box 12, folder 195.

4. Ibid.

5. For accounts of the controversy and its political origins, see Cahan, *Bleter fun mayn leben*, 4 (1928): 358–66; Marmor, *Yankev gordin*, 134–38; Warnke, "Reforming the New York Yiddish Theater," 143–202; and Zylbercweig, *Di velt fun yankev gordin*, 233–39.

6. Mark Arnstein, "Gordins 'Yesoyme' in varshe," *Der veg*, [1906], Jacob Gordin Papers, box 10, folder 193.

7. Voliner, "Fun idishen teater: 'Khasye di yesoyme,'" *Telegraf*, [1906], Jacob Gordin Papers, box 10, folder 193.

8. Yitskhok Leybush Peretz, "'Khasye di yesoyme.' A drama in fir aktn fun yankev gordin (Amerika)," *Veg*, [1906], Jacob Gordin Papers, box 10, folder 193. For more reviews and a description by Avrom Reizen (1876–1953) of Peretz's response to the play, see also Zalmen Zylbercweig, *Di velt fun ester rokhl kaminska* (Mexico: Imprenta Moderna Pintel, 1969), 53–63.

9. A Teatral, "'Khasye di yesoyme,'" *Odeser folksblat*, September 27, 1906, Jacob Gordin Papers, box 10, folder 193.

10. Untitled clipping from *Der Fraynd*, [St. Petersburg, 1907], Jacob Gordin Papers, box 11, folder 192.

11. Charles Isenberg, *Telling Silence: Russian Frame Narratives of Renunciation* (Evanston, Ill.: Northwestern University Press, 1993), 145. On the divided self in the *Künstlerroman*, see also Maurice Beebe, *Ivory Towers and Sacred Founts: The Artist as Hero in Fiction from Goethe to Joyce* (New York: New York University Press, 1964).

12. Costlow, *Worlds within Worlds*, 59.

13. Leo Marx, *The Machine in the Garden: Technology and the Pastoral Ideal in America* (1964; repr., Oxford: Oxford University Press, 2000), 11. The citation is to the 2000 edition.

14. See Nikolai Chernyshevsky, "Russkii chelovek na *rendez-vous*. Razmyshleniya po prochtenii povesti g. Turgeneva 'Asya,'" *Atenei* 3, no. 18 (1858): 65–89. Reprinted in Chernyshevsky, *Literaturnaya kritika v dvukh tomakh* (Moscow: "Khudozhestvennaya literatura," 1981), 2: 190–211.

15. See Costlow, *Worlds within Worlds*, 82–104.

16. Geoffrey H. Hartman, *Wordsworth's Poetry, 1787–1814* (New Haven, Conn., and London: Yale University Press, 1964), 12.

17. Eva Kagan-Kans, *Hamlet and Don Quixote: Turgenev's Ambivalent Vision* (The Hague and Paris: Mouton, 1975), 18. The phrase comes from a review by Turgenev of the German writer Berthold Auerbach's stories of peasant life.

18. On this recurring element of Turgenev's treatment of romantic love and infatuation, see George S. Pahomov, *In Earthbound Flight: Romanticism in Turgenev* (Rockville, Md.: Victor Kamkin, 1983), especially 89–99.

19. Joseph L. Conrad argues persuasively that N.N.'s initial attraction, both intellectually and sexually, is to Gagin, rather than to Asya. His affinity with her brother is natural, easy, and effortlessly intimate. In contrast, a greater distance must be bridged for the narrator to find a more "appropriate" love-interest in Asya. He must fight the currents (literally, in his daily river-crossings to their town) in order to realign his romantic feelings in Asya's direction. See Joseph L. Conrad, "Turgenev's 'Asja': Ambiguous Ambivalence," *Slavic and East European Journal* 30, no. 2 (Summer 1986): 215–29.

20. Jacob Gordin, *Khasye di yesoyme*, in *Dray drames*, ed. Shmuel Rozhansky (Buenos Aires: Literatur gezelshaft baym YIVO in argentine, 1973), 28. All subsequent quotations are from this edition. The manuscript, dated October 1, 1901 (Jacob Gordin Papers, box 3, folder 39), does not differ substantially from this edition.

21. "[. . .] Forndik mitn veg, vi ikh fleg derzen oyfn feld kveytn, fleg ikh aropshpringen fun vogn un loyfn oysraysn . . . di goyim hobn derfar nisht gelozt dem tatn mikh shlogn. Bay im iz dokh alts a khet! Az a yidish meydl rayst-oys a kveytl, iz zi shoyn a shikse bay im . . . Un ikh hob lib kveytn . . . Ir zet, dos iz lyubistok, dos iz tsheptshik, barvizok, romashkes, shtshebrets, vasilki, kashka, sviripka un dos iz ivan-da-mariya . . . Ikh ken ale kveytn un ale grozn in feld." Only *lyubistok* and *barvizok* are standard Yiddish; *romashkes* has an established Yiddish term in *margaritkelekh*; the standard Yiddish for "cornflower" is *korn-shvesterl*, and for "clover," *kaneshine* or *klever*. *Kveytl* is from the Russian *kvetok* or *kvitok*. See Mordkhe Schaechter, *Di geviksen velt in yidish* (New York: YIVO Institute for Jewish Research, 2005).

22. "[. . .] Ikh hob gehat simenim in veg: hoykhe vayse topoln. Dort a krenitse mit a tseylem . . . a bergele . . . vint miln . . . di zun hot geshaynt, bin ikh gengangen un gezungen . . . (*Fartrakht.*) Nokh dem iz gekumen di nakht. Di finsternish iz mir gegangen antkegn: vi a shvartser galekh mit braytn, shvartsn mantl, un hot alts ayngeviklt, alts ayngeviklt . . . Un es iz gevorn azoy shtil. Do hob ikh zikh ongehoybn shrekn: fun vaser, hob ikh gemeynt, krikhn tsu mir rusalkes mit grine hent . . . fun vald hot gesheptshet der alter valdgayst . . . funem groz hobn geblishtet fayerdike oygn . . . ikh bin gegangen azoy shtil, az ikh hob gehert, vi di zangen funem korn zogn epes tsum feld, vi der himl dertseylt a sod tsu der erd un di shtern vinken un sheptshen: yo, yo! Mayn shotn iz geven azoy groys az ikh hob moyre gehat tsu umkukn zikh . . . Ikh hob afilu moyre gehat hoykh tsu veynen . . . mayne trern hobn zikh gegosn in der shtil . . . Keyner darf nisht hern vi a yesoyme veynt . . . di nakht hot geshvign un di finsternish hot fardekt mayne trern."

23. "Nokh in dorf fleg ikh trakhtn fun dir. Un az ikh bin geforn aher, ikh

veys nisht far vos, fleg ikh fartsitert vern, az men flegt dermonen dayn nomen. Ikh hob ober bald farshtanen, vos far a tsore du bist un hob zikh gegebn a vort, hitn zikh far dir vi farn malekh-hamoves . . . Ikh hob alts dervart, vest tsu mir zikh shatkhnen, vi di andere khazeyrim krikhn, un du gor nisht . . . Hob ikh ongehoybn vartn. Nokh dem hot es mikh fardrosn. Nokh dem hob ikh etlekhe mol in der shtil geveynt. Yo, geveynt, vos ikh bin aza umgliklikhe, az demolt ven ikh vil shoyn yo, dos umglik zol tsu mir krikhn, iz dafke nisht . . . nu *(farshemt)*. Endlekh iz dos umglik gekumen tsu khrikhn un ikh bin a gliklekhe."

24. Peretz, "'Khasye di yesoyme.' A drama in fir akten fun yankev gordin (Amerika)."

25. The possibility that Khasye is already pregnant is more obvious in the manuscript text, but was omitted in this published version.

26. "Oy, ikh gedenk, az ikh bin geven a kind, fleg ikh zitsn aleyn baym taykh, araynvarfn a shteyn in vaser un fleg vartn . . . Der shteyn flegt farzunken vern, vi ikh zink itst in dem opgrunt fun toyt . . . Un a vintele flegt loyfn fun di alte beymer tsu dem trukenem kamish un mir flegt zikh oysvayzn, vi emetser sheptshet dortn: Asya, nishto shoyn . . . *shtiler* Asya nishto shoyn . . . *gants shtil* Asya nishto . . . shoyn. . . *shtarbt*."

27. Joseph Leo Koerner, *Caspar David Friedrich and the Subject of Landscape* (New Haven, Conn., and London: Yale University Press, 1990), 243.

28. See Nina Warnke's discussion of this motif in "The Child Who Wouldn't Grow Up: Yiddish Theatre and Its Critics," in Berkowitz, *Yiddish Theatre: New Approaches*, 201–16.

29. For an excellent summary of the diverse origins of and theories related to symbolist theatre, see Marvin Carlson, *Theories of the Theatre: A Historical and Critical Survey, from the Greeks to the Present* (1984; repr., Ithaca, N.Y.: Cornell University Press, 1996), 302–37. The citation is to the 1996 edition.

30. Anton Chekhov, *Chaika*, in *Dramaticheskie proizvedeniya v dvukh tomakh* (Leningrad: "Iskusstvo," 1986), 2: 113.

31. Ibid., 2: 114.

32. See Fyodor Sologub, "Teatr odnoi voli," in *Teatr. Kniga o novom teatre* (St. Petersburg: Izdatel'stvo "Shipovnik," 1908), 179–98. Reprinted in *Russian Dramatic Theory from Pushkin to the Symbolists: An Anthology*, ed. and trans. Laurence Senelick (Austin: University of Texas Press, 1981), 132–48.

33. Edward Braun, *Meyerhold: A Revolution in Theatre*, rev. and expanded (1979; repr., London: Methuen, 1995), 57. The citation is to the 1995 edition.

34. See excerpts, Jacob Gordin, "Der unbekanter," *Di tsukunft* 4, no. 3

(1905): 147–50; and Gordin, "Oyf di berg (Prolog)," *Di tsukunft* 11, no. 10 (1906): 598–601.

35. "Gordin's 'On the Mountains': New Drama by the Yiddish Playwright," *American Hebrew*, [1907], Jacob Gordin Papers, box 11, folder 193; Pinski quoted in Zylbercweig, *Di velt fun yankev gordin*, 303.

36. Andrei Bely, "The Cherry Orchard," originally published in *Vesy* 5 (1904), reprinted in *Arabeski* (Moscow, 1911), and translated by Laurence Senelick in *Russian Dramatic Theory*, 89.

37. Henri Bergson, *Laughter: An Essay on the Meaning of the Comic*, trans. Cloudesley Brereton and Fred Rothwell (London: Macmillan, 1911; repr., Copenhagen and Los Angeles: Green Integer, 1999), 34. The citation is to the 1999 edition.

38. "Khasye: Vos zhe shvaygn zey vi fremde? (*Kukt zikh aroys.*) Likhtik do un freylekh . . . Men zingt, me shpilt, un bay undz, dort, azoy shpet bay nakht, iz shtil un finster . . . oder men shloft shoyn lang, oder men krigt zikh, oder di kinder veynen . . . (*Freylekh*) Dos zaynen undzere? Un ikh hob zikh far zey dershrokn, vi a nar . . . Ikh hob gemeynt, gebildete mentshn zitsn mit groyse bikher, azoy vi gemore, un men lernt . . . Un zey shpiln gor in kortn . . . Ha, ha, ha! In mitn mitvokh in kortn shpiln! Vos zhe, in katerinslav falt-oys hanukah zumer gor? (*Gelekhter.*)"

39. "Oy, der tate iz avek un ikh bin vider geblibn tsvishn fremde . . . (*Ziftst. Shtelt zikh presn.*) Dort, in korotshikrak, zaynen itst klor, kalte frimorgns. Men zet vayt ibern taykh a dorf in an ander gubernie . . . a vaser-kloyster . . . stolbes roykh geyen fun di koymens tsu di himlen . . . (*Prest un zingt shtil 'Oy, mama, mama, ne vydai mne zamuzh.'*)"

40. Bely, "The Cherry Orchard," 89.

CHAPTER 6: HOMECOMING

1. Gordin, "Di tsukunft fun idishen teater," 85.

2. Letter from Eva Lioznova to Jacob Gordin, postmarked April 19, 1905, Jacob Gordin Papers, box 9, folder 178.

3. For discussion of this period see Sheila Fitzpatrick, *The Russian Revolution* (Oxford and New York: Oxford University Press, 1994); Robert Service, *The Russian Revolution, 1900–1927*, 2nd ed. (Houndmills, Basingstoke, Hampshire, and London: Macmillan Press, 1991); and Peter Waldron, *The End of Imperial Russia* (New York: St. Martin's Press, 1997).

4. For recent analyses, see Anthony J. Heywood and Jonathan D. Smele, eds., *The Russian Revolution of 1905: Centenary Perspectives* (Abingdon, U.K.: Routledge, 2005); and Stefani Hoffman and Ezra Mendelsohn, eds., *The Revolution of 1905 and Russia's Jews* (Philadelphia: University of Pennsylvania Press, 2008).

5. Letter from Eva Lioznova to Jacob Gordin, autumn 1905, Jacob Gordin Papers, box 9, folder 178.

6. "The Spirit of Little Russia: What They Think Who Hope the Czar Will Lose to Japan; a Look into Revolutionary Russia through the Eyes of Jacob Gordin, Who Has Felt the Heavy Hand of Her Tyranny—It Seeks to Rule the World, He Says," undated clipping, Jacob Gordin Papers, box 11, folder 193.

7. "Our New York Letter: Jewish Nationalism vs. Assimilation—Mr. Cortelyou and Yom Kippur—the Stokes Flat—Goldfogle in Hot Water—Jottings," *Jewish Exponent*, October 13, 1905, Jacob Gordin Papers, box 11, folder 193.

8. Zylbercweig, *Di velt fun yankev gordin*, 329–30.

9. "Our New York Letter: Jewish Nationalism vs. Assimilation."

10. Zylbercweig, *Di velt fun yankev gordin*, 263.

11. On the economics of immigrant entertainment in Jewish New York, see Judith Thissen, "Reconsidering the Decline of the New York Yiddish Theatre in the Early 1900s," *Theatre Survey* 44, no. 2 (November 2003): 173–97; Nina Warnke, "Immigrant Popular Culture as Contested Sphere: Yiddish Music Halls, the Yiddish Press, and the Processes of Americanization, 1900–1910," *Theatre Journal* 48 (1996): 321–35; and Warnke, "Theater as Educational Institution: Jewish Immigrant Intellectuals and Yiddish Theater Reform," in *The Art of Being Jewish in Modern Times*, ed. Barbara Kirshenblatt-Gimblett and Jonathan Karp (Philadelphia: University of Pennsylvania, 2008), 23–41.

12. *Di dramatishe velt* published theoretical and review articles by Gordin and his friends and associates from the Educational League, such as Hillel Zolotarov and Joel Entin. It lasted only a year.

13. "Interesting Symposium on Modern Drama—Methods of Philanthropic Work," *Jewish Assembly Summer Supplement*, July 24, 1904: 1. Clipping, Jacob Gordin Papers, YIVO, box 11, folder 193.

14. Ibid.

15. For an account of the controversy surrounding *Tares hamishpokhe* and a summary of the play itself, see Warnke, "Reforming the New York Yiddish Theater," 184–94.

16. In fact, Jewish immigration from the Russian empire to the United States increased after 1905, although it did not help the fortunes of the Yiddish theatre. As Rebecca Kobrin notes, nearly 78 percent of all Jewish emigrants left Russia not after 1881 but between 1903 and 1914. By 1920, more than 35 percent of Jews in the United States (and 70 percent in Argentina) had arrived after 1905. Rebecca Kobrin, "The 1905 Revolution Abroad: Mass Migration, Russian Jewish Liberalism, and American Jewry, 1903–1914," in Hoffman and Mendelsohn, *The Revolution of 1905 and Russia's Jews*, 227–44.

17. Gordin, "Di tsukunft fun idishen teater," 82–83.

18. On the much-repeated history of Cahan's and Gordin's differences, see Cahan, *Bleter fun mayn leben*, especially 4: 344–97, 499–529; Ronald Sanders, *The Downtown Jews: Portraits of an Immigrant Generation* (New York; Evanston, Ill.; and London: Harper and Row, 1969), 301–26, 387–90; and Zylbercweig, *Di velt fun yankev gordin*, 240–69.

19. Gordin, "Di tsukunft fun idishen teater," 84–85.

20. Ibid., 84.

21. Ibid., 82. This comment is clearly a dig at Cahan, who was an accomplished English-language journalist and novelist.

22. Ibid., 85.

23. "Malen'kaya khronika," *Teatr i iskusstvo*, no. 43 (1913): 810.

24. This figure is based on a survey of advertisements and reviews in *Teatr i iskusstvo*, *Rech'* [Speech], *Birzhevye vedomosti* [Stock Exchange News], *Obozrenie teatrov* [Theatre Revue], and other newspapers between 1903 and 1917.

25. There is a parallel tradition of Yiddish "pogrom" plays, with Gordin's *Der pogrom in rusland* (1891) being one of the earliest, followed by *Di familye tsvi* [The Zvi Family, 1904], by Dovid Pinski, who protested that his play was not of this genre, and *Shema, Yisroel / Slushai, Izrail.'* [*Hear, O Israel!* 1907], by Osip Dymov.

26. Alekseev, "Teatr i muzyka—Novyi teatr (direktsiya L. B. Yavorskoi), 'Evrei'," *Novaya zhizn'*, November 27, 1905. *Novaya zhizn'* [New Life] was issued by the Russian Social Democrat Worker's Party, which in 1903 gave rise to the Bolshevik and Menshevik parties.

27. See Aleksandr Kugel', "Teatral'nye zametki," *Teatr i iskusstvo*, no. 31 (1910): 583–86; Kugel', "Teatral'nye zametki," *Teatr i iskusstvo*, no. 11 (1911): 239–40; and Homo Novus [Aleksandr Kugel'], "Zametki," *Teatr i iskusstvo*, no. 17 (1915): 292–93. Kugel', the editor of *Teatr i iskusstvo*, a leading theatre critic, a cofounder of the Krivoe Zerkalo theatre, and the organizer of the Jewish Theatre Studio in Petrograd in 1920, was one of the tiny minority of Jews from the Pale who had won the right to study and to stay in St. Petersburg.

28. For discussion of Yiddish theatre in Russia during the years of the "ban," see Klier, "Exit, Pursued by a Bear"; Barbara J. Henry, "Jewish Plays on the Russian Stage: St. Petersburg, 1905–1917," in Berkowitz, *Yiddish Theatre: New Approaches*, 61–75; Nokhem Oyslender, "In di yorn funem teater-farbot," in *Yidisher teater, 1887–1917* (Moscow: Melukhe-farlag "Der emes," 1940), 7–53; and Nina Warnke, "Going East: The Impact of American Yiddish Plays and Players on the Yiddish Stage in Czarist Russia, 1890–1914," *American Jewish History* 92, no. 1 (March 2004): 1–29.

29. On Spivakovski, see Evgenii Binevich, *Evreiskii teatr v peterburge.*

Opyt istoricheskogo ocherka (St. Petersburg: Evreiskii obshchinnyi tsentr Sankt-Peterburga, 2003), 31–58; and Zylbercweig, *Leksikon fun yidishn teater,* 2: 1533.

30. As Warnke notes ("Going East," 12), not even Lateiner, Hurwitz, and Shomer, or the playwrights who succeeded them, such as Leon Kobrin and Zalmen Libin, had their plays printed in such widely available and inexpensive copies.

31. Warnke ("Going East," 16–17) lists the following titles and their clearance dates from the censor's collection at the St. Petersburg Theatrical Library: *Der yidisher kenig lir* (cleared in 1902); *Got, mentsh, un tayvl* (cleared in 1904); *Di gebrider lurye* [The Brothers Lurie; cleared in 1905], *Khasye di yesoyme, Mirele efros,* and *Di vilde printsesin, oder Medeas yugend* [The Wild Princess, or Medea's Youth], Gordin's adaptation of Franz Grillparzer's (1791–1872) *Medea,* all cleared in (1905); and "eighteen more separate titles by Gordin," cleared between 1906 and 1908.

32. See Warsaw and Odessa reviews of *Khasye* from 1906, in chapter 6. There is also correspondence between Gordin and various entrepreneurs in Russia in this period. See a letter from the actor and impresario Julius Adler (b.1880) dated October 20, 1907, in which are included reviews of Adler's productions in Russia of *Got, mentsh, un tayvl; Kreytser sonata; Safo;* and *Di shkhite* (Jacob Gordin Papers, box 9, folder 112).

33. See Gordin's correspondence with his Lemberg representative, Gershom Bader, in Zylbercweig, *Di velt fun yankev gordin,* 457–74; and Kaplan, *Finding the Jewish Shakespeare,* 205.

34. Cahan, *Bleter fun mayn leben,* 4: 372–73.

35. Spivakovski's company was actually the first to perform Gordin's plays in St. Petersburg in 1907. The Gordin plays performed on the Kaminsky company's 1908 tour were *Di shkhite, Mirele efros, Der fremder* [The Foreigner, 1906], *Di kreytser sonata, Der yidisher kenig lir, Khasye, Di emese kraft* [The True Power, 1904] and *Di vilde printsesin, oder Medeas yugend.*

36. See Oyslender's extensive treatment of the Kaminsky's "literary troupe," its repertoire, reception, and effects, in *Yidisher teater,* especially 176–235. See also Zylbercweig, *Di velt fun ester rokhl kaminska.*

37. Pinski's schema puts Goldfaden, Lateiner, and Hurwitz in the first act, Gordin in the second, and the newer playwrights like Sholem Asch and Peretz Hirshbein, who represented original and aesthetically coherent Jewish plays, in the third. Pinski envisioned the "fourth act" as combining the theatricality of the "second act" Yiddish dramas with the more "independent," original, and uniquely Jewish content of the "third" act. See Pinski, *Dos idishe drama,* "Sof-vort," 57–58.

38. S. Gen [S. M. Ginnerman], "Evreiskaya stsena i evreiskii balagan," *Teatr i iskusstvo,* no. 15 (1907): 252, 254.

39. Aleksandr Kugel', "Evreiskii teatr," *Teatr i iskusstvo*, no. 17 (1908): 314.

40. Ibid.

41. Victor [pseud.], "Evreiskii teatr," *Teatr i iskusstvo*, no. 16 (1908): 237–38.

42. Homo Novus [Aleksandr Kugel'], "Evreiskii teatr," *Teatr i iskusstvo*, no. 19 (1908): 335.

43. See Jacob Gordin, *Dramy* (St. Petersburg: Izdatel'stvo "Teatr," 1910).

44. *Mirele efros, Di gebrider lurye, Khasye, Kreytser sonata*, and *Got, mentsh, un tayvl* were performed in 1909.

45. I. A. Klei[ma]n, "Teatr i muzyka—Evreiskii teatr, 'Mirele Efros' Ya. Gordina," *Rech'*, March 11, 1909.

46. The reproach was from Victor, "Evreiskii teatr," *Teatr i iskusstvo*, no. 15 (1909): 272. See remarks of praise in N. R., "Teatr i muzyka—Evreiskii teatr," *Rech'*, March 18, 1909; March 20, 1909; "Teatr i muzyka," *Rech'*, April 22, 1909; "Teatr i muzyka—Ekaterinskii teatr, 'Satana' Ya. Gordina," *Rech'*, December 20, 1909; "Ekaterinskii teatr," *Teatr i iskusstvo*, no. 52 (1909): 965–66; "Novyi teatr," *Teatr i iskusstvo*, no. 14 (1910): 300–301; and "Teatr i muzyka—Novyi teatr—'Mirra Efros' Ya. Gordina," *Rech'*, April 1, 1910. See also Oyslender, *Yidisher teater*, 92–101.

47. Arnstein quoted in Zylbercweig, *Di velt fun ester-rokhl kaminska*, 53.

48. See the following articles by Abraham Cahan: "Di perzonen in gordins piesen," *Forverts*, February 15–16, 1908; "Vos heyst an origineles verk?" *Forverts*, February 22, 1908; "A por perzenlekhe verter," *Forverts*, March 10–11, 1908; "Vos men denkt in rusland vegn gordinen," *Forverts*, March 15, 1908; and "Fun vanen hot gordin genumen 'zayne' artiklen," *Forverts*, April 4–11, 1908.

49. Cahan, *Bleter fun mayn leben*, 4: 526.

50. Norman Hapgood, "The Theatres," *Commercial Advertiser* (undated), Jacob Gordin Papers, box 11, folder 193.

51. Kin [pseud.], "Teatr i muzyka: Evreiskii literaturnyi teatr—'Zaklanie' drama v 4 d. soch. Ya. Gordina," *Rech'*, April 17, 1908.

52. Ibid.

53. Kin, "Teatr i muzyka: Evreiskii literaturnyi teatr, 'Mirele Efros,' drama v 4-kh deistviyakh, soch. Ya. Gordina," *Rech'*, April 19, 1908. Kean is the pseudonym in English translation, Kin [Кин] in Russian transliteration.

54. Kin, "Teatr i muzyka: Evreiskii literaturnyi teatr, 'Yankel' kuznets,' zhiznennaya kartina v 4-kh deistviyakh D. Pinskogo," *Rech'*, April 24, 1908.

55. Kin, "Mirele Efros."

56. Ibid.

57. "Mr. Gordin and His Friends," [1903], *American Hebrew*, Jacob Gordin Papers, box 11, folder 193.

58. Kin, "Mirele Efros."
59. "Preniya o Ya. Gordine. Sobranie 'Evr. Literaturnogo Obshchestva v. S. Peterburge," *Russko-Amerikanskoe Ekho*, November 11, 1909, Jacob Gordin Papers, box 11, folder 192.
60. Skitalets [S. G. Petrov], "Kaminskaya," *Obozrenie teatrov*, April 12, 1909, quoted in Binevich, *Evreiskii teatr v Peterburge*, 92–93.
61. Oyslender, *Yidisher teater*, 238.
62. Productions of Gordin's plays in Yiddish and Russian, in St. Petersburg and Petrograd, were *Der yidisher kenig lir*: February 22, 1918, "Komediya i Drama" theatre; *Der unbekanter*: January 27–29, 1922, "Komediya i Drama" theatre; *Di gebrider lurye*: April 14, 1909, Ekaterinsky theatre; March 1, 1916, "Komediya" theatre; July 1, 1916, Bol'shoi Siverskii theatre; October 10, 1922, "Mramornyi" theatre; *Der meturef*: April 12, 1917, Ekaterinsky theatre; *Di shkhite*: April 12, 1911, Ekaterinsky theatre; January 24–26, 1922, "Komediya i Drama" theatre; June 9, 11, 1922, "Teatr dlya vsekh"; *Di shvue*: April 26, 1923, Petrogradskii evreiskii teatr; *Got, mentsh, un tayvl*: December 16, 1909, Ekaterinsky theatre; November 10, 1910, Adler and Rivesman, Pavlova Hall; April 1, 1912, Blagorodnoe sobranie; February 12, 1913, "Komediya i Drama" theatre; August 15, 1922, Gosudarstvennoi tipografii; April 20, 1923, Petrogradskii evreiskii teatr; *Khasye di yesoyme*: March 3, 1912 (in Ukrainian), Teatr Passazh; March 3, 1916, "Komediya" theatre; April 15, 1917, Ekaterinsky theatre; February 15, 1918, "Komediya i Drama" theatre; *Di kreytser sonata*: January 12, 1916, "Pollak" theatre hall; April 9, 1917, Ekaterinsky theatre; November 27, 1922, Teatr muzykal'noi komedii; *Mirele efros*: March 30, 1910, Novyi theatre; February 20, 1912, Pavlova Hall; October 13, 1916, Intimnyi theatre; February 13, 1923, Petrogradskii evreiskii teatr; and *Safo*: March 14, 1913, Ekaterinsky theatre. Productions in Moscow, at the Korsh theatre (all productions in Russian), were *Di shkhite* (translated as Uboi), opened February 28, 1911; *Got, mentsh, un tayvl* (as Satana): opened December 11, 1909; *Kapital, libe, un mord* (as Lyubov' i smert'): opened February 13, 1915; *Di kreytser sonata* (as Za okeanom): October 14, 1911; *Mirele efros* (as Mirra Efros): opened February 12, 1910; and *Safo* (as Sof'ya Fingergut): opened October 12, 1912.
63. On film adaptations of Gordin's plays, see J. Hoberman, *Bridge of Light: Yiddish Film between Two Worlds* (New York: Museum of Modern Art, 1991; Philadelphia: Temple University Press, 1995), 16–19, 21, 209–11, 293, 295, 336–37. References are to the 1995 edition.
64. "Later, when his plays became known in Russia, they all laughed at them; but, as it was soon noted, in the ten-year period of which we're speaking here, they weren't even aware of him in Russia. His American followers had believed that there they would have just as high opinion of him as they had." Cahan, *Bleter fun mayn leben*, 4: 372–73.

65. Gordin could not have entered Russia without a visa issued by the Russian government. The government was reluctant to admit Jews of any nationality, but Gordin's case was further complicated by the fact that after sixteen years in the United States he had at last applied for, but not yet been granted, American citizenship. On Gordin's immigration status, see Zylbercweig, *Di velt fun yankev gordin*, 308; and Kaplan, *Finding the Jewish Shakespeare*, 194–95.

66. Yakov Mikhailovich, "Strannyi portnoi," *Knizhki nedeli*, no. 9 (1890): 29.

67. Ibid., 31 (italics in original).

68. Ibid., 32.

69. Jacob Gordin, "A yidishe shtetl baym rusishen grenets," in *Ale shriftn fun yankev gordin*, 3: 220–21.

70. For accounts of Gordin's last days, see Winchevsky, *A tog mit yankev gordin*, 107–12; "Yankev gordin's abshied un zayn tsavoe," *Di tsukunft* 7 (July 1909): 379–80; and Cahan, *Bleter fun mayn leben*, 4: 571–74. See Beth Kaplan's excellent treatment of the funeral in *Finding the Jewish Shakespeare*, 1–6, 210–15. See also "Jacob Gordin Dead; Yiddish Dramatist," *New York Times*, June 12, 1909; "Thousands Honor Gordin's Memory," *New York Times*, June 14, 1909.

71. See B. Gorin's theories on the "decline" of the Yiddish theatre in this period, which he attributed to the untutored tastes of the newest, post-1905 immigrants, in "Der fal fun der beserer drame," in *Di geshikhte fun idishen teater*, 2: 171–89.

72. Pinski, *Dos idishe drama*, 50.

73. Ibid., 54.

74. Ibid., 55.

75. On the preference for Jewish cultural and educational autonomy in this period, see especially Mikhail Krutikov, *Yiddish Fiction and the Crisis of Modernity, 1905–1914* (Stanford, Calif.: Stanford University Press, 2001); and Kenneth B. Moss, "1905 as a Jewish Cultural Revolution? Revolutionary and Evolutionary Dynamics in the East European Jewish Cultural Sphere, 1900–1914," in Hoffman and Mendelsohn, *The Revolution of 1905 and Russia's Jews*, 185–98.

76. Nina Warnke argues that this period's popular plays, which celebrate a Jewishness that is stalwart in its opposition to antisemitism but very secular in its expression of that sentiment, are an American response to the pogroms and unrest in Russian-Jewish life after 1905. See Warnke, "Theater as Educational Institution," 39.

77. Walter Benjamin, "The Storyteller: Reflections on the Works of Nikolai Leskov," *Illuminations: Essays and Reflections*, ed. and with an introduction by Hannah Arendt (New York: Schocken Books, 1988), 86.

78. Ibid.

BIBLIOGRAPHY

ARCHIVAL SOURCES

Gordin, Jacob. Papers. YIVO Institute for Jewish Research, New York.

"Ob obshchestve Elizavetgradskom Dukhovno-bibleiskom bratstve" [On the Elisavetgrad society the Spiritual-Biblical Brotherhood]. Fond 102, 3-e deloproizvodstvo, opis' 87, ed. khr. 606 (1, 2). Gosudarstvennyi Arkhiv Rossiiskoi Federatsii, Moscow.

PRIMARY SOURCES

Chekhov, Anton. *Dramaticheskie proizvedeniya v dvukh tomakh* [Dramatic works in two volumes]. Leningrad: "Iskusstvo," 1986.

Gordin, Jacob. *Ale shriftn fun yankev gordin* [Complete works of Jacob Gordin]. 4 vols. New York: Hebrew Publishing Company, 1910.

———— [Ivan Kolyuchii, pseud.]. "Berkova koza (Fantaziya)" [Berkov's goat (A fantasy)]. *Elisavetgradskii vestnik*, July 3, 1888.

———— [Ivan Kolyuchii, pseud.]. "Bezbrachniki (Etyud)" [The celibates (A study)]. *Elisavetgradskii vestnik*, June 10, 1890.

———— [Ivan Kolyuchii, pseud.]. "Dovol'no! Dovol'no!" [Enough! Enough!] *Elisavetgradskii vestnik*, June 11, 1889.

————. *Dramy* [Dramas]. St. Petersburg: Izdatel'stvo "Teatr," 1910.

————. *Dray drames* [Three dramas]. Edited by Shmuel Rozhansky. Buenos Aires: Literatur gezelshaft baym YIVO in Argentine, 1973.

————. "Dva slova pravdy v pol'zu 'brat'ev-bibleitsev'" [Two words in defense of the biblical brothers]. *Russkii evrei* 36 (September 3, 1881): 1424–26.

————. "Erinerungen fun yankev gordin: Vi azoy ikh bin gevorn a dramaturg?" [Reminiscences of Jacob Gordin: How I became a playwright]. In *Di yidishe bine* [The Yiddish stage], edited by Chanan Minikes. Vol. 1. New York: J. Katzenelenbogen, 1897.

———— [Ivan Kolyuchii, pseud.]. "*Evgenii Onegin* na elisavetgradskoi stsene" [*Evgenii Onegin* on the Elisavetgrad stage]. *Elisavetgradskii vestnik*, June 4, 1889.

————. *Evreiskii Lir. Drama v chetyrekh deistviyakh* [The Jewish Lear. Drama in four acts]. Translated by D. Rozenblit. Odessa: Izdatel'stvo "Odesskikh Novostei," 1912.

———— [N., pseud.]. "Evreiskie siluety" [Jewish silhouettes]. Pts. 1–4. *Knizhki nedeli* 5 (1885): 1–12; 8 (1885): 13–34; 10 (1885): 35–65; 11 (1885): 67–93.

———— [N., pseud.]. "Evreiskie siluety." *Knizhki nedeli*, no. 2 (1886): 120–42.

———— [Yakov Mikhailovich, pseud.]. "Evreiskie siluety." *Knizhki nedeli*, no. 9 (1890): 1–32.

———— [Yakov Mikhailovich, pseud.]. "Evreiskie siluety." *Knizhki nedeli*, no. 6 (1891): 29–50.

———— [Ivan Kolyuchii, pseud.]. "Fel'eton. Peterburg-Odessa (Nechto v rode putyovoi zametki)" [Feuilleton. Petersburg-Odessa (Something like travel notes)]. *Odesskie novosti*, February 21, 1887.

———— [Yakov Mikhailovich, pseud.]. "Fel'eton. Po nashim yuzhnym palestinam" [Feuilleton. Around our southern Palestines]. *Odesskie novosti*, March 11, 1887.

————. "Fel'eton. Prazdnovanie godovshchiny 'Dukhovno-bibleiskogo bratstva' v Elisavetgrade" [Feuilleton. A celebration in Elisavetgrad of the anniversary of the "Spiritual-Biblical Brotherhood"]. *Odesskie novosti*, January 10, 1887.

———— [Ivan Kolyuchii, pseud.]. "Fel'eton. Sutoloka odesskoi zhizni" [Feuilleton. The bustle of Odessa life]. *Odesskie novosti*, April 26, 1887.

————. [Ivan Kolyuchii, pseud.]. "Fel'eton. Sutoloka odesskoi zhizni" [Feuilleton. The bustle of Odessa life]. *Odesskie novosti*, May 24, 1887.

————. [Ivan Kolyuchii, pseud.]. "Fel'eton. Sutoloka odesskoi zhizni" [Feuilleton. The bustle of Odessa life]. *Odesskie novosti*, May 31, 1887.

————. *The Jewish King Lear: A Comedy in America*. Translated by Ruth Gay, with notes and essays by Ruth Gay and Sophie Glazer. New Haven, Conn., and London: Yale University Press, 2007.

————. *Kreitserova sonata. Drama v chetyrekh deistviyakh* [The Kreutzer sonata. Drama in four acts]. In *Polveka evreiskogo teatra, 1876–1926. Antologiya evreiskoi dramaturgii* [A half century of Jewish theatre, 1876–1926. An anthology of Jewish dramaturgy], edited by Boris Entin, translated by Ruth Levin, 151–219. Moscow: Izdatel'stvo "Paralleli," 2003.

————. *Kreytser sonate: A drame in fir aktn* [The Kreutzer sonata: A drama in four acts]. New York: M. Mayzel, 1907.

———— [Yakov Mikhailovich, pseud.]. "Liberal i narodnik" [The liberal and the populist]. Pts. 1–2. *Knizhki nedeli*, no. 8 (1886): 29–94; no. 9 (1886): 1–90.

——— [Ivan Kolyuchii, pseud.]. "M. G. Savina na Elisavetgradskoi stsene (Pis'mo v redaktsiyu)" [M. G. Savina on the Elisavetgrad stage (Letter to the editor)]. *Elisavetgradskii vestnik*, July 3, 1888.

——— [Alfei, pseud.]. "Malen'kii fel'eton: Real'nyi roman v sovremennom dukhe" [Little feuilleton: A realist novel in the contemporary spirit]. *Elisavetgradskii vestnik*, January 8, 1889.

——— [Ivan Kolyuchii, pseud.]. "Neskol'ko slov po povodu melodeklamatsionnogo vechera" [A few words about an evening of *melodeklamatsiya*]. *Elisavetgradskii vestnik*, March 27, 1888.

———."Di oblave. Oys dem yidishn lebn in rusland" [The Raid. From Jewish life in Russia]. *Di arbayter tsaytung*, September 4, 1891.

——— [Ivan Kolyuchii, pseud.]. "Pis'mo k chitatelyam" [Letter to readers]. *Elisavetgradskii vestnik*, December 17, 1889.

———. "Pis'mo v redaktsiyu (Ot Yakova Gordina)" [Letter to the editor (From Jacob Gordin)]. *Elisavetgradskii vestnik*, July 22, 1881.

——— [Yakov ben Mikhl, pseud.]. "Der pogrom in elizavetgrad (Oys a privat-brif)" [The pogrom in Elisavetgrad (From a private letter)]. *Di arbayter tsaytung*, August 21, 1891.

——— [Yakov Mikhailovich, pseud.]. "Po povodu odnoi retsenzii" [In response to a review]. *Elisavetgradskii vestnik*, March 19, 1886.

——— [Ivan Kolyuchii, pseud.]. "Progulka po Elisavetgradu" [A stroll around Elisavetgrad]. *Elisavetgradskii vestnik*, January 29, 1889.

——— [Yakov Mikhailovich, pseud.]. "Putyovaya zametka" [Notes on the road]. *Elisavetgradskii vestnik*, November 8, 1885.

——— [Ivan Kolyuchii, pseud.]. "Razgovory" [Conversations]. *Elisavetgradskii vestnik*, July 9, 1889.

——— [Ivan Kolyuchii, pseud.]. "Rody razlichnykh rodov (Eskiz)" [Varieties of birth (A sketch)]. *Elisavetgradskii vestnik*, November 6, 1888.

——— [Yan, pseud.]. "Teatr" [Theatre]. *Elisavetgradskii vestnik*, December 4, 1888.

——— [Yan, pseud.]. "Teatr i muzyka" [Theatre and music]. *Odesskie novosti*, June 27, 1887.

——— [Yan, pseud.]. "Teatr i muzyka: Russkii teatr" [Theatre and music: The Russian theatre]. *Odesskie novosti*, November 18, 1886.

——— [Yan, pseud.]. "Teatr i muzyka: Russkii teatr" [Theatre and music: The Russian theatre]. *Odesskie novosti*, November 20, 1886.

——— [N.N., pseud.]. "Teatr v derevne" [Theatre in the countryside]. *Elisavetgradskii vestnik*, August 3, 1889.

———. "Tipy shtundistov" [Stundist types]. *Nedelya*, no. 15 (April 6, 1884): 518–24; no. 20 (May 13, 1884): 679–86; no. 35 (August 26, 1884): 1158–62.

———. "Di tsukunft fun idishen teater" [The future of the Yiddish theatre]. *Di tsukunft* 2 (February 1906): 81–85.

———. "V zashchitu dukhovno-bibleiskogo bratstva—Pis'mo v redaktsiyu" [In defense of the Spiritual-Biblical Brotherhood—Letter to the Editor]. *Nedelya*, no. 45 (November 4, 1884): 1535–36.

———. *Yankev gordin's dramen* [Jacob Gordin's dramas]. 2 vols. New York: Ferlag fun dem "Soyrkl fun yankev gordin's fraynt," 1911.

———. *Yankev gordins ertseylungen* [Jacob Gordin's stories]. 3rd ed. New York: International Library Publishing Company, 1909.

———. *Yankev gordins eyn-akters* [Jacob Gordin's one-act plays]. New York: "Tog," ca. 1917.

———. *Di yesoyme. Drama in 4 akten fun yankev gordin. Spetsiel geshriben fir madam K. liptsin* [The Orphan. Drama in four acts by Jacob Gordin. Written especially for Madame K. Liptzin]. New York: Madame K. Lipzin, 1911.

———. *Der yudisher kenig lir. Drama in 4 akten fun y. gordin* [The Jewish King Lear. Drama in four acts by J. Gordin]. Warsaw: Starovol'sky Typography, 1907.

Shakespeare. *King Lear.* Edited by R. A. Foakes. 1997. Reprint, London: Arden Shakespeare, Thomson Learning, 1997.

Tolstoy, Lev. *Polnoe sobranie sochinenii v 90-i tomakh. Akademicheskoe yubileinoe izdanie* [Complete collected works in ninety volumes. Academic jubilee edition]. Edited by Vladimir G. Chertkov. Moscow: Gosudarstvennoe Izdatel'stvo Khudozhestvennoi Literatury, 1928–58.

Turgenev, Ivan. *Polnoe sobranie sochinenii i pisem v dvadtsati vos'mi tomakh* [Complete collected works and letters in twenty-eight volumes]. Edited by Mikhail P. Alekseev. Moscow and Leningrad: Izdatel'stvo "Nauka," 1960–68.

SECONDARY SOURCES

Aleksandrov, Kh. "Tkhies hameysim: Tolstoys letster roman" [*Resurrection*: Tolstoy's last novel]. *Di arbayter tsaytung*, March 11, 1900.

Alekseev. "Teatr i muzyka—Novyi teatr (direktsiya L. B. Yavorskoi), 'Evrei'" [Theatre and music—the New Theatre (under the direction of L. B. Yavorskaya), "The Jews"]. *Novaya zhizn'*, November 27, 1905.

Allen, Elizabeth Cheresh. *Beyond Realism: Turgenev's Poetics of Secular Salvation.* Stanford, Calif.: Stanford University Press, 1992.

Alter, Iska. "King Lear and *1000 Acres*." In *Transforming Shakespeare: Contemporary Women's Re-visions in Literature and Performance*, edited by Marianne Novy, 145–58. New York: St. Martin's Press, 1999.

Aronson, I. Michael. "The Attitudes of Russian Officials in the 1880s toward Jewish Assimilation and Emigration." *Slavic Review* 34 (March 1975): 1–18.

———. *Troubled Waters: The Origins of the 1881 Anti-Jewish Pogroms in Russia*. Pittsburgh: University of Pittsburgh Press, 1990.

Auerbach, Nina. "The Rise of the Fallen Woman." *Nineteenth-Century Fiction* 35, no. 1 (1980): 29–52.

Baker, Zachary M., ed. *Judaica in the Slavic Realm, Slavic in the Judaic Realm: Repositories, Collections, Projects, Publications*. New York, London, Oxford: Haworth Information Services, 2003.

Bakhtin, Mikhail. *The Dialogic Imagination: Four Essays by M. M. Bakhtin*. Edited by Michael Holquist. Translated by Caryl Emerson and Michael Holquist. Austin: University of Texas Press, 1981.

———. *Problemy poetiki Dostoevskogo*. Moscow: Sovetskii Pisatel', 1963. Edited and translated by Caryl Emerson as *Problems of Dostoevsky's Poetics* (Minneapolis and London: University of Minnesota Press, 1984).

Barish, Jonas. *The Anti-theatrical Prejudice*. Berkeley, Los Angeles, and London: University of California Press, 1981.

Barnett, Vincent. *The Revolutionary Russian Economy: 1890–1940; Ideas, Debates, and Alternatives*. London and New York: Routledge, 2004.

Bartal, Israel. *The Jews of Eastern Europe, 1772–1881*. Translated by Chaya Naor. Philadelphia: University of Pennsylvania Press, 2002.

Beebe, Maurice. *Ivory Towers and Sacred Founts: The Artist as Hero in Fiction from Goethe to Joyce*. New York: New York University Press, 1964.

Belkin, Ahuva. "The 'Low' Culture of the *Purimshpil*," in Berkowitz, *Yiddish Theatre: New Approaches*, 29–43.

Benjamin, Walter. *Illuminations: Essays and Reflections*. Edited and with an introduction by Hannah Arendt. New York: Schocken Books, 1988.

Bentley, Eric, ed. *The Theory of the Modern Stage: An Introduction to Modern Theatre and Drama*. 1968. Reprint, London: Penguin Books, 1992.

Bergson, Henri. *Laughter: An Essay on the Meaning of the Comic*. Translated by Cloudesley Brereton and Fred Rothwell. London: Macmillan, 1911. Reprint, Copenhagen and Los Angeles: Green Integer, 1999.

Berkowitz, Joel. *Shakespeare on the American Yiddish Stage*. Iowa: University of Iowa Press, 2002.

———, ed. *Yiddish Theatre: New Approaches*. Oxford and Portland, Ore.: Littman Library of Jewish Civilization, 2003.

Berkowitz, Joel, and Jeremy Asher Dauber, eds. and trans. *Landmark Yiddish Plays: A Critical Anthology.* Albany: State University of New York Press, 2006.

Berkowitz, Peter, ed. *Varieties of Progressivism in America.* Stanford, Calif.: Hoover Institution Press, Stanford University, 2004.

Binevich, Evgenii. *Evreiskii teatr v Peterburge. Opyt istoricheskogo ocherka* [Jewish theatre in Petersburg. A historical essay]. St. Petersburg: Evreiskii obshchinnyi tsentr Sankt-Peterburga, 2003.

———. "Nachalo evreiskogo teatra v Rossii" [Origins of the Jewish theatre in Russia]. 1994 Preprint 3 of the Jewish Heritage Society. http://www.jewish-heritage.org/prep3.htm.

Boyarin, Daniel. "Old Wine in New Bottles: Intertextuality and Midrash." *Poetics Today* 8, nos. 3–4 (1987): 539–56.

Brandes, Joseph, in association with Martin Douglas. *Immigrants to Freedom: Jewish Communities in Rural New Jersey since 1882.* Philadelphia: University of Pennsylvania Press, 1971.

Brands, H. W. *The Reckless Decade: America in the 1890s.* 1995. Reprint, Chicago: University of Chicago Press, 2002.

Braun, Edward. *Meyerhold: A Revolution in Theatre.* 1979. Revised and expanded, London: Methuen, 1995.

Brook, Peter. *There Are No Secrets: Thoughts on Acting and the Theatre.* London: Methuen, 1993.

Brown, John. *The Stundists: The Story of a Great Religious Revolt; with photographs of Typical Stundists, and a Map of Southern Russia, showing distribution of the body.* London: James Clark, 1893.

Bryusov, Valerii. "Nenuzhnaya pravda" [The unnecessary truth]. *Mir iskusstva* 8, no. 4 (1902): 67–74.

Bukhbinder, Nikolai A. "Iz istorii sektantskogo dvizheniya sredi russkikh evreev. Dukhovno-bibleiskoe bratstvo" [From the history of a Russian-Jewish sectarian movement. The Spiritual-Biblical Brotherhood]. *Evreiskaya starina* 11 (1918): 238–65.

Burshtein, Lev. "K istorii 'Dukhovno-bibleiskogo bratstva'" [Toward a history of the "Spiritual-Biblical Brotherhood"]. *Perezhitoe* 1 (1908): 38–41.

Butkevich, Anatolii. *Vospominaniya L. N.* [Memories of Lev Nikolaevich]. Moscow: Izdatel'stvo Gosudarstvennogo literaturnogo muzeya, 1938.

Cahan, Abraham. *Bleter fun mayn leben* [Pages from my life]. 6 vols. New York: Forverts Association, 1926–31.

———. "A por perzenlekhe verter" [A few personal remarks]. *Forverts*, March 10, 1908; March 11, 1908.

———. "Di perzonen in gordins piesen" [The characters in Gordin's plays]. *Forverts*, February 15–16, 1908.

———. "Di yidishe bine: *Sibirya* in yunyon teater" [The Yiddish stage: *Siberia* at the Union Theatre]. *Di arbayter tsaytung*, November 20, 1891.

———. "Fun vanen hot gordin genumen 'zayne' artiklen" [Where Gordin got "his" articles from]. *Forverts*, April 4–11, 1908.

———. "Realistishe literatur. Zol der shrayber zikh araynmishn in bild?" [Realist literature. Should the writer put himself in the picture?] *Forverts*, December 17, 1903.

———. "Vos heyst an origineles verk?" [What is an original work?] *Forverts*, February 22, 1908.

———. "Vos men denkt in rusland vegn gordinen" [What they think of Gordin in Russia]. *Forverts*, March 15, 1908.

Camfield, Graham P. "From Tolstoyan to Terrorist: The Revolutionary Career of Prince D. A. Khilkov, 1900–1905." *Revolutionary Russia* 12, no. 1 (June 1999): 1–43.

Carlson, Marvin. *Theories of the Theatre: A Historical and Critical Survey, from the Greeks to the Present.* 1984. Reprint, Ithaca, N.Y.: Cornell University Press, 1996.

Cassedy, Steven, ed. and trans. *Building the Future: Jewish Immigrant Intellectuals and the Making of "Tsukunft."* New York: Holmes and Meier, 1999.

———. *To the Other Shore: The Russian Jewish Intellectuals Who Came to America.* Princeton, N.J.: Princeton University Press, 1997.

Chernyshevsky, Nikolai. *Literaturnaya kritika v dvukh tomakh* [Literary criticism in two volumes]. Moscow: "Khudozhestvennaya literatura," 1981.

———. "Russkii chelovek na *rendez-vous*. Razmyshleniya po prochtenii povesti g. Turgeneva 'Asya'" [A Russian on a *rendez-vous*. Thoughts on reading Turgenev's novella "Asya"]. *Atenei* 3, no. 18 (1858): 65–89.

Cohen, Jocelyn, and Daniel Soyer, eds. and trans. *My Future Is in America: Autobiographies of Eastern European Jewish Immigrants.* New York and London: New York University Press, 2008.

Conrad, Joseph. L. "Turgenev's 'Asja': Ambiguous Ambivalence." *Slavic and East European Journal* 30, no. 2 (Summer 1986): 215–29.

Conybeare, Frederick C. *Russian Dissenters.* Harvard Theological Studies. Cambridge, Mass.: Harvard University Press; London: Humphrey Milford, Oxford University Press, 1921.

Cory, Herbert Ellsworth. "The Sublime, the Beautiful, and the Good." *International Journal of Ethics* 37, no. 2 (January 1927): 159–72.

Costlow, Jane T. *Worlds within Worlds: The Novels of Ivan Turgenev.* Princeton, N.J.: Princeton University Press, 1990.

Danilov, Sergei. *Ocherki po istorii russkogo dramaticheskogo teatra* [Essays on the history of the Russian dramatic theatre]. Moscow and Leningrad: "Iskusstvo," 1948.

Dauber, Jeremy Asher. *Antonio's Devils: Writers of the Jewish Enlightenment and the Birth of Modern Hebrew and Yiddish Literature.* Stanford, Calif.: Stanford University Press, 2004.

Deryugin, A. A. "Soderzhanie perevodcheskogo priema 'Sklonenie na nashi (russkie) nravy.'" [Elements of the translation device "Adaptation to our (Russian) ways"]. *Seriya literatury i yazyka* 54, no. 5 (1995): 61–64.

Diner, Hasia R. *Lower East Side Memories: A Jewish Place in America.* Princeton, N.J., and Oxford: Princeton University Press, 2000.

Dubnow, Simon. "Kakaya samoemansipatsiya nuzhna evreev" [The type of self-emancipation the Jews need]. *Voskhod*, nos. 5–6 (May–June 1883): 219–46.

Dubrovsky, Gertrude Wishnick. *The Land Was Theirs: Jewish Farmers in the Garden State.* Tuscaloosa and London: University of Alabama Press, 1992.

"Dukhovno-bibleiskoe bratstvo" [The Spiritual-Biblical Brotherhood]. *Odesskii vestnik*, November 13, 1882.

Edgerton, William B. "The Artist Turned Prophet: Leo Tolstoj after 1880." In *American Contributions to the Sixth International Congress of Slavists*, 2: 61–85. The Hague and Paris: Mouton, 1968.

Eisenberg, Ellen. *Jewish Agricultural Colonies in New Jersey, 1882–1920.* Syracuse, N.Y.: Syracuse University Press, 1995.

"Ekaterinskii teatr" [Ekaterinsky Theatre]. *Teatr i iskusstvo*, no. 52 (1909): 965–66.

Eliasberg, Galina A. "I. Teneromo—provintsial'nyi korrespondent L. N. Tolstogo" [I. Teneromo—L.N. Tolstoy's provincial correspondent]. *Filologicheskie nauki* 5 (2009): 45-55.

"Elisavetgrad (Korrespondentsiya 'Russkogo Evreya'): Materialy dlya istorii novoobrazovsheisya sekty" [Elisavetgrad (Reporting by "Russian Jew"): Materials for a history of a newly formed sect]. *Russkii evrei* 29 (July 14, 1881): 1137–38.

Emerson, Caryl. "*What Is Art?* and the Anxiety of Music." *Russian Literature* 40 (1996): 433–50.

———. "Tolstoy's Aesthetics: A Harmony and Translation of the Five Senses." *Tolstoy Studies Journal* 12 (2000): 9–17.

Epstein, Melech. *Profiles of Eleven.* Detroit: Wayne State University Press, 1965.

Firer, A. "Vozniknovenie novogo tolka" [Emergence of a new creed]. *Razsvet* 15 (1881): 574–76.

Fitzpatrick, Sheila. *The Russian Revolution*. Oxford and New York: Oxford University Press, 1994.

Frankel, Jonathan. *Prophecy and Politics: Socialism, Nationalism, and the Russian Jews, 1862–1917*. Cambridge: Cambridge University Press, 1981.

Friedman, Max Paul. "Beyond 'Voting with Their Feet': Toward a Conceptual History of 'America' in European Migrant Sending Communities, 1860s to 1914." *Journal of Social History* 40, no. 3 (Spring 2007): 557–75.

Garrett, Leah. *Journeys beyond the Pale: Yiddish Travel Writing in the Modern World*. Madison: University of Wisconsin Press, 2003.

Ginnerman, S. M. [Gen, pseud.]. "Evreiskaya stsena i evreiskii balagan" [The Jewish stage and the Jewish fairground show]. *Teatr i iskusstvo*, no. 15 (1907): 252–54.

Gitelman, Zvi. *A Century of Ambivalence: The Jews of Russia and the Soviet Union, 1881 to the Present*. Bloomington: Indiana University Press, 2001.

Goering, Orlando J., and Violet Goering. "The Agricultural Communes of the Am Olam." *Journal of Communal Studies* 4 (1984): 74–86.

Goldberg, Isaac. *The Drama of Transition: Native and Exotic Playcraft*. Cincinnati: Stewart Kidd, 1922.

Gorin, B. [Yitskhok Goydo]. *Di geshikhte fun idishen teater. Tsvey toyzend yohr teater bay iden* [The history of the Yiddish theatre. Two thousand years of Jewish theatre]. New York: Spetsiele oyflage fun "Forverts," 1929.

"Graf tolstoy in kheyrem" [Count Tolstoy excommunicated]. *Di arbayter tsaytung*, March 10, 1901.

Gusev, N. *Letopis' zhizni i tvorchestva L. N. Tolstogo, 1828–1919* [Chronicle of the life and work of L. N. Tolstoy, 1828–1919]. Moscow and Leningrad: Akademiya, 1936.

Gustafson, Richard F. *Leo Tolstoy, Resident and Stranger: A Study in Fiction and Theology*. Princeton, N.J.: Princeton University Press, 1986.

Haberer, Erich. *Jews and Revolution in Nineteenth-Century Russia*. Cambridge: Cambridge University Press, 1995.

Hamburg Passenger Indirect Lists. Staatsarchiv Hamburg, Film no. S 13162, Auswanderungsamt I, VIII B1, Bd 91, Verkleinerung 18(6) July 1–July 30, 1891.

Hapgood, Hutchins. *The Spirit of the Ghetto*. 1902. Reprint. Edited by Moses Rischin. Cambridge, Mass.: Belknap Press of Harvard University Press, 1967.

Hartman, Geoffrey H. *Wordsworth's Poetry, 1787–1814*. New Haven, Conn., and London: Yale University Press, 1964.

Henry, Barbara J. "Jewish Plays on the Russian Stage: St. Petersburg, 1905–1917." In Berkowitz, *Yiddish Theatre: New Approaches*, 61–75.

Herman, David. "Stricken by Infection: Art and Adultery in *Anna Karenina* and *Kreutzer Sonata*." *Slavic Review* 56, no. 1 (1997): 15–36.

Herscher, Uri D. *Jewish Agricultural Utopias in America, 1880–1910*. Detroit: Wayne State University Press, 1981.

Heywood, Anthony J., and Jonathan D. Smele, eds. *The Russian Revolution of 1905: Centenary Perspectives*. Abingdon, U.K.: Routledge, 2005.

Hoberman, J. *Bridge of Light: Yiddish Film between Two Worlds*. Philadelphia: Temple University Press, 1995. First published 1991 by the Museum of Modern Art.

Hoffman, Stefani, and Ezra Mendelsohn, eds. *The Revolution of 1905 and Russia's Jews*. Philadelphia: University of Pennsylvania Press, 2008.

Hofstadter, Richard. *The Age of Reform: From Bryan to F.D.R*. New York: Alfred A. Knopf, 1966.

Howe, Irving. *World of Our Fathers: The Journey of the East European Jews to America and the Life They Found and Made*. 1976. Reprint, New York: New York University Press, 2005.

Hughes, Alan. "Henry Irving's Tragedy of Shylock." *Educational Theatre Journal* 24, no. 3 (October 1972): 248–64.

Hutcheon, Linda. *A Poetics of Postmodernism: History, Theory, Fiction*. New York and London: Routledge, 1988.

———. *A Theory of Parody: The Teachings of Twentieth Century Art Forms*. Urbana and Chicago: University of Illinois Press, 2000. Originally published 1985 by Methuen in New York.

"Interesting Symposium on Modern Drama—Methods of Philanthropic Work." *Jewish Assembly Summer Supplement* 29, no. 15 (1904): 1.

"In vos beshteyt tolstoys groskayt?" [In what does Tolstoy's greatness lie?] *Forverts*, November 23, 1910.

Isenberg, Charles. *Telling Silence: Russian Frame Narratives of Renunciation*. Evanston, Ill.: Northwestern University Press, 1993.

Kachuk, Rhoda S. "Entering *King Lear* with Shakespeare and His Yiddish Adapter." In *Entering the Maze: Shakespeare's Art of Beginning*, edited by Robert F. Willson, Jr., 145–53. New York: Peter Lang, 1995.

———. "The First Two Yiddish Lears." In *The Globalization of Shakespeare in the Nineteenth Century*, edited by Krystyna Kujawińska Courtney and John Mercer, 55–67. Lewiston, N.Y.: Edwin Mellen Press, 2003.

Kagan-Kans, Eva. *Hamlet and Don Quixote: Turgenev's Ambivalent Vision.* The Hague and Paris: Mouton, 1975.

Kaplan, Beth. *Finding the Jewish Shakespeare: The Life and Legacy of Jacob Gordin.* Syracuse, N.Y.: Syracuse University Press, 2007.

———. *The Shakespeare of the Jews.* Ottawa: National Library of Canada, 1988.

Karp, Abraham J. *Haven and Home: A History of the Jews in America.* New York: Schocken Books, 1985.

Katsenel'son, Lev. I, and Baron David G. Gintsburg, eds. *Evreiskaya entsiklopediya. Svod znanii o evreistve i ego kul'ture v proshlom i nastoyashchem* [The Jewish encyclopedia. A repository of knowledge of Jewry and its culture in the past and present]. 16 vols. St. Petersburg: Brockhaus-Efron, 1908–13.

Kean [pseud.]. *See* Kin [pseud.].

"Khronika" [Chronicle]. *Elisavetgradskii vestnik,* March 7, 1886.

"Khronika." *Elisavetgradskii vestnik,* May 31, 1889.

"Khronika." *Elisavetgradskii vestnik,* October 1, 1889.

"Khronika." *Elisavetgradskii vestnik,* December 1, 1889.

Kin [pseud.]. "Teatr i muzyka: Evreiskii literaturnyi teatr—'Zaklanie' drama v 4 d. soch. Ya. Gordina" [Theatre and music: The Jewish literary theatre—"The Slaughter," a drama in four acts by J. Gordin]. *Rech',* April 17, 1908.

———. "Teatr i muzyka: Evreiskii literaturnyi teatr, 'Mirele Efros,' drama v 4-kh deistviyakh, soch. Ya. Gordina" [Theatre and music: The Jewish literary theatre, "Mirele Efros," a drama in four acts by J. Gordin]. *Rech',* April 19, 1908.

———. "Teatr i muzyka: Evreiskii literaturnyi teatr, 'Yankel' kuznets,' zhiznennaya kartina v 4-kh deistviyakh D. Pinskogo" [Theatre and music: The Jewish literary theatre, "Yankel the Smith," scenes from life in four acts by D. Pinski]. *Rech',* April 24, 1908.

Kirshenblatt-Gimblett, Barbara, and Jonathan Karp, eds. *The Art of Being Jewish in Modern Times.* Philadelphia: University of Pennsylvania, 2008.

Klei[ma]n, I. A. "Teatr i muzyka—Evreiskii teatr, 'Mirele Efros' Ya. Gordina" [Theatre and music—Jewish theatre, J. Gordin's "Mirele Efros"]. *Rech',* March 11, 1909.

Klibanov, A. I. *Istoriya religioznogo sektantstva v Rossii: 60-e gody XIX v.–1917 g.* [A history of religious sectarianism in Russia: 1860s–1917]. Moscow: Izdatel'stvo "Nauka," 1965.

Klier, John. "'Exit, Pursued by a Bear': Russian Administrators and the Ban on Yiddish Theatre in Imperial Russia." In Berkowitz, *Yiddish Theatre: New Approaches,* 159–74.

———. "From Elisavetgrad to Broadway: The Strange Journey of Iakov Gordin." In *Extending the Borders of Russian History: Essays in Honor of Alfred J. Rieber*, edited by Marsha Siefert, 113–25. Budapest and New York: Central European University Press, 2003.

———. *Imperial Russia's Jewish Question, 1855–1881*. Cambridge: Cambridge University Press, 1995.

———. *Russia Gathers Her Jews: The Origins of the "Jewish Question" in Russia, 1722–1825*. De Kalb: Northern Illinois University Press, 1986.

Knapp, Liza. "Tolstoy on Musical Mimesis: Platonic Aesthetics and Erotics in *The Kreutzer Sonata*." *Tolstoy Studies Journal* 4 (1991): 25–42.

Kobrin, Leon. *Erinerungen fun a yidishn dramaturg: A fertl yorhundert yidish teater in amerika* [Reminiscences of a Yiddish playwright: A quarter century of Yiddish theatre in America]. 2 vols. New York: Komitet far Kobrins shriftn, 1925.

Kobrin, Rebecca. "The 1905 Revolution Abroad: Mass Migration, Russian Jewish Liberalism, and American Jewry, 1903–1914." In Hoffman and Mendelsohn, *The Revolution of 1905 and Russia's Jews*, 227–44.

Koerner, Joseph Leo. *Caspar David Friedrich and the Subject of Landscape*. New Haven, Conn., and London: Yale University Press, 1990.

Kopper, John. M. "Tolstoy and the Narrative of Sex: A Reading of *Father Sergius*, *The Devil*, and *The Kreutzer Sonata*." In McLean, *In the Shade of a Giant*, 158–86.

"Korrespondentsii 'Nov.Tel.': Elisavetgrad" [Reports from the Novorossiysk Telegraph: Elisavetgrad]. *Novorossiiskii telegraf*, April 24, 1881.

Kristeva, Julia. *Desire in Language: A Semiotic Approach to Literature and Art*. Edited by Leon S. Roudiez. Translated by Thomas Gora, Alice Jardine, and Leon S. Roudiez. Oxford: Basil Blackwell, 1980.

———. *The Kristeva Reader*. Edited by Toril Moi. New York: Columbia University Press, 1986.

———. *La révolution du langage poétique*. Paris: Seuil, 1974.

Krutikov, Mikhail. *Yiddish Fiction and the Crisis of Modernity, 1905–1914*. Stanford, Calif.: Stanford University Press, 2001.

Kugel', Aleksandr [Homo Novus, pseud.]. "Evreiskii teatr" [Jewish theatre]. *Teatr i iskusstvo*, no. 17 (1908): 314.

———. "Evreiskii teatr" [Jewish theatre]. *Teatr i iskusstvo*, no. 19 (1908): 335.

———. *List'ya s dereva* [Leaves from a tree]. Leningrad: "Shipovnik," 1927.

———. "Teatral'nye zametki" [Theatre observations]. *Teatr i iskusstvo*, no. 31 (1910): 583–86.

———. "Zametki" [Observations]. *Teatr i iskusstvo*, no. 17 (1915) 292–93.

Kuznitz, Cecile E. "'Who Is to Guide the Destiny of the East Side Russian Masses?' The Educational Alliance, the Educational League, and the Struggle to Become 'Good Americans.'" Unpublished paper, April 1994.

Landau, A. E. "Vnutrenee obozrenie" [Internal survey]. *Voskhod*, no. 7 (1881): 33–38.

LeBlanc, Ronald D. "Tolstoy's Way of No Flesh: Abstinence, Vegetarianism, and Christian Physiology." In *Food in Russian History and Culture*, edited by Musya Glants and Joyce Toomre, 81–102. Bloomington: Indiana University Press, 1997.

Levine, Lawrence W. *Highbrow/Lowbrow: The Emergence of Cultural Hierarchy in America*. Cambridge, Mass.: Harvard University Press, 1988.

Levitats, Isaac. *The Jewish Community in Russia, 1844–1917*. Jerusalem: Posner and Sons, 1981.

Lifschutz, Ezekiel. "Jacob Gordin's Proposal to Establish an Agricultural Colony." In *The Jewish Experience in America; Selected Studies from the Publications of the American Jewish Historical Society*, edited by Abraham J. Karp, 252–64. Waltham, Mass.: American Jewish Historical Society, 1969.

Lifson, David. S. *The Yiddish Theatre in America*. New York: Thomas Yoseloff, 1965.

Link, Arthur S., and Richard L. McCormick. *Progressivism*. Arlington Heights, Ill.: Harland Davidson, Inc., 1983.

Lotman, L. M. "Turgenev i Fet." In *Turgenev i ego sovremenniki* [Turgenev and his contemporaries]. Edited by M. P. Alekseev, 25–47. Leningrad: Izdatel'stvo "Nauka," 1977.

"Malen'kaya khronika" [Little chronicle]. *Teatr i iskusstvo*, no. 43 (1913): 810.

Mandelker, Amy. *Framing Anna Karenina: Tolstoy, the Woman Question, and the Victorian Novel*. Columbus: Ohio State University Press, 1993.

Marker, Lise-Lone. *David Belasco: Naturalism in the American Theatre*. Princeton, N.J.: Princeton University Press, 1975.

Marmor, Kalmon. *Yankev gordin*. New York: YKUF, 1953.

Marx, Leo. *The Machine in the Garden: Technology and the Pastoral Ideal in America*. 1964. Reprint, Oxford: Oxford University Press, 2000.

Mazower, David. "Stories in Song: The *Melo-deklamatsyes* of Joseph Markovitsh." In Berkowitz, *Yiddish Theatre: New Approaches*, 119–37.

McConachie, Bruce A. *Melodramatic Formations: American Theatre and Society, 1820–1870*. Iowa City: University of Iowa Press, 1992.

McGeer, Michael E. *A Fierce Discontent: The Rise and Fall of the Progressive Movement in America*. New York: Free Press, 2003.

McLean, Hugh, ed. *In the Shade of a Giant: Essays on Tolstoy*. Berkeley: University of California Press, 1989.

Mendes-Flohr, Paul, and Jehuda Reinharz, eds. *The Jew in the Modern World: A Documentary History*. 2nd ed. Oxford: Oxford University Press, 1995.

Menes, Abraham. "The *Am Oylom* Movement." *YIVO Annual of Jewish Social Science* 4 (1949): 9–33.

Meyer, Michael A. "The German Model of Religious Reform and Russian Jewry." In *Danzig between East and West: Aspects of Modern Jewish History*, edited by I. Twersky, 67–86. Harvard Judaic Texts and Studies 4. Cambridge, Mass.: Harvard University Press, 1985.

Michels, Tony. *A Fire in Their Hearts: Yiddish Socialists in New York*. Cambridge, Mass.: Harvard University Press, 2005.

Miron, Dan. *A Traveler Disguised: The Rise of Modern Yiddish Fiction in the Nineteenth Century*. 2nd ed. Syracuse, N.Y.: Syracuse University Press, 1996.

Montefiore, C. G. "Unitarianism and Judaism in Their Relations to Each Other." *Jewish Quarterly Review* 9, no. 2 (January 1897): 240–53.

Morgulis, M. G. *Voprosy evreiskoi zhizni* [Questions of Jewish life]. St. Petersburg: Tipo-Litografiya A. E. Landau, 1889.

Moss, Kenneth B. "1905 as a Jewish Cultural Revolution? Revolutionary and Evolutionary Dynamics in the East European Jewish Cultural Sphere, 1900–1914." In Hoffman and Mendelsohn, *The Revolution of 1905 and Russia's Jews*, 185–98.

———. "Not *The Dybbuk* but *Don Quixote*: Translation, Deparochialization, and Nationalism in Jewish Culture, 1917–1919." In Nathans and Safran, *Culture Front: Representing Jews in Eastern Europe*, 196–240.

N. R. "Teatr i muzyka—Evreiskii teatr" [Theatre and music— Jewish theatre]. *Rech'*, March 18, 1909; March 20, 1909.

"Nam pishut: Iz Elisavetgrada (Khersonskoi gubernii)" [They write to us: From Elisavetgrad (Kherson province)]. *Nedelya*, no. 39 (September 27, 1881): 1298–99.

"Nam pishut: Iz Elisavetgrada" [They write to us: From Elisavetgrad]. *Nedelya*, no. 3 (January 15, 1884): 102.

Nasaw, David. *Going Out: The Rise and Fall of Public Amusements*. Cambridge, Mass., and London: Harvard University Press, 1999. First published by Basic Books, 1993.

Nathans, Benjamin. *Beyond the Pale: The Jewish Encounter with Late Imperial Russia*. Berkeley: University of California Press, 2002.

———. ed., with Gabriella Safran. *Culture Front: Representing Jews in Eastern Europe*. Philadelphia: University of Pennsylvania Press, 2008.

"Nedel'nye zametki" [Observations of the week]. *Nedelya*, no. 7 (February 14, 1887): 235–36.

New York Passenger Lists, 1820–1957. Year: *1891*; Arrival: *New York, United States*; Microfilm serial: M237; Microfilm roll: M237_572; Line: 41; List number: 1112. Provo, Utah: Generations Network, Inc., 2006. http://www.ancestry.com.

Newman, Louis Israel. *Jewish Influence on Christian Reform Movements*. New York: Columbia University Press, 1925.

Niger, Shmuel, and Jacob Shatzky, eds. *Leksikon fun der nayer yidisher literature* [Encyclopedia of the new Yiddish literature]. New York: Altveltlekhn yidishn kultur-kongres, 1956–81.

Nikitin, V. N. *Evrei zemledel'tsy. Istoricheskoe, zakonodatel'noe, administrativnoe i bytovoe polozhenie kolonii so vremeni ikh vozniknoveniya do nashikh dnei. 1807–1887* [Jewish agrarians. The historical, legal, administrative and daily circumstances of colonies from the time of their emergence until the present day. 1807–1877]. St. Petersburg: Tipografiya Gazety "Novosti," 1887.

"Novyi teatr" [New Theatre]. *Teatr i iskusstvo*, no. 14 (1910): 300–301.

"N'yu-Iork (Iz nashego korrespondenta)" [New York (From our correspondent)]. *Voskhod*, no. 4 (January 24, 1902): 30.

Oberdeck, Kathryn J. *The Evangelist and the Impresario: Religion, Entertainment, and Cultural Politics in America, 1884–1914*. Baltimore and London: Johns Hopkins University Press, 1999.

Orwin, Donna Tussing. *Consequences of Consciousness: Turgenev, Dostoevsky, and Tolstoy*. Stanford, Calif.: Stanford University Press, 2007.

Oyslender, Nokhem. *Yidisher teater, 1887–1917* [Yiddish theatre, 1887–1917]. Moscow: Melukhe-farlag "Der emes," 1940.

Pashutin, A. N. *Istoricheskii ocherk g. Elisavetgrada* [A historical essay on the city of Elisavetgrad]. Elisavetgrad: Lito-Tipografiya Vr. Shpolyanskikh, 1897.

Pahomov, George S. *In Earthbound Flight: Romanticism in Turgenev*. Rockville, Md.: Victor Kamkin, 1983.

Peiss, Kathy. *Cheap Amusements: Working Women and Leisure in Turn-of-the-Century New York*. Philadelphia: Temple University Press, 1986.

Pike, David L. *Metropolis on the Styx: The Underworlds of Modern Urban Culture, 1800–2001*. Ithaca, N.Y., and London: Cornell University Press, 2007.

Pinski, Dovid. *Dos idishe drama: Eyn iberblik iber ihr entviklung* [The Yiddish drama: A survey of its development]. New York: S. Drukerman, 1909.

Portugalov, Venyamin. "Nezhdannaya pomekha" [An unexpected obstacle]. *Nedelya*, no. 39 (September 23, 1884): 1293.

————. *Znamenatel'nye dvizheniya v evreistve* [Notable movements in Jewry]. St. Petersburg: Izdatel'stvo avtora, Tipografiya Dr. M. A. Khana, 1884.

Prager, Leonard. "Of Parents and Children: Jacob Gordin's *The Jewish King Lear.*" *American Quarterly* 18, no. 3 (1966): 506–16.

Prelooker, Jaakoff. *Under the Czar and Queen Victoria: The Experiences of a Russian Reformer.* London: James Nisbet, 1895.

————. *See also* Priluker, Yakov.

"Preniya o Ya. Gordine; Sobranie 'Evr. Literaturnogo Obshchestva v. S. Peterburge'" [The debate on Jacob Gordin. Meeting of the "Jewish Literary Society in St. Petersburg"]. *Russko-Amerikanskoe Ekho,* November 11, 1909.

Priluker, Yakov [Emmanuel Ben-Sion, pseud.]. *Evrei-reformatory: "Novyi Izrail'" i "Dukhovno-Bibleiskoe Bratstvo." Opyt sotsial'no-religioznoi reformy evreistva I novoi postanovki evreiskogo voprosa v Rossii* [Jewish reformers: "New Israel" and the "Spiritual-Biblical Brotherhood"; an experiment in the socioreligious reform of Jewry and a new approach to the Jewish question in Russia]. St. Petersburg: Tipografiya i khromolitografiya A. Transhelya, 1882.

———— [Emmanuel Ben-Sion, pseud.]. "Novye idei sredi evreev" [New ideas among the Jews]. *Nedelya,* no. 12 (March 20, 1883): 379–80.

Prugavin, Aleksandr S. "Dukhovno-bibleiskoe bratstvo (Ocherk evreiskogo religioznogo dvizheniya)" [The Spiritual-Biblical Brotherhood (An essay on a Jewish religious movement)]. *Istoricheskii vestnik* 18, no. 11 (1884): 398–410; no. 12 (1884): 632–49.

Quint, Alyssa. "The Botched Kiss: Abraham Goldfaden and the Literary Origins of the Yiddish Theatre." Ph.D. diss., Harvard University, 2002.

Rapport, Nigel, and Andrew Dawson, eds. *Migrants of Identity: Perceptions of Home in a World of Movement.* Oxford and New York: Berg, 1998.

Ravage, Marcus E. *An American in the Making: The Life Story of an Immigrant.* New York and London: Harper and Brothers Publishers, 1917.

Rischin, Ruth. "*Allegro Tumultuosissimamente*: Beethoven in Tolstoy's Fiction." In McLean, *In the Shade of the Giant,* 12–60.

Robbins, Richard G. *The Tsar's Viceroys: Russian Provincial Governors in the Last Years of the Empire.* Ithaca, N.Y., and London: Cornell University Press, 1987.

Rose, Margaret. *Parody: Ancient, Modern, and Post-modern.* Cambridge: Cambridge University Press, 1995.

Roskies, David G. *The Jewish Search for a Usable Past.* Bloomington: Indiana University Press, 1999.

Rozenfeld, M. "Ruslands neyr-tomed. Gedanken iber graf tolstoy" [Russia's eternal light. Thoughts on Count Tolstoy]. *Forverts,* November 29, 1910.

Safran, Gabriella. *Rewriting the Jew: Assimilation Narratives in the Russian Empire*. Stanford, Calif.: Stanford University Press, 2000.

Sanders, Ronald. *The Downtown Jews: Portraits of an Immigrant Generation*. New York; Evanston, Ill.; and London: Harper and Row, 1969.

Sandrow, Nahma. "Romanticism and the Yiddish Theatre," in Berkowitz, *Yiddish Theatre: New Approaches*, 47–59.

———. *Vagabond Stars: A World History of Yiddish Theater*. New York: Harper and Row, 1977. Reprint, Syracuse, N.Y.: Syracuse University Press, 1996.

Schaechter, Mordkhe. *Di geviksen velt in yidish* [Plant names in Yiddish]. New York: YIVO Institute for Jewish Research, 2005.

Schapiro, Leonard. *Turgenev: His Life and Times*. Cambridge, Mass.: Harvard University Press, 1982.

Seeley, Frank Friedeberg. *Turgenev: A Reading of His Fiction*. Cambridge: Cambridge University Press, 1991.

Seidman, Naomi. *A Marriage Made in Heaven? The Sexual Politics of Hebrew and Yiddish*. Berkeley: University of California Press, 1997.

Seiger, Marvin. "A History of the Yiddish Theatre in New York City to 1892." Ph.D. diss., Indiana University, 1960.

Senelick, Laurence. "Anti-Semitism and Tsarist Theatre: The *Smugglers* Riots." *Theatre Survey* 44, no. 1 (May 2003): 68–101.

———. ed. and trans. *Russian Dramatic Theory from Pushkin to the Symbolists: An Anthology*. Austin: University of Texas Press, 1981.

Service, Robert. *The Russian Revolution, 1900–1927*. 2nd ed. Houndmills, Basingstoke, Hampshire, and London: Macmillan Press, 1991.

Shatzky, Jacob, ed. *Arkhiv far der geshikhte fun yidishn teater un drama* [Archival documents on the history of Yiddish theatre and drama]. Vilna and New York: YIVO Institute for Jewish Research, 1930.

———. ed. *Hundert yor Goldfadn* [A hundred years of Goldfaden]. New York: YIVO Institute for Jewish Research, 1940.

Schedrin, Vassili. "No More Cries! History of the Reform Jewish Congregation in St. Petersburg in the 1900s." News Update of the Jewish Heritage Society, December, 1997. http://www.jewish-heritage.org/vspres.htm.

Sherman, Joseph, and Ritchie Robertson, eds. *The Yiddish Presence in European Literature: Inspiration and Interaction*. Oxford: Legenda, 2005.

Shklovsky, Viktor. *O teorii prozy* [On the theory of prose]. Moscow: Izdatel'stvo "Federatsiya," 1929.

"Sholem aleykhem un tolstoy" [Sholem Aleichem and Tolstoy]. *Forverts*, July 19, 1903.

Shtarkman, Moyshe. "Yankev Gordins debyut af yidish" [Jacob Gordin's Yiddish debut] *YIVO Bleter* 3 (February 1932): 180–85.

Silbajoris, Rimvydas. *Tolstoy's Aesthetics and His Art.* Columbus, Ohio: Slavica, 1991.

Slobin, Mark. *Tenement Songs: The Popular Music of the Jewish Immigrants.* Urbana: University of Illinois Press, 1982.

Stanislawski, Michael. *Tsar Nicholas I and the Jews.* Philadelphia: Jewish Publication Society, 1983.

Stein, Sarah Abrevaya. *Making Jews Modern: The Yiddish and Ladino Press in the Russian and Ottoman Empires.* Bloomington: Indiana University Press, 2004.

Suvenir tsu yankev gordins tsen-yorikn yubileyum [Souvenir of Jacob Gordin's ten-year anniversary]. New York: n.p., 1901.

Swift, E. Anthony. "Fighting the Germs of Disorder: The Censorship of Russian Popular Theatre, 1888–1917." *Russian History / Histoire Russe* 18, no. 1 (1991): 1–49.

"Teatr i muzyka" [Theatre and music]. *Rech'*, April 22, 1909.

"Teatr i muzyka—Ekaterinskii teatr, 'Satana' Ya. Gordina" [Theatre and music— the Ekaterinsky Theatre, J. Gordin's "Satan"]. *Rech'*, December 20, 1909.

"Teatr i muzyka—Novyi teatr—'Mirra Efros' Ya. Gordina" [Theatre and music—the New Theatre—J. Gordin's "Mirra Efros"]. *Rech'*, April 1, 1910.

Thissen, Judith. "Film and Vaudeville on New York's Lower East Side." In Kirshenblatt-Gimblett and Karp, *The Art of Being Jewish in Modern Times*, 42–56.

———. "Reconsidering the Decline of the New York Yiddish Theatre in the Early 1900s." *Theatre Survey* 44, no. 2 (November 2003): 173–97.

"Tolstoy in kampf" [Tolstoy's struggle]. *Forverts*, March 18, 1901.

"Tolstoy tsum tsar" [Tolstoy to the tsar]. *Forverts*, April 21, 1901.

"Tolstoy vegn amerike—an intervyu" [Tolstoy on America—an interview]. *Forverts*, October 2, 1901.

"Tolstoys groskayt als a shrayber" [Tolstoy's greatness as a writer]. *Forverts*, November 24, 1910.

"Tolstoys protest-briv" [Tolstoy's letter of protest]. *Di arbayter tsaytung*, August 16, 1901.

Turgaev, A. S., ed. *Vysshie organy gosudarstvennoi vlasti i upravleniya rossii IX–XX vv. Spravochnik* [The highest organs of state power and administration in Russia in the nineteeth and the twentieth centuries. A guide]. St. Petersburg: Izdatel'stvo Severo-zapadnoi Akademii Gosudarstvennoi Sluzhby, 2000.

Turkow-Grudberg, Isaac. *Goldfaden un gordin. Eseyen un biografies* [Goldfaden and Gordin. Essays and biographies]. Tel Aviv: "Urli," 1969.

Twelfth Census of the United States. Schedule No. 1: Population. State of New York, City of New York, Kings County, Brooklyn, Ward 22, Enumeration district 368, roll T628_1059, page 17 A, June 12, 1900. http://www.ancestry.com.

Tynyanov, Yuri. *Arkhaisty i novatory* [Archaists and innovators]. Ann Arbor, Mich.: Ardis Publishers, 1985. Originally published 1929 in Prague by Priboi.

———. *Mnimaya poeziya: Materialy po istorii poeticheskoi parodii xviii i xix vv.* [Fleeting poetry: Materials on the history of poetic parody of the eighteenth and the nineteenth centuries]. Moscow-Leningrad: "Akademiya," 1931.

———. *Poetika. Istoriya literatury. Kino* [Poetics. Literary history. Cinema]. Moscow: Izdatel'stvo "Nauka," 1977.

Van de Stadt, Janneke. "Narrative, Music, and Performance: Tolstoy's *Kreutzer Sonata* and the Example of Beethoven." *Tolstoy Studies Journal* 12 (2000): 57–69.

"Ver grobt di kvorim. Di zelbstmord epidemie unter yidn" [Who digs the graves. The suicide epidemic among Jews]. *Jewish Daily News / Yidishes tageblat*, October 20, 1903.

Victor [pseud.]. "Evreiskii teatr" [Jewish theatre]. *Teatr i iskusstvo*, no. 15 (1909): 272.

"Vnutrennaya khronika: Evreiskii pogrom" [Local chronicle: Jewish pogrom]. *Nedelya*, no. 17 (April 26, 1881): 573.

"Vysochaishie Prikazy: Po Ministerstvu Vnutrennykh Del, 7-go sego iyunya" [Supreme Commands: From the Ministry of Internal Affairs, June 7]. *Pravitel'stvennyi vestnik*, June 9, 1890.

Waldinger, Albert. "Jewish Groundlings, Folk Vehemence, and *King Lear* in Yiddish." *Yiddish* 10 (1996): 121–39.

Waldron, Peter. *The End of Imperial Russia.* New York: St. Martin's Press, 1997.

Warnke, Bettina. "Reforming the New York Yiddish Theater: The Cultural Politics of Immigrant Intellectuals and the Yiddish Press, 1887–1910." Ph.D. diss., Columbia University, 2001.

Warnke, Nina. "The Child That Wouldn't Grow Up: Yiddish Theatre and Its Critics." In Berkowitz, *Yiddish Theatre: New Approaches*, 201–16.

———. "Going East: The Impact of American Yiddish Plays and Players on the Yiddish Stage in Czarist Russia, 1890–1914." *American Jewish History* 92, no. 1 (March 2004): 1–29.

———. "Immigrant Popular Culture as Contested Sphere: Yiddish Music Halls, the Yiddish Press, and the Processes of Americanization, 1900–1910." *Theatre Journal* 48 (1996): 321–35.

———. "The Jewish Drama Collection at the St. Petersburg State Theatrical Library." *Yiddish Theatre Forum* 2, no.1 (March 12, 2003). http://www2.trincoll.edu/~mendele/tmrarc.htm.

———. "Theater as Educational Institution: Jewish Immigrant Intellectuals and Yiddish Theater Reform." In Kirshenblatt-Gimblett and Karp, *The Art of Being Jewish in Modern Times*, 23–41.

———. *See also* Warnke, Bettina.

Waugh, Patricia. *Metafiction: The Theory and Practice of Self-Conscious Fiction*. London and New York: Methuen, 1984.

Weiner, Miriam. *Jewish Roots in Ukraine and Moldova: Pages from the Past and Archival Inventories*. Secaucus, N.J.: Miriam Weiner Routes to Roots Foundation and the YIVO Institute for Jewish Research, 1999.

Wiener, Leo. *The History of Yiddish Literature in the Nineteenth Century*. New York: Charles Scribner's Sons, 1899.

Winchevsky, Morris. "Gordin un lilienblum." *Di tsukunft*, 14, no. 8 (1909): 447–55.

———. *A tog mit yankev gordin* [A day with Jacob Gordin]. New York: M. Mayzel, 1909.

———. "Yankev gordin's abshied un zayn tsavoe" [Jacob Gordin's farewell and his testament]. *Di tsukunft* 7 (July 1909): 379–80.

Wirtschafter, Elise Kimerling. "Legal Identity and the Possession of Serfs in Imperial Russia." *Journal of Modern History* 70, no. 3 (September 1998): 561–87.

Wishnia, Kenneth. "Yiddish in Amerike: Translating Multilingual Texts; Jacob Gordin's 'Moses, Jesus Christ, and Karl Marx Visit New York.'" *MELUS* 28 (Summer 2003): 203–15.

Yachnin, Paul. "The Jewish King Lear: Populuxe, Performance, and the Dimension of Literature." *Shakespeare Bulletin* 21 (Winter 2003): 5–18.

Yarmolinsky, Abraham. *A Russian's American Dream: A Memoir on William Frey*. Kansas: University of Kansas Press, 1965.

Zhuk, Sergei. I. *Russia's Lost Reformation: Peasants, Millennialism, and Radical Sects in Southern Russia and Ukraine, 1830–1917*. Washington, D. C: Woodrow Wilson Center Press; Baltimore: Johns Hopkins University Press, 2004.

Zipperstein, Steven J. "Heresy, Apostasy, and the Transformation of Joseph Rabinovich." In *Jewish Apostasy in the Modern World*, edited by Todd M. Endelman. New York: Holmes and Meier, 1987.

————. *The Jews of Odessa: A Cultural History, 1794–1881*. Stanford, Calif.: Stanford University Press, 1986.

Zolotaroff, Hillel [Zolotarov, Zolotareff, Solotaroff]. "Der onfang fun der yidisher drame in rusland" [The origins of Yiddish drama in Russia]. In *Suvenir tsu yankev gordins tsen-yoriken yubileyum* [Souvenir of Jacob Gordin's ten-year anniversary], 23–30.

————. "Yankev gordin un di 'bibleiskoe bratstvo' (an entfer dem h'lilienblum)" [Jacob Gordin and the "Biblical Brotherhood" (A response to Mr. Lilienblum)]. *Der fraynd*, July 23, 1909; July 24, 1909.

Zylbercweig, Zalmen, ed. *Leksikon fun yidishn teater* [Encyclopedia of the Yiddish theatre]. 6 vols. New York, Warsaw, Mexico City: Farlag "Elisheva," 1931–70.

————. *Di velt fun ester rokhl kaminska* [The world of Esther Rokhl Kaminska]. Mexico: Imprenta Moderna Pintel, 1969.

————. *Di velt fun yankev gordin* [The world of Jacob Gordin]. Tel-Aviv: Hadfus "Orli," 1964.

INDEX

Page numbers in italic refer to figures.